D1758173

ANTHROPOLOGICAL PAPERS

OF

THE AMERICAN MUSEUM OF NATURAL HISTORY

VOLUME XXXIV, PART II

KINSHIP IN THE ADMIRALTY ISLANDS

By Margaret Mead

By Order of the Trustees

OF

THE AMERICAN MUSEUM OF NATURAL HISTORY

New York City

1934

SN2   A 27

KINSHIP IN THE ADMIRALTY ISLANDS
By Margaret Mead

PREFACE

I have called this paper *Kinship in the Admiralty Islands*, and thereby exercised a certain amount of license, as fully nine-tenths of it deals with one Admiralty Island tribe, the sea-dwelling Manus people of the southern lagoons and adjacent islands. The appended notes on five other Admiralty Island kinship systems, while fragmentary, are nevertheless good proof that the Manus system is one special development of a type which is characteristic of other parts of the Admiralties. I plead, in further extenuation, that the accident of having worked consecutively in Manu'a (Samoa)[1] and Manus (Admiralty Islands) opens the way for endless confusion, and the use of the phrase Admiralty Islands will make for bibliographical clarity.

The task of isolating certain elements of a culture for separate discussion is always a difficult one, for one part of it cannot be completely understood without a knowledge of the other parts; a truism which leads, however, no further than a logical impasse. When two people work together in the same culture the task becomes infinitely more complicated. For the kind of field-work which Mr. Fortune and I do, a general knowledge of the whole culture pattern is essential; upon a base of such general knowledge, we then proceed to specialize to some extent. But, in spite of such specialization, it is inevitable that each should continually contribute new items of information to the special subject of investigation to which the other has devoted maximum attention, the more so, when the field-workers are of opposite sex and so draw for information on different sections of the primitive community. In our work among the Manus from November 1928 to June 1929 I specialized on a study of primitive education and child thought; Mr. Fortune specialized in a study of the intricate functioning of the religious system. To make these separate investigations, we both required a sound working knowledge of the social organization, the economic organization, and the language. But, while I learned the language for purposes of communication with the natives, I did not take long native texts, and while Mr. Fortune learned the social structure and the kinship system, he did not collect the minutiæ of kinship behavior and kinship function which form a large part of the present study. Such minute studies of the personal relations of individuals as lie back of the statements in the following pages were more relevant to my study of child life, as were texts of seances and myths more relevant to his study of the functioning of the

---

[1]Mead, Margaret, Social Organization of Manua (*Bulletin 76, Bernice P. Bishop Museum, Honolulu, 1930*).

religion. As therefore, I had this bulk of detail upon the kinship system, it has been decided between us that I should write the description of the kinship system, as at some later time Mr. Fortune will write a description of the Manus language. It is to be hoped that other ethnologists will refrain from cavilling over a division of the rather bulky task of recording our material, if for no other reason, in appreciation of the usefulness of having material on one culture gathered simultaneously from two different points of view. Our previous publications upon the Manus culture include Mr. Fortune's study of the religion,[1] my study of the education, a paper on child thought, and a brief paper on Admiralty Island trade.[2]

My part of the Admiralty Island field-work was conducted as a Fellow of the Social Science Research Council, in 1928–1929. I wish to express my appreciation to that body for the opportunity to do this field-work. I am indebted to the American Museum of Natural History, and to the kind interest of Doctor Clark Wissler, in particular, for the opportunity to work up and publish this material. I owe special thanks to my husband, Mr. Reo Fortune, for his invaluable coöperation, both in the field and in collaboration and criticism of my results. I have to thank Professor A. R. Radcliffe Brown and Professor Ruth Benedict for most illuminating and stimulating assistance in the understanding of the general problems of kinship and social organization and, more particularly, for a criticism of this manuscript. I have also to thank Miss Bella Weitzner and Miss Paula Glotzer for their patient and valuable work in the preparation of the manuscript.

[1]Fortune, R. F., Manus Religion (*Oceania*, vol. 2, no. 1, 74–108, Sydney, 1931).
[2]Mead, Margaret, Growing up in New Guinea (New York, 1930). An Investigation of the Thought of Primitive Children, with Special Reference to Animism (*Journal of the Royal Anthropological Institute of Great Britain and Ireland*, vol. 62, pp. 173–190, London, 1932); Melanesian Middlemen (*Natural History*, vol. 30, 115–130, New York, 1930).

CONTENTS

ILLUSTRATIONS

TEXT FIGURES

THE MANUS TRIBE

SKETCH OF MANUS CULTURE

The Manus people are a fishing and navigating group who build their houses in the shallow lagoons adjacent to the south coast of the Great Admiralty and to a series of small islands off the south coast. They construct their own houses and canoes, the materials for which, however, they must obtain by trading fish with the land peoples. For all raw materials and for vegetable foods they are entirely dependent upon these neighboring tribes. Due to their superior seamanship and determined efforts they have succeeded in dominating the sea on the south coast. Their large two-masted, single-outrigger dug-out canoes are the carriers for the various artifacts manufactured on the southern islands. With the exception of the Manus settlement near the island of Mbuke, on which pottery vessels are made, the Manus manufacture nothing for trade but depend entirely upon fishing and marine transportation to obtain all the other manufactured products of the archipelago. They supplement their fish diet with taro, sago, coconuts, yams, papayas, and mud hens' eggs. They depend upon trade for bast for thread, string, and rope, for wood, for obsidian for knives and spears, for paraminium nut which they use as a caulking and binding material, for betel nut, for carved wooden bowls, for the paraminium gum covered basketry used as everyday utensils, and for the more elaborate objects of ornament and ceremonial such as the frigate bird war charms with the carved wooden heads, the tortoise shell breast ornaments and delicately worked ornaments of gold lip shell, elaborate combs carved of wood and ornamented with bas relief in paraminium nut, carved daggers with sting-ray points, lime gourds with burned-in designs, and the carved lime spatulas. The carved dancing poles, sometimes as much as thirty feet in length, the slit gongs with carved ends, the large table-like beds with carved legs—all these must be obtained by trade. Their position of dependency upon the manufactures of other tribes, the extreme meagerness of their natural resources and the day-by-day nature of a continuous traffic in fish are all important factors in understanding the general orientation of the Manus culture towards trade and the accumulation of material wealth. The Manus are essentially middlemen in a complicated system of intertribal exchange; they are ever under the necessity of being alert, active, unremittingly industrious and enterprising.

The economic organization which provides for the exchange and accumulation of a very considerable amount of property for a primitive people to possess is threefold. It consists of a system of daily markets in which a Manus village and a group of land-dwellers meet and barter fish for vegetable products of the land; a system of affinal exchanges within each tribal group which binds one village to another and serves a double purpose in stimulating the production of the objects required for the extensive systems of validation of births, marriages, deaths, etc., and also provides for the distribution of foreign products within a tribe; and a system of trade partnerships sometimes between members of quite distant tribes through which agency large articles of trade such as dugong, turtle, carved beds, large drums, etc., pass from one tribe to another. There is a double currency in Manus, dogs' teeth and strings of shell money; this currency in large amounts forms the principal permanent element in the Manus affinal exchanges and is also used in the major transactions between trade partners. In the daily market, barter, rather than money purchase, is the rule. The affinal exchanges among the Manus require the collection of large amounts of pots, grass skirts, sago, pigs, and oil, to meet the advances of dogs' teeth and shell money which are made by the kin group of the husband to the kin group of the wife. Either the raw materials, or the finished products of the wife's kin's share of the exchange must be obtained in the local market. Because about twenty-five per cent of the marriages are inter-village, these products then find their way to villages far distant from the point of manufacture. The knowledge that neighboring tribes provide a ready outlet for surplus manufactures combines with a desire to make a fine display in the affinal exchanges at home to encourage surplus production. Whenever there is a scarcity of any kind of manufacture, or in those cases where an intermittent failure of supply is to be feared, as in the supply of fish or of betel nut, compulsive barter,—that is, a refusal to sell a desired article for any valuable except a particular desired one—becomes the rule.

The Manus man has then a continuous call to commercial activity; he must fish for his family and for a surplus to trade at the market, he must plan for and accumulate sufficient native property for the large affinal exchanges (which often necessitates long overseas trips and elaborate negotiations with his trade partners in distant parts). This whole system has become too complex and too difficult to be handled by every adult male in Manus society. Instead, all the important planning is carried out by a few entrepreneurs, men of means, intelligence, and leadership. For these men, their young and dependent relatives fish and trade and undertake long journeys. The affinal exchanges them-

selves have been keyed to an individual emphasis. They do not represent the pooled wealth of the entire kinship group involved in a particular
marriage, or ear-piercing, or birth ceremony, but the aggregate of
individual contributions, each one of which is made to an individual
recipient on the opposite side of the exchange, and returned precisely.
Thus efficiently have the Manus eliminated the familiar type of commu-
nism within a kin group which permits the lazy and the inept to batten
upon the intelligent and the vigorous in so many primitive societies.

The religious system of the Manus is a special variant of ancestor
worship, combined with a system of communication with the spirits
of the dead through two sets of oracles—female mediums and male
diviners. Each house is guarded by a guardian ghost of a recently deceased male relative; the householder gives shelter and honor to the
dead man's skull and renders him lip service on festival occasions; the
ghost in return protects his ward's family, guards its health and safety
and prospers its fishing. Mr. Fortune has designated the guardian
ghost of a man, (whom the Manus refer to as *Moen Palit*) as *Sir Ghost*
while all other ghosts, from the standpoint of any given individual are
merely *ghosts*, often malicious and never actively enlisted in the interests
of other than their own wards. The Sir Ghost acts in a disciplinary rôle
towards his wards, extending help and protection to them only so long as
they are free from sin. The principal sin is any violation of the rigid
sexual code which supports the child betrothals and the stability of
marriage; sins also are failure to pay debts, failure to use one's economic
resources wisely, failure to provide for the betrothal and marriage of
young relatives, failure to assist other relatives in economic matters,
failure to obey the economic dictates of the head of the family, failure to
keep one's house in repair, etc. In other words, the spirits enforce, by a
withdrawal of aid and by punitive measures which are felt in failure of
fishing devices, hurricanes, and, most particularly, in sickness and accident, a stern puritanical moral code of saving, working, and abstinence
from all unlawful fleshly indulgence. The ward in his turn expects his
Sir Ghost to chasten for sin, but not to kill, and to protect all the members of his household from death at the hands of revengeful and malicious
ghosts. The death of a householder usually results in the destruction of
his house, which has sheltered an unfaithful Sir Ghost, the expulsion of
the Sir Ghost by throwing his skull in the sea, and the installation of the
recently deceased householder as the Sir Ghost of his heir. Deaths of
women and children result in strained relations between Sir Ghosts and
wards, but usually not in eviction, as neither women's nor young children's

ghosts would make satisfactory substitutes. Every illness results in a searching for sin, for full confession and expiation is believed to mitigate ghostly wrath. The cautious will also seek, through divination and seance, the advice of their Sir Ghosts before entering on any important undertaking or making any momentous choice. Another religious cult, the cult of the male ancestors in the male line and the female ancestors in the female line, is administered by the women, and is principally directed towards the regulation of pregnancy, the conferring of moral and spiritual blessings upon the young at various occasions of crisis, and the release of individuals from periods of ritual segregation. This cult which Mr. Fortune has described under the head of the *tandritanitani* cult will be discussed at greater length later as it is most intimately integrated with the kinship system.

With these few introductory remarks concerning the economic and religious aspects of Manus life,[1] I can proceed to a detailed consideration of the social organization. The peculiar nature of Manus society necessitates a somewhat special division of the discussion of the social organization. This paper will deal with the structure of Manus society, the village organization, gentile organization, the kinship system, and the way in which this structure functions in the community. Those periods in the life history of the individual, birth, puberty, marriage, parenthood, and death, which are usually regarded as an aspect of social organization assume a particular cast in Manus because they are the pivots upon which the economic activity of the society is balanced. They therefore belong more accurately in the discussion of economics and will be reserved for a future publication.

THE MANUS TRIBE

The Manus all speak one language with a single slight phonetic variation in the medial r-1 sound between two different sets of villages. They also recognize themselves as members of one tribal group, speaking of themselves as *yoya Manus* (we, plural exclusive, Manus), in contradistinction to the peoples of the Great Admiralty of whom they speak collectively as *ala Usiai* (they, plural, people of the land), and to the land-dwelling people of the surrounding islands they also apply a collective term, *ala Matankor* (which literally translated is "they, the eye of the land," more generally as "the face of the land"). Parkinson[2]

[1]For a full discussion see R. F. Fortune's forthcoming study of the Manus religion, still in manuscript. The opening sections of this study also contain somewhat more extended summaries of the economic and social organization. For a brief description of the trading system of the Admiralties see my *Melanesian Middlemen, op. cit.*

[2]Parkinson, R., *Dreissig Jahre in der Südsee.* Stuttgart, 1907.

followed the Manus usage in discussing the people of the Admiralties. This division is, however, hardly an ethnographic one, but is rather a reflection of the typical sea-dwellers' point of view towards people land-bound and wholly without canoes, the Usiai, and those who live on land but who use canoes with more or less frequency, the Matankor. As a matter of fact, those Matankor peoples who live near the Manus use canoes very infrequently, while the Matankor of the north coast seem to be as habitual and fearless sailors as are the Manus themselves.

The Manus are distinguished also by common custom. There are slight variations in behavior between settlements; the method of possession of a medium in Papitalai, the only Manus settlement on the north coast, has more in common with extra-Manus practice; the Taui bride may not sit beside her husband as may the brides from other settlements, but must remain with her back to him; the Mbuke widow is not permitted to face a stranger during mourning, but must present her buttocks to him. With the exception of a few such minor points which are conspicuous because of their rarity, the Manus people may be regarded as they regard themselves, as one people.

This unity of custom and language does not however indicate any sort of political unity. There is no indication that the Manus ever acted as a body and there is abundant evidence of inter-village wars, raids, and reprisals. Each Manus village has a regular trading relationship with some gardening land people. The Peri[1] people, for instance, speak of "our Usiai" as distinguished from the Mbunei or Pomatchau Usiai; and between these different groups of Usiai there was not only frequent hostility, but also considerably greater apparent divergence in language and custom. If reports are to be trusted, Manus and landspeople sometimes joined in war against another similar combination of Manus and neighboring landspeople.

There are some two thousand Manus natives living at the present time in eleven villages: Papitalai, Pomatchau, Mbunei, Tchalalo, Peri, Patusi, and Loitcha are all coastal lagoon villages; there are also Manus settlements near the islands of Mok, Mbuke, Taui, and Rambutchon. Parkinson's map shows several more villages in the Mok, Balowan, and Lou region. Although all of these villages are not remembered today, there is one circumstance which would seem to confirm this suggestion of a previous larger population in this region. The present Mok people, the only Manus left in that locality, are of a very distinct local physical type. It is possible to identify Mok people almost unfailingly in an

---

[1] Spelled with the terminal *i* to distinguish the village from the gens, Pere.

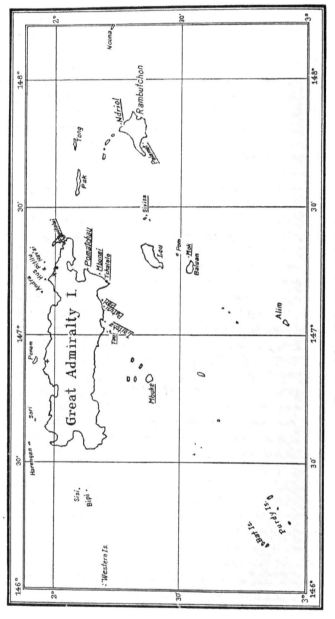

Fig. 1. Map of the Admiralty Islands.

194

assembly of Manus from other villages. This peculiar physical type owes part of its individuality to greater height and weight, which may alternatively be attributed to the superior quality of the foods which are grown on the island of Balowan and traded to the Mok people.

It is not possible to get any very accurate information from the Manus themselves concerning their past. They are a people essentially uninterested in history of any sort; they have only a few of the slightest and scantiest of origin myths to which they hardly ever refer. The only war stories which are told are events which occurred in the lifetime of living men; past events, instead of being reworked into the miraculous and the legendary, tend to be pared down to anecdotes which finally lose their individuality. The Peri people declare that they are now fewer than they were on account of the defection of certain gentes—notably Tchokani, a section of Matchupal gens which emigrated to Mok, and the ranking section of the present gens of Lo. They also comment upon the influenza epidemic of 1918 when one whole gens was decimated within a few days. This is the only epidemic of which there is any record. Conversely, the very slight differentiation of the Manus groups does not argue for an immensely extended population, nor does there seem to be evidence for the loss of more than three or four villages.

Inter-village contacts were of two types, the formal and exceedingly rare inter-village feasts given by the *luluai* or head man of a particular village, assisted by the entire village, and the continual movements, exchanges, adoptions, shifts of residence, visits incidental to intermarriage, etc., between individuals. Of the inter-village feast it was not possible to obtain very detailed information, as none occurred during our stay in Manus, but it seems to have been of that type so familiar in Nuclear Polynesia,[1] in which a kinship pattern is elaborated for political purposes. The Manus type of affinal exchange in which the two parties to an exchange each have an organizer who enlists the aid of the individual participants was translated into an inter-village affair with the *luluai* of each village as organizer. The collection of the necessary property, especially the necessary amount of coconut oil, took several years and one such affair was regarded as sufficient for a lifetime.[2]

---

[1] *Social Organization of Manua*, 9, and 26–30.
[2] At present Mbunei is preparing to give one of these large intervillage feasts, which are known as *tchinal*. They take their name from the raised dancing pole which is used at smaller feasts without, however, the features reported to be characteristic of inter-village affairs; they attempt to break the *tchinal* by a number of dancers and the use of public magic between head men. The Mbunei feast was scheduled three or four years in advance. Christian mission converts from Papitalai, the only christianized Manus village, were attempting to gain a foothold in Mbunei, but the Mbunei leaders insisted that they would not admit Christianity until after they had made their *tchinal*, then, as neither another *tchinal*, nor anything as important, would ever be made in their lifetimes, the mission might come in if it wished.

Informal contact between villages is governed only by distance and the number of intermarriages, which themselves reflect distance. So contact between Peri and Patusi, between Peri and Tchalalo was daily; with Loitcha and Mbunei at least bi-weekly; the arrival of a canoe from Taui, Mbuke, or Mok was an event; trips to and from Rambutchon occurred even more rarely, and there was only one contact in six months with Papitalai (when the husband of a sick woman went there to fetch a magician).

Gentes are prevailingly local; a member of one village will usually be unable to name more than one or two of the gentes of another village. In only one case did I receive an account of a gens which was represented in three villages. In several instances there are theoretical equivalences between gentes of different names which are claimed to be due to a past split in a gens. So a Mok gens is said to be a part of the gens of Matchupal. But these equivalences in a gens are the exception to the general rule of purely local gentes. Within a village, other village membership is considered as analogous to the local gens membership, so that in any question about an individual's affiliations, a Peri native will answer, "He belongs to Pontchal" (a Peri gens), but "His wife belongs to Mok" (a village). Gentile privileges and gentile taboos are also local and when the same fishing right is owned by different gentes in different villages, this fact is not regarded as of extra-village significance.

A village is spoken of as a *kor*, literally *place*. *"Oi pati tcha kor,"* literally, "You belong to what place," calls forth an answer in village terms, while *"Oi pati te?"* "You belong at what," receives an answer in terms of gens if asked within the speaker's village, but is likely to receive a village answer also if asked outside the village. If two villages are not at war, one village can go *en masse* to fish at the other during the periods of the monthly runs of fish, but trapping sites on the reefs are strictly owned and fished by residents of the adjacent village.

When an individual moves permanently from one village to another, the move is usually phrased in terms of going to live with relatives. So two youths left Patusi forever after a disturbance in which one of them was accused of having committed adultery with and so caused the death of the wife of the *luluai*. The youth protested his innocence and refused to confess, although this entailed a court case and a jail sentence; on his return from jail he and his brother went to live in his sister's husband's house in Peri. When these two young men marry, they will probably live first in the houses of the older men of Peri who are their financial backers and eventually build houses in Peri.

Moving from one village to another is also a variant of the pattern of moving house sites and village sites. The theory of localized spirit residence results in a Manus moving his house whenever there has been a death of importance (i.e., a house will not always be moved for a young child's death). After a series of deaths in a group of adjacent houses, which usually, but not necessarily, will be houses of members of one gens, sometimes half the village will move to some little distance, as much as a quarter of a mile, from the old site. An alternative to moving one's house to a more healthy spiritual locality within the village, is to move oneself and one's family to another village. At one time quite recently several families in Patusi moved to Peri and lived there for several months, so frightened were they of the spirits which were believed to be decimating Patusi. At the same time that this happened, a number of other householders in Patusi were moving their houses away from the old site—near the shore and so near mosquitoes and malaria[1]—out to a site further to seaward which had formerly been occupied by their ancestors. Or a disgruntled gens, or part of a gens may leave a village in a body and either move to another or start a new village, as was the history of the present village of Tchalalo, which was composed of the ranking members of the gens of Lo of Peri village. The commoners, however, remained in Peri. The small coral rubble platforms (*arakeu*) and the little islets which are gentile owned are sometimes referred to their former gentile owners who have fled the village.

Although a split in a gens or a quarrel between members of a family may be solved by one party moving to another village, flight to another village does not offer a solution for lovers, adulterers, and individuals in disgrace, as it does in some other parts of the world. This is primarily due to the religious system under which the guardian ghost of each house oversees jealously the behavior of all who live within it, even the temporary stranger within the walls. No runaway lovers would be received in any Manus house, for fear that the guardian ghost of that house would punish the inmates. As most quarrels, like most other events in Manus, have a spiritual side, the runaway is often of such bad spiritual odor that he cannot be received. This only applies, however, where the runaway is himself likely to be regarded as a moral leper. If he or she is merely fleeing the unreasonable malice of some ghost—as for example a widow and her new husband must flee the malice of the dead ghostly

---

[1]House moving may sometimes be to more healthful sites, sometimes to less healthful ones, as residence shifts within a small lagoon.

husband—then flight to another village is highly desirable as a way of putting distance between the fugitives and the pursuing ghosts.[1]

Similarly, individuals suffering from long and lingering illnesses, which are not provided for in the Manus theology with its doctrine of confess, repent, atone, and recover, will sometimes be moved from one village and its unfriendly or, at least, most unhelpful ghosts, to a relative in another village, the services of whose Sir Ghost will then be enlisted in his favor as a prestige point of the house owner.[2]

To a moral leper, that is, a man who has just committed a sex offense, another Manus village cannot offer a refuge, but another-tribal village may. So there is a case in Peri of a pair of eloping lovers who fled to the house of a trade friend among the Usiai, a people without such exacting views on sex questions, and another of a young man who had gotten an unmarried girl with child, who confessed his sin to his cross-cousin and made him promise to hold the confession until he could get well away towards the Matankor village of Bipi. Today, going away to work for the white man provides the safest refuge for a man who has transgressed the Manus code and who could not at any time find shelter in another Manus village.

There is also a certain amount of that type of residence which has been called in ethnographic literature, with loose inexactness, matrilocal, but which is merely residence in the wife's place for a certain period of time. There were eight such cases in Peri, almost all of them men of very little importance. But this latter fact, that it is only the inept and the unimportant who live in their wives' places, applies to intra-village residence arrangements also, and may be regarded as an extension of them. In fact, no one of the moves under discussion is regarded by the Manus in strictly village terms except that of the type of the two Patusi youths who had publicly proclaimed that they were leaving Patusi

---

[1] Manus theory and Manus practice are very inconsistent in this respect. Theoretically, a ghost can go wherever it wishes; in the seances, in popular belief, ghosts are constantly said to be moving about, either accompanying their wards or going on their own or their ward's business. See for instance (in Fortune, Chapter V, Section VIII) the account of the man who suggested that his Sir Ghost go to Patusi on an errand during a seance over a sick child, and then repented in fear of having his house left without a guardian and suggested that another ghost go instead. Similarly I once asked Paliau where Pwanau, his Sir Ghost was, as I was surprised that both Paliau and his wife and children had come to sleep in my house during Mr. Fortune's absence, leaving their own house unattended, which is a gross insult to a Sir Ghost. Paliau replied airily, "Oh, he is not here, I sent him to Lorengau with Moeyap (Mr. Fortune) to twist the *Kiap's* (district officer's) neck,"—i.e., to help influence the *Kiap* to grant a native request which he knew Mr. Fortune was carrying to Lorengau.

Nevertheless, a widow fleeing her dead husband does feel safer in another village. It is probable that this is merely a translation into ghostly terms of the fact that she feels safer away from the angry and frightened relatives of her dead husband, and her own relatives who, frightened of her ghostly husband, are angry at her for exposing them to his vengeful rage. It is a common habit in Manus to translate happenings on one plane into happenings on the other plane; so, for instance, if two families living in one house quarrel, the quarrel and resultant hasty removal of one family will be phrased as the fact that the Sir Ghosts of the respective households stole each other's betel nut.

[2] For an account in which a host exhorts his Sir Ghost to exert himself on behalf of a guest from another village, see Fortune, *l.c.*, Chapter V, Subsection 10.—ED.

forever. But movements on account of quarrels, fear of ghosts, dis-
gruntlement with particular ghosts, search for ghosts of greater potency,
residence with one's wife's people, are indifferently intra-village or inter-
village, the second, like the first, being phrased in terms of moving among
relatives.

The feeling of strangeness which is so prominent in the attitudes of
Melanesian natives towards members of other tribes or other villages, is
seen even among members of different Manus villages who are in fairly
close contact with one another. So in a canoe full of Mok people coming
into Peri, they will stay together, wait a long time on their canoe, enter
the house of relatives only, and generally behave in a shy and embarrassed
fashion. The only time when this type of behavior is not manifested is
upon occasions of general festivity, like a house building, a canoe race,
or a very large affinal exchange, when several canoes from each village
are present. When there is a dispute between members of different
villages, the party from the complaining village remains in its canoe or
canoes and the village owners speak from their house platforms. Here
again, an intra-village type of behavior is merely extended. In a Mánus
quarrel between individuals whose houses are too far apart for ease in
shouting, it is customary for one to approach the house of the other and
speak from the platform of a canoe. The canoe is as much a proper
platform from which to assail an opponent verbally as is the pile-dwelling.
Quarrels such as these are not, strictly speaking, between villages, only
a few members of either village will be concerned in a broken betrothal
engagement or a theft of coconuts,[1] but the fact that the contestants
belong to different villages, while it does not necessarily involve their
respective villages in the quarrel, adds to the strain of the situation, and
probably formerly was intensified by the greater possibility of war.

There is one other way in which all the members of a village are
classified together in Manus behavior. During the term of a betrothal,
the betrothed pair must avoid every member of the opposite sex in the
village of the betrothed. Here there is a clear equivalence between
gens within one's own village and other villages. Within Peri, if a boy
from the gens Kalat is betrothed to a girl from the gens Matchupal, he
will have to avoid only the women of Matchupal and other own relatives
of his betrothed; she will have to observe like avoidances only towards
Kalat. But if a girl of Matchupal gens is betrothed to a boy from Patusi,
then she avoids, not only the gens of her betrothed, but all Patusi. This
behavior seems to flow from the fact that it is difficult to follow gentile

---

[1] See Fortune, *l.c.*, Chapter V, Subsection 7.

membership or relationship in another village and it is a safer rule for a girl or boy to dive under a mat whenever a canoe from the forbidden village hails in sight. Within one's own village, on the other hand, where every individual is known, it is possible to make finer distinctions.

THE MANUS VILLAGE

Before discussing the organization of a Manus village, it may be useful to give some picture of its physical aspect. The Manus house is built upon stout piles, driven into the silt bottom of the lagoon. The house is dome-shaped, thatched with sago-leaf thatch from ridge pole to floor, with verandas with overhanging roofs at one or both ends. At either end of the house are landing platforms, some of them well built, others mere crossed sticks. The houses range from thirty to sixty feet in length and fifteen to twenty feet in width. They are arranged in long rows, in an almost exactly parallel formation; however, there seems to be no rule as to the number of rows which a village should comprise, but a feeling for parallel lines prevails throughout. Most of the houses in a row are set within four or five feet of each other; sometimes, but not by any means invariably, two adjacent houses will be connected by a narrow plank. Plank walks of this type had been developed into a regular system in the village of Mok[1]. But in Peri and Patusi, this is a casual, house-to-house type of inter-communication, which does not form any regular thoroughfare throughout the village. All inter-communication between other than adjacent houses (and often even between adjacent houses) is by canoe. At low tide in Peri, it is possible to walk about some parts of the village but not about other parts, which makes inter-communication at these periods difficult.

Although the Manus village is laid out in water, it relies upon a certain amount of land for social and industrial purposes. Sometimes it is located near enough to the shore so that the beach can be utilized for feasts, canoe building, etc., but in Mok, where the village is built adjacent to an uninhabited island of some size, with a long shallow shelf along the shore at the foot of the precipitous central part, the Mok people nevertheless have been at pains to build a rubble platform (*arakeu*) which is so new that it still bears the marks of recent construction.[2] It therefore seems safe to infer that the construction of these

---

[1]This was probably due to the fact that the village of Mok lay so close to the shore of a small island that the village must have been frequently dry and unnavigable at low tide.

[2]These platforms are built up with coral rubble, and were originally kept in place by a series of stakes set at intervals in the muddy bottom of the lagoon. Leaves, bits of wood, bark, the refuse from canoe building and fish-trap making, old pieces of trees which have been used in the dances, etc., are then expressly piled or allowed to accumulate on top of this groundwork of coral rubble. The people understand very clearly that such materials will eventually rot and make a top soil. The *arekeus* in Peri are of such different ages, that one of them boasts a whole grove of palm trees, while another has a single decrepit tree, and two others several trees of varying ages.

earthen platforms is an integral part of the village plan, as it practically survives any real need. The recent shift in village situation of Patusi has necessitated leaving the shore, where a beach served the purposes of a platform, and moving out to sea, where there are old platforms, with trees upon them, which will again be useful. Similarly, a former site of Peri, near the land, would have been more accessible to the land than to its *arakeus;* but a comparison of the age of house posts at the old house sites and the trees on the *arakeus* leaves no doubt that the *arakeus* are older and that the Peri site must have been moved in shore and out again at least once and probably many times. Old as are the *arakeus,* the villagers still maintain a constructive attitude towards them; at high tide, part of the supporting rubble tends to wash away and the women go out with small canoes and fill the interstices with the dislodged stones which they replace on the *arakeu,* at the same time clearing out near the *arakeus* the channels which have become choked.

Arakeus are used for all purposes for which a large flat floor is needed; for building canoes, making the fish trap fences which must be laid down over a length of twenty-five to thirty feet; for firing pots or firing tortoise shell to make *kopkops,*[1] for feeding pigs, for setting out pots of sago or bowls of food for feasts, for erecting the lines upon which strings of shell money and dogs' teeth are hung up at affinal exchanges, and for erecting the long carved dancing poles. Upon the occasions of very large feasts, when a tremendous amount of sago is displayed in an affinal exchange, there are villages with *arakeus* which are insufficient and then temporary piers have to be built out into the lagoon. This was done at Taui while we were in Peri.

The ceremonial use of the small precipitous islets which dot the lagoon is also a well integrated aspect of Manus life. These little islands are densely covered with a stunted type of foliage and have practically no level surfaces. Here are localized the ancestral spirits of each gens; to their shores are brought individuals who are to be released from periods of segregation and the ceremony of release is accompanied by throwing a handful of food against the shore. Similarly the bones of the fish which an adolescent girl has eaten during her puberty segregation are placed on her gentile island. The dead are also laid upon more distant islands; this follows a desire to remove them from the close proximity of the village, rather than gentile lines. In the village of Peri there is some further specialization of island sites; one of them is regarded as a woman's island, here the little girls may dance without their grass skirts, and here

---

[1] The breast ornaments of *Tridacna* shell discs with tortoise shell filigree work superimposed.

women go to dry leaves which are to be used for making mats and grass skirts. The lee side of a further island is used as a latrine by the men.

A further use for the islets is as a place where canoes may be placed in drydock. Some slight outcrops towards Patusi which it is now impossible to define as either *arakeu* or islet, and which are said to have belonged either to departed gentes or to Patusi gentes when Patusi was located nearer to Peri, are also used in this way. There are only four *arakeus* in Peri and their allocation is peculiar; two belong to the gens Pere, one to the gens of Pontchal, which is an offshoot of Pere, and which may possibly have taken unto itself an *arakeu* which was the property of a former gens, or else may have appropriated an *arakeu* which belonged to its parent gens of Pere. The fourth *arakeu* is now heavily dotted with palm trees and is used by the men of the entire village as a shipyard and a sort of adult men's club. This *arakeu* formerly belonged to the gens of Lo, but with the departure of the ranking members of that gens, close ownership seems to have lapsed.

A gens asserts its right over an *arakeu* by building the house of its ranking member adjacent to it. This is, strictly speaking, only the privilege of those families who claim the rank of *lapan*.

Ghosts who have been evicted from the houses of their descendants by having their skulls thrown into the sea tend to haunt the edges of the *arakeus* and islets. The Manus have particularly definite feelings of awe towards the trees on the islets. It is at the edge of the gentile islet that all the invocations to the ancestral lines of spirits are pronounced; these words are believed to linger in the trees which, therefore, become invested with a peculiarly sacred character. The scraggly trees on the *arakeus* are feared on another count, because they are inhabited by tree spirits. However, tree spirits, as something belonging to the land, are not regarded very seriously.

The Manus make a genuine distinction between the land which is inhabited by alien peoples and the fresh water which collects in pools or runs in streams on those alien lands, and their own little islets and *arakeus* in the lagoon. If a Manus falls to the ground, on alien land, some of the earth and some of the leaves and other rubbish which lay upon the spot where he fell must be gathered up carefully and brought home with him—otherwise part of his soul will remain on the alien land. No such precautions are necessary, however, when a child falls upon the friendly *arakeu* or village islet. The fresh water of foreign lands is equally dangerous. If one looks into it, one's soul remains there. But puddles of rain on the *arakeu* hold no such traps for the unwary.

The open spaces between the rows of houses, although usually conceived of as part of the village and so, friendly, may, if there is sickness
and unfriendly ghosts are believed to be abroad, assume the hostile,
ambiguous character of the open sea or the empty lagoon stretches
between villages, which are known as "the middle spaces." These middle
spaces are inhabited by vague, partially depersonalized ghosts who have
lost wards and shelter and are conceived of as indiscriminately inimical.
In ordinary times the Manus do not take these shadowy inhabitants of
their waterways very seriously; they think very little of night journeys,
or solitary long expeditions from one village to another. But in times of
fear, a traveler will prepare for a journey by painting his face with
protective paint against the "spirits of the middle spaces," and canoes
may make detours within the village itself, because a certain part of the
watery stretches between house rows may be temporarily conceived as
dangerous.

The water underneath a house is regarded as a part of the property
of that house. It would be unlicensed prying for a man to walk, as is
possible at low tide, beneath the house of another. A child who picks up
a banana floating several yards from a house will be branded as a thief,
unless a round of the neighboring houses is first made to see if ownership
is claimed.

Ordinarily, the village is a unit, except to those who have avoidance
relatives in one section of it. A quarrel, a serious charge that the ghosts
of one gens have been responsible for a death in another gens, an accusation of sin between a boy of one gens and a girl of another, an elopment
of a widow—events of this sort may lead to a temporary development of
a strong sense of locality which may even spread to the children as one
small part of the village huddles in upon itself in rage, chagrin, or fear.

Former residents of other villages who come to live in a new village,
will be spoken of in terms of their old village, Moen Taui, Moen Mbuke.
The prefix Moen meaning "man of" or "sir" serves to select out from a
large number, anyone towards whom one stands in a definite, and usually
pleasant relationship. So, the Manus will say of a canoe load of Mbuke
people, "*ala* Mbuke" "they of Mbuke," but of a Mbuke friend or a
Mbuke man resident in Peri they will say "*Moen* Mbuke."

According to accounts received, the village acted as a unit in serious
warfare, although raiding parties to obtain a human body for the termina-
tion of first mourning, or for the release of a man from a vow taken when
he assumed the peculiar neck ornament of human hair, or raids to obtain
a prostitute for the men's house, were sometimes carried out by a few of

the young men only. In the retaliatory measures which followed these raids the whole village was likely to be involved under the leadership of the *luluai*, the hereditary war leader.

RANK

The Manus preserve marked traces of rank which, however, is not functionally stressed in the society. There are two groups: *lapan*, or those of noble blood, and *lau*, commoners. There is the *lapan* family in each old village which furnishes a *luluai*, hereditary war leader. (The village of Tchalalo, a new and very small village had no *luluai*). There is no correlation between gens and rank except that the gens which furnishes the *luluai* gains a little prestige thereby. In the village of Peri there were two gentes which numbered no *lapan* among them. Pere gens, the gens of the *luluai*, which gave its name to the village, contained both *lau* and *lapan* families as well as the family from which the *luluai* came. There is reason to believe that claims to *lapan* blood which cannot be supported by conspicuous affinal exchange lapse and that rich *lau* in a few generations come to be regarded as *lapan*. There is the saying that "if a *lau* man is strong he will purchase for his son a *pilapan*[1], a female *lapan*".

In Peri were two brothers whose father was a *lapan* of Taui. The father died and the brothers were both adopted, the younger by a *lapan* and the elder by a *lau*. The younger brother had a son, who was adopted by the elder. Subsequently, the younger brother had a daughter. Now he dresses his daughter in the distinctive costume of a *lapan*, but his elder brother does not so dress his adopted son. The shadow of his *lau* adoption and his own modest economic position deters the elder brother from making any claims to *lapan*ship, even for his adopted son whose blood father is acknowledged to be a *lapan*.

PRIVILEGES OF PERI LAPAN

To build a house near the *arakeu* of the gens.

To hang *ovalis* shells, which are called *mana*,[2] on their belts, their houses, and their canoes.

To string one hundred dogs' teeth on a string in an affinal exchange.

To wear a string of dogs' teeth transversely across the breast.

To build a large house.[3]

To eat from wooden bowls while *lau* were supposed to eat only from the cruder paraminium gum covered basketry.

---

[1] On the island of Lou the *pilapan* is the daughter of the *luluai* and seems to hold a slightly honorable position in the regard of the whole community.

[2] Compare *mana* of Polynesian chiefs. Manus *ta-mana*, literally to make or put *mana* refers to the dance in which the participants wear *ovalis* shells as a phallic ornament.

[3] House size is reckoned in terms of number of piles. Compare Samoa where the highest chief builds a house with the largest number of cross beams.

It is probable that there are additional local *lapan* privileges in other villages. The *luluai* has the right to build a larger house than any other *lapan* and to build it next to the best *arakeu*. And there is a prohibition against drinking water which falls off the roof of the *luluai's* house. In the light of the distribution of taboos regarding anything which has been over the head of a chief, this slight prohibition is probably important. The *luluai* keeps a bundle of sticks or a frame into which sticks are thrust which is a record of every man killed in war by any member of the community. He is permitted to boast of this collection of sticks as other men vaunt their individual exploits.   According to the accounts which we received, the feast called *tchinal* is only given by a *luluai*, but Parkinson[1] states that this feast was formerly celebrated with one for the skull of the dead. This suggests that the feast for the skull of the dead *luluai* may have once been the occasion of a *tchinal* feast and possibly a community homage to the skull and Sir Ghost of the *luluai*. But we found no present custom to confirm this. In civil affairs the *luluai* had no power beyond that inspired by wealth and personal authority. A small boy could be impertinent to him with impunity in peace time.

It is possible that the feast for hair cutting for a boy, *kan tchinitchini poenpalan*, and the second late marriage payment, *metcha*, were once privileges of a *lapan*. But today anyone who makes these feasts is so rich that there seems a fair chance of his descendants being classed as *lapan*. However, a *lau* who makes a *metcha* must ask permission to use an *arakeu* from the ghosts of former *lapans* of that *arakeu*. The people said of one man, Pomat, in Peri, "His father was a *lapan*, but he is nothing at all. He is just a *lau* of Mbosai." In other words, he is a man of no wealth, no economic initiative nor distinction, who serves Mbosai. Mbosai was a rich man, his mother was a *lapan*, his father a very insignificant *lau*. But he built a large house in his mother's brother's place, and with his wealth was able to validate a slight claim through his mother, while Pomat, a waster, was no longer accorded any recognition of his position as his father's son.

The most important use of rank is in quarrels; here a *lapan* can always score verbally over a *lau*.

There is a tendency to use the term *lau* to mean economic dependents, applied indiscriminately to younger brothers, younger sons, etc., but technically, every son of a *lapan* is a *lapan*. This suggests that in the formal ideology there was some suggestion of mutual obligation between *lapan* and *lau*, which survives in this use of the word, *lau*.

---

[1]Parkinson, *o.c.*, 404–406.

As rank, with the exception of the *luluai*ship, is non-functioning in Manus, and does not even, like the kinship system, provide a pattern for new and anomalous activities, it gives every evidence of being a survival of an institution analogous to those found in other Oceanic societies, but which is of little real importance in Manus culture.

The Gens[1]

The Manus gens is patrilineal, localized, limited in most cases to one village. It is exogamous and there are gentile taboos, but no indications of totemism. There are no legends of gentile origin beyond recent history comments upon the breakdown of a particular gens, or its division into several different gentes. Nor is there a word for *gens* in the language. The question of gentile membership is merely, "To what do you belong"? There is a term *sowal* which is sometimes used descriptively for gens. Its literal meaning is "side," as "north side"; as a social simile its more exact meaning is "parties to one side of an affinal exchange," which always involves more than one gens. The people of Balowan and Lou translate the concept gens into pidgin English as "*liklik* (small) place belong me," in contradistinction to "place belong me" which is merely village. Although the Manus do not respond as readily to questions of this sort, they too seem to connect the gentile concept with a subdivison of space. As the subdivision is merely a part of the lagoon, not jealously bounded and guarded as a land site would be, it has not come to the attention of government and there has been no need to translate the concept, which is without a term in Manus, into pidgin English. It is significant, however, that neither has it seemed necessary to use the term in inter-tribal contacts in which pidgin English is used extensively.

As the gentes are so local, they can be discussed best in terms of concrete instances. Below I give a table of the Peri gentes and the number of adult males in each.

The Manus apply kinship terms to all members of their own gens on the supposition that all are closely related as descendants from a recent common ancestor. When the gens is large and has become subdivided into several smaller groups who act more or less independently of one another under different leadership, there is a tendency to use kinship terms only within this smaller group, although terms for members of the other groups within the gens can be supplied on request. To understand

---

[1]In *Growing up in New Guinea* I used the more familiar term *clan* to describe the patrilineal unilateral grouping in Manus, but here I shall adhere to the more technical Americanist usage which reserves the term clan for matrilineal unilateral organization only.

the composition of a gens, it is necessary to bear in mind that there are
roughly three economic classes in Manus: the rich *entrepreneurs,* their
dependents who are men whose marriages the entrepreneurs have financed
and who work for their financial backers, and a class of poor middle-aged
men who neither coöperate with some leader, nor engage in affinal
exchanges on a large scale on their own account. This last group I have
called *independents.* About each entrepreneur is formed an economic
constellation consisting of his dependents and a few independents who
contribute slightly to the affinal exchanges which the leader is financing.
The entrepreneurs assume the responsibility of initiating and supervising
the affinal exchanges of their dependents; their dependents in turn fish
and trade for them. As the reward of his organizing and foresight, an
entrepreneur receives freedom from daily fishing in middle age and the
prestige of a man of large affairs. The poor independents, on the other
hand, must fish from day to day to provide their households with food
and other necessities.

In the following table of membership of Peri gentes, economic status
and coöperation is indicated.

TABLE OF PERI GENS MEMBERSHIP[1]

PERE GENS

This was the leading gens in Peri village. It contained the family of the *luluai,*
and several other *lapan* families. It owned two *arakeus.*

Korotan, retiring *luluai*

Talikai, half-brother of Korotan, just entering on prerogatives of *luluai,* a
    leader

Ngamel, a *lapan* of a different family line, a leader

Pwisieu, adopted brother of Ngamel, as his own gens, Tchokanai was
    extinct in Peri, a leader

Paliau, *lapan* of a third family line, a leader

Tunu, younger foster brother of Paliau, and a dependent of his

Ndrosal, younger brother of Talikai, a dependent of his, partially

Talikawa, younger brother of Talikai, a dependent of his

Bonyalo, a *lau,* a dependent of Paliau

Tcholai, adopted son and heir of Korotan

Saot, son of the father of Tunu, dependent of Ngamel and Pwisieu

Acting with Pere gens, but not yet reckoned of it:—

    The two brothers of Pwisieu's Patusi wife, who fled from Patusi and came
    to live with Pwisieu. Both unmarried

[1]This table will be found to differ in a few respects from that included in Appendix V of *Growing up in New Guinea.* The latter was provided as a framework against which the children's comments might be understood. Only one gentile affiliation, that which was popularly attributed to him by the community, was given for each householder. Young men who were away at work at the time the children's comments were collected, or during our entire stay, were omitted. For a detailed consideration of gentile affiliations it is necessary, however, to recognize that one man may act with as many as three gentes: it is also desirable to include the young men away at work in the estimate of relative gentile strengths.

Kala, a middle-aged unimportant man of Kamatatchau (a practically extinct Peri gens) who lived in the rear of Talikawa's house

Polin, son of a Peri mother and a Rambutchon father, who coöperates with Talikai and also with Talikai's brother-in-law, Kemwai, of Lo

PONTCHAL GENS

This gens is said to have split off from Pere gens about three generations ago. The split is not complete as members of each gens still sometimes use kinship terms appropriate within a gens, to one another. Has one small *arakeu*. Since the official[1] split of the village of Peri into two administrative units, Peri and Pontchal,—owing to the younger men of Pontchal abducting the daughter of a trade partner of Korotan, *luluai* of Peri—the gens of Pontchal considers itself as the chief gens of a new village unit. The artificial break in the village unity did not entail any change in house sites.

Pokanau, a *lapan*, but poor and unenterprising

Pataliyan, a native of Nauna (a Matankor island), taken captive as a child by Pokanau's grandfather and brought up as a member of the family, a widower

Ndropal, an unimportant man with a half-Usiai wife, independent

Selan, the son of a Taui father who had been adopted by a *lapan* of Pontchal. Selan acts sometimes with Pontchal, sometimes with Matchupal and sometimes with his elder brother, Ngandiliu, who belongs to Lo, a leader

Kalowin, the son of a Lo mother, now domiciled in the house of Nane of Lo, and acting, unimportantly, with Lo. His father had been Pontchal

Nganidrai, the son of Kalowin, married to the daughter of Pope of Lo, resident in Pope's house. Unimportant, acts with Lo when he acts at all

Kampwen, an unimportant man

MATCHUPAL GENS

This gens is said to be a remnant of a much larger gens, most of whose members fled to Mok about three or four generations ago. It is at present in a particularly impoverished condition as eleven adult members died in the influenza epidemic of 1918.

Mbosai, the most prominent man in Matchupal, a *lapan* through his Matchupal mother, had built his house in his mother's brother's place and acted partly with Matchupal and partly with Kalat, his father's gens

Pomat, the unimportant son of a *lapan* father, a dependent of Mbosai's

Tchaumutchin, a sturdy, unenterprising man, coöperates with Paliau of Pere

Pomalat, heir of a *lapan*, but unimportant himself

Luwil, sister's son of a Matchupal *lapan*, but dependent of Paliau, his foster brother, of Pere

Topas, acts with Mbosai for either Matchupal or Kalat, as his mother belongs to Kalat

Polau, father's elder brother's son of Topas, a dependent of Topas, lives in the back of his house

---

[1]For governmental purposes.

Pope, mother belonged to Lo, his marriage was financed by Lo, but the
    funeral ceremonies for his wife were performed by Pondramet of
    Matchupal
Pondramet, an insignificant man who married an ex-prostitute
Pomo, his mother had belonged to Matchupal, husband of Pondramet's
    daughter, insignificant
Poiyo, a middle-aged, independent man, with two wives
Samal, son of Mbosai, away at work

KALO GENS

This gens, very small itself, is in process of absorbing the surviving members of
three other gentes.
    Tuain, *lau*, but head of the gens
    Ngamasue, stupid ortho-cousin of Tuain, acts with him
    Songan, an old widower
    Manawei, just returned from work, married
Acting with Kalo:—
    Pokanas, a substantial man with a clever Pere wife, himself a member of the
        vanishing gens of Lopwer
    Poli, unimportant member of Lopwer. (The mother of Tuain belonged to
        Lopwer and formed the link with Pokanas and Poli)
    Kea, unimportant survivor of Kamatatchau gens
    Malean, only survivor of Kapet gens, a young, just married dependent of
        Pokanas
    Sali, younger brother of Tuain, unmarried, just returned from work
    Ndroi, younger brother of Ngamasue, away at work, unmarried

LO GENS

This gens is the remainder of a split in which all the *lapan* left Peri and founded
a separate village of Tchalalo.
    Kemwai, head of the gens, a *lau*, who has completed the feasts of a *lapan*
    Nane, parallel cousin of Kemwai, a *lau* who has completed the feasts of a
        lapan
    Kali, widowed old father of Nane
    Ngandiliu, son of a Taui father, whose mother married Kali. He was
        adopted by Kali and usually acts with Lo, but sometimes with his
        younger brother Selan of Pontchal
    Pomele, son of a Lo mother, acts with Lo part of the time, but more often
        with Paliau of Pere, his wife's older sister's husband
Acting with Lo:—
    Kalowin, who now lives in Nane's house
    Nganidrai, son of Kalowin, son-in-law of Pope
    Pope, a useless widower, son of a Lo mother
    Polin, sister's son of Kemwai's wife, really belonging to Rambutchon, acts
        also with Talikai, Kemwai's Pere brother-in-law

KALAT GENS

Tchanan, *lapan* and leader of Kalat, to which his mother belonged
Sanau, acts with Tchanan
The three sons of Polyon, dead mother's brother of Tchanan, all away at
    work
Acting with Kalat:—
    Mbosai
    Moen Taui, a Taui man, husband of a Kalat woman, resident in Kalat
    Nyapo, a native of Loitcha village, resident in Peri, husband of a Kalat
        woman
Not assimilated to any gens were two old men from Patusi, who lived in the
houses of their wives' relatives, one young man from Patusi who lived in the house of
his mother, and one young man of Loitcha who lived in the house of his wife's brother.

From this table certain points will be immediately apparent; the
gens of Pere, which is the ranking gens of the village, as it contains the
largest number of *lapan*, the family line which furnishes the *luluai*, and
owns two of the four *arakeus*, is also, by far, the most numerous, and the
one within which it is hardest to trace actual blood relationships. From
this gens there has been one historical split-off, four generations ago,
into the present gens of Pontchal. At present there are three distinct
factions within the gens Pere, led by Talikai, Ngamel, and Paliau;
these operate almost like sub-gentes, and it is possible that they may at
any time break off from the parent stem. The lack of cohesion in a
Manus gens of any size, coupled with the small number and actual blood
relationship of members of most gentes, leads to the suspicion that this
had been of frequent occurrence. It is possible that Pere is so much
larger and more unwieldly than the other gentes for the same causes which
obtain in Polynesia, where chiefs tend to have more *soi-disant* relatives than do unimportant people. The list also reveals the fact that
three gentes are in process of disappearance, Lopwer, Kapet, and
Kamatatchau.

A glance at the present house groundplan[1] (Fig. 2) reveals that while
there is a tendency to localization of house sites, this is not by any means
adhered to carefully. In popular conception, the village is allocated
between gentes according to the plan in Fig. 3, with the provenience of
the disappearing gentes no longer present in the popular mind. This
localization is indicated by a jerk of the head when *"ala Kalo"* or *"ala
Kalat"* ("they of Kalo" or "they of Kalat") are mentioned collectively,
a gesture which tends to ignore the presence of scattered members of
these gentes in inappropriate living quarters.

---

[1]As Manus houses are all rectangular, and arranged in rows, there seems little profit in inserting a
map containing little squares rather than numbers here. Photographic impressions of the village may
be obtained from the illustrations in *Growing Up In New Guinea*. The purpose of this plan is to present
structure, not pictorial setting.

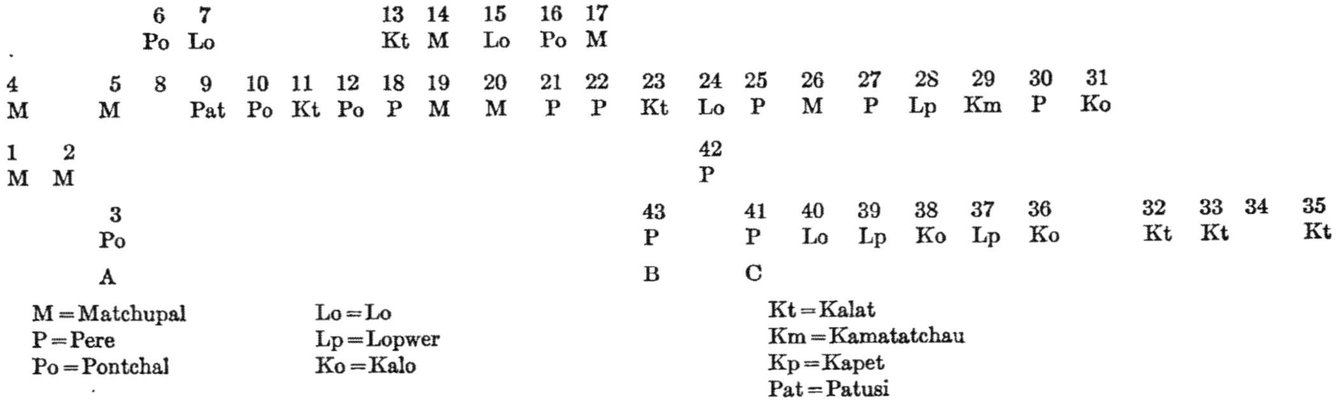

Fig. 2. Diagram of the Village showing House Ownership, Gentile Membership, and Residence

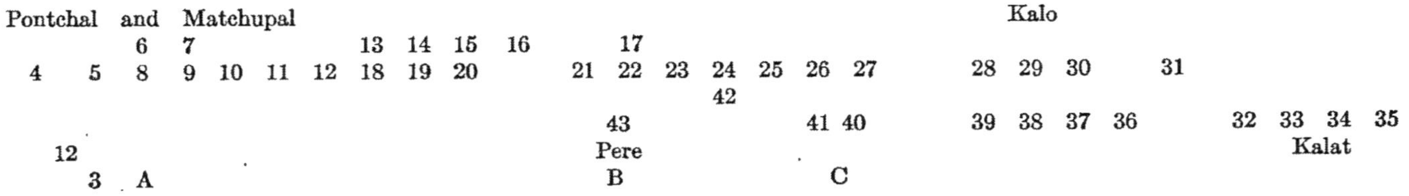

```
                              6   7
                              Po  Lo
                              13  14  15  16  17
                              Kt  M   Lo  Po  M
      5                                                     23  24  25  26  27  28  29  30  31
      M                                                     Kt  Lo  P   M   P   Lp  Km  P   Ko
1  2                                                                                              32  33  34  35
M  M                                                                                              Kt  Kt      Kt
      4      8   9   10  11  12  18  19  20  21  22
      M      Pat Po  Kt  Po  P   P   M   M   P   P
                        3                                   42
                        Po                                  P
                                                            43      41  40  39  38  37  36
      A                                                     P       P   Lo  Lp  Ko  Lp  Ko

                                                            B
                                                            C
```

M = Matchupal   Lo = Lo   Kt = Kalat
P = Pere   Lp = Lopwer   Km = Kamatatchau
Po = Pontchal   Ko = Kalo   Kp = Kapet
                                        Pat = Patusi

Fig. 3. Diagram of the Village of Peri as its Inhabitants conceptualize the Localization of Gentes within the Village.

```
Pontchal  and  Matchupal
                          6   7
                          13  14  15  16  17
      5   8   9   10  11  12  18  19  20                    Kalo
4                                                           28  29  30  31
1  2                                                        32  33  34  35
      3   A                                                     Kalat
      12                                                    39  38  37  36
                                                            41  40
                                        43                      C
                                        Pere
                                        B
                          21  22  23  24  25  26  27
                                          42
```

A. Pontchal Arakeu Barrack (our residence for two months).
B. Pere Arakeu (our house site).
C. Pere Arakeu.

211

Fig. 4 is a diagrammatic representation of a Matankor village on the island of Lou which shows strict and undeviating localization of house site and men's house for each gens. It is possible that the Manus village is a rough and never complete attempt to approximate a plan in which in

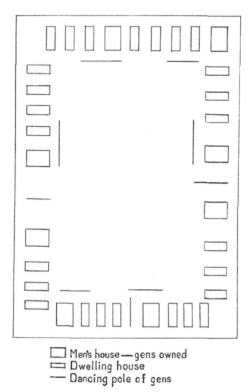

☐ Men's house — gens owned
⊏⊐ Dwelling house
— Dancing pole of gens

Fig. 4. Diagrammatic Representation of a Matankor Village on the Island of Lou, showing Formal Arrangement of House Sites, Gentile Men's Houses, and Gentile Dancing Poles.

each gens there would be both *lapan* and *lau*, the house of the principal *lapan* would be built adjacent to an *arakeu* which would be gentile property and correspond to the sections of village green which lie in front of the house sites in a Lou village, while each gens would have its men's house, built exclusively for the young men of that gens. In actual

House No.	House Owner	Gens	Head Subsidiary Household	Gens
1	Pomalat	Matchupal		
2	Topas	Matchupal	Polau	Matchupal
3	Pokanau	Pontchal		
4	Luwil	Matchupal	Saot	Pere
5	Tchaumutchin	Matchupal		
6	Ndropal	Pontchal		
7	Ngandiliu	Lo	Ndrauga	Patusi
8	(Deserted. Temporarily occupied by one of Poiyo's wives)			
9	Maku	Patusi		
10	Kampwen	Pontchal		
11	Ngapo	Loitcha, acts with Kalat		
12	Selan	Pontchal		
13	Ngamoto (a widow)	Kalat	Pongi	Patusi
14	Pope	Matchupal and Lo	Nganidrai	Pontchal and Lo
15	Pomele	Lo		
16	Kalowin	Pontchal (removed to 24, acting with Lo)		
17	Poiyo	Matchupal (another wife of No. 8)		
18	Tunu	Pere		
19	Mbosai	Matchupal and Kalat		
20	Pomat	Matchupal		
21	Pwisieu	Pere (two unmarried brothers of wife)		Patusi
22	Paliau	Pere		
23	Ngapatchalon (widow)	Kalat		
24	Nane	Lo (Kalowin now lives in rear of his house)		Pontchal
25	Bonyalo	Pere		
26	Pondramet	Matchupal	Pomo	Matchupal
27	Ndrosal	Pere (gens sister's husband, Sisi)		Loitcha
28	Pokanas	Lopwer	Malean	Kapet
29	Kea	Kamatatchau		
30	Talikawa	Pere	Kala	Kamatatchau
31	Young men's house belonging to the gens of Kalo			
32	Tchanan	Kalat		
33	Nyapolyon (widow)		Moen Taui	Taui
34	Small girls play house belonging to Kalat			
35	Sanau	Kalat		
36	Tuain	Kalo		
37	Poli	Lopwer	Manawai	Kalo
38	Ngamasue	Kalo		
39	Ndrantche (widow)	Lopwer	Sali	Kalo
40	Kemwai	Lo	Polin	Rambutchon
41	Talikai	Pere		
42	Korotan	Pere	Tcholai	Pere
43	Ngamel	Pere		

practice, possibly because of the difficulties of obtaining materials and building in the sea, the arduous labor of constructing *arakeus*, and certainly because of the tendency to build as few men's houses as possible (Peri has only one, which belongs to Kalo gens), and the habit of moving houses at a death, which could not be followed under the Lou system with any such freedom, no Manus village conforms to any such perfect plan.

Members of a gens are spoken of as *ato*[1] *ndriasi*, "they brothers," and where more minute inquiries are made regarding relationship, unless it is very close, the inquiry will be dismissed with "*aru pati Kalat,*" "they two, belong to Kalat," which implies merely gentile relationship.

Gentile taboos (*nambu* –*n*) are of very slight importance and of the greatest variety; e.g., to the gens of Matchupal it was forbidden to spill red sago on the threshold of the house; members of Pere gens were not permitted to burn coconut shells in their house fires, and the members of the gens of Kamatatchau were forbidden to rescue a pig which escaped from a canoe on the way to a feast.

Because the distinction between patrilineal family lines and gentes is so shifting, some gentes shrinking into single lines, other gentes breaking up into family lines, various types of taboos which originally descended in family lines may come to be regarded as gens-wide. These include tabooed fish which descend in patrilineal family lines and are spoken of as "the taboo which belongs to the house"[2] and taboos associated with canoe-building charms which originally pass from owner to owner either through descent or purchase. Also omen birds (*kendrol*) or omen fish which are primarily family property, even passing from one family to another as part of an affinal exchange, may sometimes come to be regarded as gentile property. This was true of the *kendrol* which Pokanau's great-grandmother had brought as part of her dowry from Mbunei, in the days when the ancestors of the present gens of Pontchal were members of Pere gens. But today this *kendrol* is spoken of as belonging to all Pontchal. Similarly, a taboo against the *pwitch* fish, originally merely a family taboo of a member of Kalo gens, was extended through a series of unfortunate happenings with which it was believed to be connected, to all of Kalo gens, then to all members of the village of Peri, and finally to include Patusi village also. In this case, eating the *pwitch* fish was believed to give offense to a powerful, recently translated ghost, named Popwitch.

---

[1]Collective reference to a group of relatives who are classified together is always preceded idiomatically by the trial third person *ato* regardless of the number mentioned. In speeches, the terms *ato yayen, ato mambun, ato ngasin,* they, the mothers, they, the grandfathers, they, the maternal grandmothers, etc., continually recur. *Ato* indicates a more restricted plural than does *ala*.

[2]A woman will speak of a child by a previous husband as belonging to "another house."

None of these taboos plays an important part in Manus life. The average adult can only name the taboo of two or three gentes besides his own. These taboos are primarily a *pis aller* for mediums and diviners who cannot or do not wish to find an explanation of illness in some moral lapse. The slightness of their importance in present-day Manus—not to be in any way attributed to white influence, but merely to the preponderant importance of the spiritistic cult—may be realized from the following facts. During six months, gentile taboos were mentioned three times, except in response to direct questions, which only too often received equivocal and doubtful answers. The circumstances were these:—

A Matchupal medium holding a seance in a Matchupal house wished to counter the charge that all Matchupal had died because of sex offenses—which was the current village view. (Actually almost all of Matchupal had been killed by the 1918 influenza epidemic). She affirmed, with considerable hesitation, as she knew that she would not be believed, that Matchupal had died out, not from sex offenses, but because they had broken the taboo against spilling red sago on the threshold. Nobody paid any attention to this lame excuse.

Our orphan school boy interpreter, Bonyalo, was taken ill with fever. He had very little allegiance to the life of the village from which he had been absent for many years. He was too young to be suspected of any sex offense of importance and one medium after another refused to take the case—which often happens when there seems no reason for illness or where the case is a particularly ticklish one. Finally, Selan, the only male medium in the village and an obliging assistant of Paliau, Bonyalo's brother-in-law and financial backer, held a seance and declared that Bonyalo was ill because, while absent in another village, he had gone fishing and built a fire with some wood which was a taboo of his Mbuke father's. This explanation was obviously a pure *tour de force.* Bonyalo himself had never been taught which wood was taboo to him.

The third instance occurred as a cause of a quarrel between a husband and wife who had been on the verge of a quarrel for weeks. Finally, the husband accused his wife of having served him with a crab which was his gentile taboo and which she had knowingly included in his evening meal, and made this an occasion for throwing lime in her eyes. But there was no further mention of the matter, nor did the husband suffer any untoward consequences from breaking his taboo.

These taboos in Manus must certainly be regarded as vestigial, practically functionless, except in their rare use as alibis. The people of Balowan and Lou, however, preserve a far more careful record of their inherited prohibitions, so that the inference that they are decayed in Manus is made that much more plausible. Mr. Fortune has shown in detail how the Manus retain magical explanation of illness or misfortune only as alibis so that the moral system enforced by the spirits may not be put to undue strain. The same thing is true, and to a far greater extent, of the taboos.

Three of the Peri gentes were named after fishing devices, *Kapet*, "net," *Lo*, a coconut leaf fish barrier, *Kalo*, a bamboo walled fish trap. Additionally, *Kalat* is probably the same word as *Karat*, turtle, as the *l* and *r* are interchangeable between dialects in Manus. This is not a sufficient proportion of gentile names associated with fish or fishing to make a rule, but the probability seems to be that names of fish, crabs, fishing devices, etc., form an alternative to place names which have lost their meaning. Mbuke, the name of a Manus village, means clam shell, which is said to have taken its name from the shape of the protecting island of Mbuke. Additionally, the gens of Pere claimed the *kau*, the two-handled, three-sided two man net, as its own, while the gens of Matchupal claimed the same net with a slight modification of form, called the *laiyo*. Lo claimed a crabbing basket used by women, in which the hand was inserted in an open space at the top, as well as the long leaf-hung fish drag. Pontchal claimed the *Ponopon*, a hand net. Kalat claimed special rights in turtle fishing. The round fish traps belonged to the village of Patusi and only Patusi men, or men with relationships which could be traced to Patusi, made them in Peri.

Examination of the meaning of these fishing device rights revealed, however, that they meant very little. Where it was a question of manufacture, the members of the gens with the hereditary claims were the expert manufacturers, but beyond this, there was little feeling of proprietorship. It was necessary to be able to supply a relationship road by which a special device was used, if challenged. One man gave me, unsolicited, a statement of the way in which he could, if he wished, lay claim to every fishing device in Pere, either through his mother, his wife, or his various brothers-in-law. Gentile claims to use (not always to manufacture) have become a mere matter of form. The custom by which brothers-in-law and cross-cousins are often fishing partners may be related to some more stringent observance of these rights at an earlier time. Brothers-in-law and cross-cousins are accustomed to participation in other exclusive property rights such as sago patches, or canoes.

The gens does not act as an economic unit except upon a few rare occasions which call for quick united action, as in bringing down a log for a canoe, or putting up the house posts for a men's house. But here also the canoe and the men's house are individually owned. It is said: "Pwisieu is building a young men's house for Manawei, his son." But it is also said: "That young men's house is for all the boys of Pere (gens)." In practice the house would be frequented by all the youths of the village, and in practice also most of the members of a village will help in any undertaking requiring many hands and be rewarded for it afterwards. There is only a very slightly greater social obligation upon a gentile relative than upon a village mate to assist in such matters. All participants, however related, are paid for such services.

But the important economic coöperation in Manus is based upon the relationship between the leaders or entrepreneurs and the young or dependent males who are their assistants; these dependents are not necessarily of the same gens as the leader, although this is more often the case. There is no strong supernatural sanction to compel coöperation within a gens, although sometimes a slight illness may be attributed to a failure to participate in the affinal exchanges of a gens relative. But behind the economic constellation of leader and dependents stands the Sir Ghost of the leader, and the Sir Ghosts of the dependents also. The Sir Ghost of the leader may be said to cast a supervisory eye over the behavior of all of his ward's dependents; their own Sir Ghosts will punish their failure to assist their leader as a sin. Furthermore, most of the dependents are young men, whipped with shame because they have not paid for their own wives; this shame serves as an efficient goad towards economic activity and fidelity. Behind gentile coöperation there are no such efficient sanctions.

In practice, if a Kalat man is the chief entrepreneur of an enterprise, other Kalat men, entrepreneurs themselves or poor independents, will tend to participate in the exchange also, as this is the most regular formal entry into the exchange system as a minor participant. But if a Kalat man is an economic dependent of a member of another gens, he is far more likely to meet with public disapproval and ghostly chastisement in his failure towards his leader than for a complete lack of coöperation with his gens. This state of affairs is ultimately righted by the tendency to class a man with the gens of a leader with whom he has coöperated for several years, so that, finally, all men may be found to be coöperating with at least a section of their own gens, because they have been transferred in their own and public feeling, if not in residence, to the gens with which they previously coöperated as a non-member. But the economic constellations, cutting as they do across gentile lines, are the effective groups in Manus, while the gentile unit is rendered lip service, but functions only slightly.

The gens has no absolute claim upon its minor members at any time. They may be adopted by men of their mother's gens, by stepfathers, by other distantly connected persons. Final gentile affiliation is not decided until a man is married, and not always then. So they say of Pope, son of a Matchupal father and a Lo mother. "Lo (that is, a prominent man of Lo) paid for his marriage so he is Lo completely"; yet others still speak of Pope as belonging to Matchupal. Often, especially if a man is financed by his mother's brother, he is said to belong to two gentes, and works now with members of one, now with the other. The gens concept in Manus is the familiar one of birth into a unilateral descent group having a name and a common taboo, all of which are conceived as being related to each other, and upon whom exogamy is enjoined. But because of the freedom of adoption, the importance of financial backing of young men by older men and the reciprocal economic obligations involved, the fluidity of residence and the late age at which gentile membership is decided, and then in other terms than birth, it is more correct to speak of gentile *affiliation* than of gentile membership. If the idea of the gens were to be lost from Manus culture, the actual functioning of the society would not be appreciably altered.

THE KINSHIP SYSTEM

THE KINSHIP TERMINOLOGY

The question of kinship in primitive society may naturally be approached from a number of different angles: from the standpoint of form, from the standpoint of function; from a consideration of the degree to which the formal demands of the system are met or contravened in the behavior of individuals; from a consideration of the way in which the kinship system dictates the behavior of individuals, or is bent to their particular uses; from a comparison with historically or functionally related forms; and from a developmental standpoint which considers the way the kinship categories gradually impinge upon the consciousness and direct the behavior of the growing individuals. However, the organization of the material from any one of these points of view means a neglect of certain detailed aspects of the system. It will therefore be my procedure to present, with a minimum of discussion, the kinship terminology, diagrammatic analyses of structure, and a traditional statement of form. After the working tools for an understanding of the system are thus acquired, the functioning of the system will be treated.

The Manus kinship structure does not present a formally clear picture. In its fundamental emphasis it is bilateral; grandparent and cross-cousin terms are used bilaterally. But it also has those features which have received so much theoretical attention as an aspect of the Crow-Omaha types of kinship terminology (Fig. 5); the classification of whole lineages under one term, regardless of generation. So the father's sister's female descent line are all called *pinpapu*, and the sons and husbands of these women are all called *papu*. In the relationships counted through the father there is the tendency to single out in this way certain lineages for terminological and functional emphasis, while in the relationships counted through the mother there is a greater tendency to emphasize each particular relationship between ego and the person addressed. Furthermore, among the Manus the descendants of brother and sister form a definite, although unnamed, social group which I have called the *Mixed Descent Group* and which is of as great functional importance as the unilateral descent group. A further complication in any attempt to reduce the Manus system to any set of clearly defined principles is the use of parent-child terms between elder and younger siblings of the same sex.

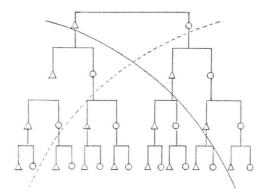

Fig. 5. Diagrammatic Representation of Crow and Omaha Types of Kinship System.

In the following list of terms it will often appear as if there were a confusion between the use of terms in a specific or in a classificatory sense. This confusion is native. Parallel cousins throughout fit into the same categories as siblings, but occasionally such terms will be used when the relationship is less definitely known, i.e., a man will call a woman of his gens *pisio* (sibling opposite sex), and his children will then, if questioned, say she is a *patieyen* (father's sister), but this latter relationship attribution will in most cases be merely a matter of form.

It has become customary to regard native categories of kinship as so alien to our own that the use of our kinship terms to define them has been interdicted. So, the assertion that a certain term means primarily "father" and that when it is applied to members of other generations the native is giving father status to the person so addressed, has been criticized on the ground that the native word does not mean father at all. I feel that, for those Oceanic systems, with the exception of Samoa, with which I have dealt, and for the Twi system which I worked with, and for Omaha, this criticism is not upheld. The natives, in all of these cases make a primary response to words like "father," "mother," "brother," "sister" in terms of the biological, or almost synonymous foster relationships, and will add for those relatives to whom the term is extended "I call him brother," thus making the distinction between one's brother and one whom one calls brother. This does not apply to the term *pinpapu*, father's father's sister and *patieye*, father's sister, for although these first meanings listed are to some extent primary in native thought, the native does think of the members of the father's father's sister's female descent line and similarly of the members of the father's sister's female descent line, as a group to all of whom one term applies. But this is *not* the case in Manus usage for the terms the primary meaning of which is "father," "mother," "grandfather," "mother's brother-sister's child," "sibling of opposite sex," and "cross-cousin of the same sex." Here the native distinguishes clearly between "my mother" and "a mother of mine," that is "one to whom I apply the term *mother*." So of a man's own or foster mother, one will say *yayem*, "mother second personal singular possessive suffix *m*," but of other women called mother, by extension, one will say: "*amo yayem e oi*" a mother—*m* of yours."

LIST OF KINSHIP TERMS[1]

In the following list of terms it will be noted that while some terms may be described as bilateral, others as unilateral, bilateral terms have been employed to make special unilateral points. The bilateral terms are *polapol*, cross-cousin, male, *pinpolapol*, cross-cousin, female, *pisio*, the term for all members of the opposite sex of own generation who are not singled out for unilateral emphasis, that is, sibling of opposite sex, parallel-cousin and one type of cross-cousin; father's sister's son w.s. and mother's brother's daughter m.s.; and *mambu*, grandparent (excluding mother's mother) reciprocal *mangambu*. Terms used unilaterally in reference to the father's line alone are *pinpapu*, father's father's sister and her female descent line, *patieye* (reciprocal *papu*, father's sister and her female descent line, reciprocal *nebonitu*, brother's son, and *asaun*, brother's daughter. Terms used unilaterally in reference to the mother's line are *ngasi*, mother's mother and women of the

---

[1] m.s. = man speaking; w.s. = woman speaking; b.s. = both sexes speaking. If no indication, means both sexes use term thus.

mother's mother's generation, reciprocal *mangambu, yaye*,[1] mother and women classed as of the mother's generation, and its reciprocal, *nat* for males, *ndrakein* for females; and *kakali*, a symmetrical term for mother's brother and sister's children. The terms which show the most confusion between these two types of usage are *mambu*, reciprocal *mangambu*, which is used also as an alternative term for the sons of the women of the father's father's female descent line, and *papu*, with its confused reciprocals, *papu* or *nat* for males addressed and *asaun* for females, which is used for the sons and husbands of the father's father's sister's female descent line.

mambu:	grandfather, paternal grandmother, father's elder brother, mother's mother's brother; alternative (optional: *papu*) term for sons of all women called *pinpapu*, all men whom father calls *papu*
ngasi:	maternal grandmother and her female siblings, mother's elder female siblings; all women whom mother calls *yaye*
pinpapu:	father's father's sister; all her female descendants in the female line; all women whom father calls *patieyen*
papu:	father, father's father's younger brother, elder brother m.s.; elder brother who finances marriage or adopts one w.s.; preferred term for father's father's sister's son; alternative term (optional: *mambu*) for all sons of other *pinpapu;* applied also to all male relatives of father who belong to father's generation; reciprocal of *pinpapu.*
yaye:	mother, mother's mother's younger sister, elder sister w.s.; elder sister who has adopted or financed one (through husband) m.s.; all mother's female relatives of mother's generation
kakali:	mother's brother; sister's son m.s.; sister's daughter m.s.; other male relatives of mother of mother's generation, and reciprocally
patieye:	father's sister; father's sister's daughter m.s.; alternative term for father's mother; father's mother's brother's daughter; all female descendants in the female line of the father's sister m.s.; father's female relatives of father's generation
pisio:	sibling of opposite sex; mother's brother's daughter m.s.; father's sister's son w.s.; parallel cousin of opposite sex; child of opposite sex of father's male cross-cousin and of all men whom father calls *polapol;* child of opposite sex of mother's female cross-cousin and of all women whom mother calls *pinpolapol;* will also be

---

[1] *yaye* also occurs as an affinal term in father's line, wives of father's male contemporaries who are called *papu.*

	applied to relatives of opposite sex and own generation towards whom exact genealogical relationship is not known.
polapol:	cross-cousin m.s.; son of all women called *patieye* (except the children of the paternal grandmother)
pinpolapol·	female cross-cousin w.s.; father's mother's brother's daughter's daughter and father's sister's daughter's daughter w.s.
nat:	son; younger brother m.s.; son of any man called *polapol* m. s.; son of any woman called *pinpolapol* w.s.; son of a parallel cousin of the same sex as speaker and near same age; much younger brother who has been adopted or financed w.s.
asaun:	daughter m.s.; brother's daughter w.s.; younger sister, younger female parallel cousin, and female parallel cousin (of same age), daughter w.s ; daughter of male parallel cousin of same age m.s.; daughter of any male called *pisio* w.s.
ndrakein:	daughter w.s.; also applied descriptively of the young daughters of men or women; primarily a term used by women for their own and their female parallel (or cross) cousin's young daughters
nebonitu:	brother's son w.s.; son of all men called *pisio* w.s.
mangambu:	grandchild, child of anyone called *nat, nrakein, asaun,* or *kakali* (as sister's son m.s.)

Terms of Consanguinity Used Descriptively Only

piloa n:	female sibling of a woman; female parallel cousin; used generally of a group of sisters, or female relatives nearly of an age
ndriasin:	male sibling of same sex, male parallel cousins of the same age, used of a group of brothers, of male relatives nearly of an age
lom kamal:	members of gens of mother of speaker
lom pein:	children of women of own gens

Example of Usage

Aru pisio aru:	They two are siblings of opposite sex
I etepe?	Why?
Yaye-aru, aru piloa aru:	The mothers of these two, they two are sisters
Similarly:	*Papu-aru, ndro amo?*: The father of these two, was one (person)? *E pwen. Pe aru ndriasi aru:* No, but, they are brothers. (i.e., members of the same gens, conceived as parallel cousins)

It is important to note that the Manus thinking proceeds in this order: two men of the same gens are so because they are ortho-cousins, *not* two men are ortho-cousins because they are members of the same gens.

Neither *ndriasi* nor *piloai* are used as terms of address, because in actual relationship parent and child terms are used instead.

Terms of Consanguinity applied to Spouses of Consanguineous Relatives of other Generations

Spouse of males in father's line called *mambu: mambu*
Spouse of males in mother's line called *mambu: ngasi*
Spouses of *kakali: kakali*
Spouse of *patieye: pauaro*
Spouse of *pinpapu: papu*
Spouse of *mangambu: mangambu*
Spouse of males called: *papu yaye*
Spouse of females called: *yaye papu*

Man Speaking

Spouse of *polapol: polapol*

Woman Speaking

Spouse of *pinpolapol: polapol*

Verbal reciprocals are used only when the behavior is identical, or virtually so, i.e., when the relationship is conceived as reciprocal. The use of *kakalin* for mother's brother and sister's son would seem to be an exception to this, but the use of the more common diminutive *kaka* for sister's son as a term of address preserves the status relationship in which respect must be shown to the mother's brother.

Collective Terms[1]

aru piloa aru:	they two are female or parallel cousins of an age
aru ndriasi aru:	they two are male siblings near of an age or (when spoken of the dead) of the same gens and the same generation
aru polapol aru:	they two are male cross-cousins
aru pinpolapol aru:	they two are female cross-cousins
aru pisio aru:	they two are siblings of the opposite sex, or parallel cousins of opposite sex, or mother's brother's daughter and father's sister's son, to one another
aru kakali aru:	they two are mother's brother and sister's son
aru kaiyo aru:	they two are brothers-in-law
aru pinkaiyo aru:	they two are sisters-in-law
aru pauaro aru:	they two are father's sister's husband and wife's brother's son, respectively

Affinal Terms Resulting from Marriages in Ego's Generation

I have given these terms in their primary meaning also. They should be read with the following extensions, *kaiyo*, wife's brother, or anyone whom wife calls *pisio*, sister's husband, or husband of anyone whom ego calls *pisio*, etc.

Man Speaking

Wife: *pati e io* (literally, belonging to me)
Wife's father and much older brother: *papu*
Wife's brother: *kaiyo;* sister's husband: *kaiyo*
Wife's much younger brother: *nat*
Wife's much younger sister: *asaun*

---

[1]These will be understood to apply to the extended relationships also.

Wife's mother and older sister: *pilanasaun*
Wife's older brother's wife: *pimandrean*
Wife's younger brother's wife: *asaun*
Spouses of all those who call wife *patieye: pauaro*
Spouses of all those whom wife calls *nat: asaun*
Spouses of all those whom wife calls *asaun: nat*
Wife of wife's *nebonitu: paluan*

Woman Speaking

Husband: *ya kamal e io* (literally, that man belonging to me)
Husband's mother and husband's much older sister; *pitumbu*
Husband's father and older brother; *timbu*
Husband's sister, brother's wife: *pinkaiyo*
Husband's younger sister's husband: *mandrean*
Husband's much younger brother: *nat*
Husband's much younger sister: *asaun*

Note on Linguistic Usage

The Manus language recognizes two types of possession, inseparable possession and more distant or separable possession. As kinship usage is intimately bound up with linguistic usage, it is necessary to make this point clear before embarking upon a discussion of kinship terms. Inseparable possession is indicated by a series of suffixes to the stem. In indicating separable possession, on the other hand, there is no such inflection, merely the addition of a prepositional phrase.

So *mata*, meaning eye, is inflected as follows:—

	Singular		Dual	Trial	Plural
1.	*mata -i*	Inc.	*mata-iotaru*	*mata-ioto*	*mata-iota*
		Ex.	*mata-ioro*	*mata-ioito*	*mata-ioia*
2.	*mata -m*		*mata-uaru*	*mata-uato*	*mata-aua*
3.	*mata -n*		*mata-aru*	*mata-ato*	*mata-ala*

But to form the same paradigm of *um*, house, *e* is the possessive:—

	Singular		Dual	Trial	Plural
1.	*um e io*	Inc.	*um e iotaru*	*um e ioto*	*um e iota*
		Ex.	*um e ioro*	*um e ioito*	*um e ioia*
2.	*um e oi*		*um e uaru*	*um e uato*	*um e aua*
3.	*um e i*		*um e aru*	*um e ato*	*um e ala*

Even all blood kinship terms do not take the inseparable suffixes.

Table of Kinship Terms Showing Form of Possession Used

Kinship terms in which inseparable possession is always used	Kinship terms in which either form is used	Kinship terms in which separable form is always used
mambu: grandfather, paternal grandmother	*nat* or *natu:* son	*polapol:* cross-cousin m.s.
ngasi: maternal grandmother	*nebonitu:* brother's son w.s.	*pinpolapol:* female cross-cousin w.s.
pau: father	*asali:* daughter m.s.	*asaun:* daughter m.s.

yaye: mother
kakali: mother's brother, sister's son
patieye: father's sister

pisio: sibling opposite sex
ndriasi: brother m.s.
piloa: sister w.s.
mangambu: grandchild

ndrakein: daughter w.s.
kaka: diminutive for sister's son m.s.
pinpapu: father's father's sisters, and their female descendants

Affinal Terms

kaiyo	pati e io
pinkaiyo	ya kamal e io
pitumbu	pilanasaun
palua	pimandrean, pauaro

The inflected form is always used for the term *paluan,* used by a man for his *nebonitu's* wife. The use of this form here is to distinguish it from *palu,* co-wife, which is never inflected.

Other Terms Important in Social Organization which are Inflected

patandrusu: taboo inherited in the female line
nambu: taboo inherited in the male line
ngara: name
molua: soul, used to make the distinction between this, the whole soul of a living person, and *mwelolo,* soul stuff, which is divisible soul stuff
tchamolua: shadow

Terms used in describing Relationships other than Kin and Affinal Relationships

pataran: the chief contracting partner in an exchange in which the speaker is chief on his side, theoretically, cross-cousins whose children are betrothed; in practice, simply those who act as chief financiers, or titular fathers, to the contracted or married couple in whose name the exchange is made
ndrengen: exchanging partner when neither are principals
tchelingen: a term which includes both *pataran* and *ndrengen.* A little more formal than *ndrengen,* implying a longer and more trusted relationship
moenkawas: literally, "man of formal trade" applied to members of other tribes with whom trade is carried on regularly, thus distinguishing a man's trade partner from the casual contacts of the market place. There is a strict rule against marriage or any sex relations between households the heads of which are *moenkawas* to each other. Secondarily a term of address meaning "friend"[1]
pikawas: literally, "women of trade," is used as a term of address between young girls and between unrelated women

---

[1]When the Manus wish to distinguish one of a group to whom they are in general antipathetic they use the prefixes *moen* or *pi* or *pin,* depending upon sex. So *palit* is ghosts, but *moenpalit* is the ghost of a speaker, or of the person addressed or spoken of (in the two latter cases implying a friendly relationship not to the speaker but to the object or subject of his remarks). Any Usiai is simply spoken of as *amo Usiai,* but a particular Usiai who is friendly to some member of one's group is *Moen Usiai e io* or *Moen Usiai e i,* my Usiai or his Usiai. So a man who changes his residence from one village to another, is spoken of by his former village prefixed by *moen.*

Age Grade Terms

Age grades in Manus are given no further recognition beyond the use of the appropriate terms. The word *aiyo* means "of the same age grade." A study of usage showed that anyone over five years younger or older than ego was spoken of as *ndre aiyo*, "of another age grade." The term is little used as it is relative age of siblings which is important, rather than equal age of gentile or village mates.

nat: boy until the age of puberty, unborn child, child used in the generic sense. To the question "who is making that noise" the answer will be "*Ndro ala nat ka pwen*," "only the children," when a mixed group of boys and girls is meant. But an individual female child may never be referred to as a *nat*.

ndrakein: girl until the age of puberty

uluo: boy from puberty until marriage

pintchuel: girl from puberty until marriage. This term is also used of married women who have as yet borne no children, thus preserving the figure, especially the breasts, of a young girl. Such women are said to be *maun pintchuel*, "still girls."

yakamal: grown man, applied to all married men and widowers. Also used generically of males. Sometimes abbreviated to *kamal* in compound expressions.

pein: grown woman, applied to married women and widows. Also used generically of females. Small boys will address a group of small girls as "*aua pein*." "You females."

mandra: old man, who is feeble, toothless, doddering. Very few men live to be called *mandra*. In Peri there were three.

pinpati: old woman. This term is used far oftener and many more women live to apparent old age.

CEREMONIAL FUNCTIONS OF RELATIVES

There are two types of relationship functions in Manus: small precise details, like the duty of the father's sister and the father's sister's daughters to eat the heads of the fish which are caught for a girl during the first menstruation segregation, and broad relationships which involve a myriad of reciprocal acts, like the relationship between brother and sister, or between brothers-in-law. Relationship functions of the latter type will occupy a large portion of the ensuing discussion and need not be noted here. In the following list are contained such definite ceremonial acts as were observed to be relationship functions. The Manus give poor accounts of ceremonies and undoubtedly many small relationship functions which are incidental to ceremonies not witnessed—particularly in connection with mourning ceremonial—are omitted here. Those recorded below are functions relating to pregnancy, birth, ear piercing, first menstruation, the *tchani* or blessing for war ceremonial, marriage, and mourning, and such others as were obtained by chance. The most important ceremonies which were not observed

were the cutting of the hair of a *lapan's* child, *kan tchinitchini poenpalan,*
the feast for a girl about to be married, *memandra,* funeral ceremonial
for an important man, and the final release of a widow from mourning.

Mother's brother, *kakali:*	Names the child. Provides for its shelter and its mother's food during the first month of its life. Kills a pig after a sister's child has escaped great danger, as in shipwreck. Cuts the hair of his sister's son at the *kan tchini tchini poenpalan.* Pierces the ears. (In this he may be assisted by his wife.) Catches the fish eaten by his sister's daughter during the first menstruation segregation. Keeps any weapon which has shed the blood of a sister's child.
Paternal grandfather, *mambu:*	Performs the ceremony known as *tchani* over his son's son which prepares him for war.
Father's father's sisters and their female descendants, *pinpapu:*	Chief mourners; must sleep with their legs over the corpse for twenty days, washing the corpse each day in the sea. Prepare the mourning decorations. Mourn also at the feast of the skull. Today bury the corpse or place it on the island where it is to desiccate.
Father's sisters and their daughters, *patieye:* (reciprocal male, *nebonitu* female, *asaun*)	Assist the *pinpapu* in performing the above rites. Mourn when a *nebonitu* or *asaun* is sick or injured. This latter mourning is called a *wari* and was especially sung over those who were injured in war. Cut the hair of an *asaun* at marriage, after delivery, and for mourning. Lead by the hand a young *nebonitu* or *asaun* who is to have the ears pierced.
Father's mother, father's sisters and father's sisters' daughters, *patieye:*	Pronounce the ceremonial invocation of the double line of male and female ancestral ghosts, known as the *tandritanitani,* on the following persons and occasions:— Girl after first menstruation segregation release Boy at ear piercing segregation release Girl at ear piercing segregation release Boy at *tchani* (war blessing ceremony) Girl at *memandra* (pre-marriage segregation) Girl at marriage Pregnant woman to determine sex of child Woman after childbirth Widow at the end of mourning Ghost immediately after death
Father's sister's son, *polapol, Lom Pein:* child of female line	Performs the *tandritanitani* to release his male cross-cousin from a period of mourning. Ceremonially blesses his male cross-cousin who is *lom kamal,* after the latter has killed his first enemy in war. As *lom pein,* child of a woman of the gens, he eats

	the funeral food which has first been tasted by the ghost on the fourth night after mourning.
Mother's brother's son, and his son, *polapol, Lom Kamal:* child of male line	As *lom kamal*, child of the male line of the mother of the dead, he tears down the house of his deceased *polapol* (father's sister's son) and plunders his property. This is called the *ngang*.

SUMMARY OF MARRIAGE RULES

The ideal marriage in Manus is arranged by child betrothal between the children of two male cross-cousins, or of two cross-cousins who are father's sister's daughter and mother's brother's son to each other. That is, a man marries his father's mother's brother's son's daughter or his mother's mother's brother's son's daughter. The cross-cousin of the female line, *lom pein,* is said to "make the road." He initiates the marriage negotiations on behalf of a male child, demanding a female child from *lom kamal.* The children of female *lom kamal* and male *lom pein* cannot marry. The children of two female cross-cousins were said to be able to marry, but we have no instances of this. The ideal marriage obtains for first marriage of women only.

For other than first marriages it is only necessary to observe the rules of exogamy; marriage is forbidden within the gens and within the female descent line, and between people who use kinship terms for other reasons. The levirate is not practised, but two instances were found of a man's marrying his deceased wife's sister. The sororate does not occur except in this form. Polygamy is permitted, but frowned upon; the obscenity permitted by custom between co-wives jars on Manus feeling.

Divorce may be initiated by either party; a woman may either flee from her husband to her brother, and refuse his attempts to win her back, or a man may chase his wife away and never send for her. Outstanding debts between the contracting kin groups have to be paid, the sanction being the fear of ghostly wrath. Widows are permitted to remarry after the ten month period of segregation in the house of the husband's kin is completed, but it is considered better form to wait until all the mourning feasts are completed, a matter of two or three years. Occasionally, a widow will even elope before the mourning is complete. The wrath of the dead husband is feared by the new husband and by the former husband's kin and the wife's kin, so that elopement rather than arranged marriage is the rule. Occasionally if a woman is a widow of some years' standing, or if the corpse of the dead husband has been charmed into impotency, the marriage will be arranged with preliminary payments like a first marriage.

STRUCTURAL EMPHASES

Under the Manus kinship organization every person stands in intimate relation to four lineages: his father's father's male descent line, his mother's father's male descent line, his father's mother's female descent line, and his mother's mother's female descent line. The first and second of these relationships are extended to include not only the direct male descent line but also the entire gens, while the third and fourth are confined to direct lines of descent. It is because of this extension of terms and function in the male descent lines, in contradistinction to the female descent lines, that Manus society can be said to be patrilineal, and uni-

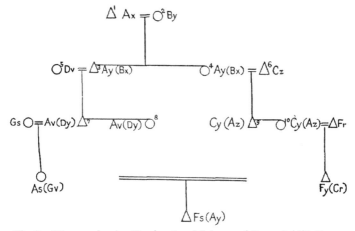

Fig. 6.   Diagram showing Dominant and Submerged Descent Affiliations.

lateral in principal emphasis. This fourfold classification of relationship may be expressed diagrammatically (Fig. 6) as follows:—

A, B, C, D, represent male descent lines, groups counted in the male line, and through which name, residence, status, and material property are inherited. v, x, y, z, represent the female descent lines, which are unnamed, have no explicit form of organization, and are only distinguished by the possession of a taboo inherited in the female line, called *patandrusun*. For purposes of this discussion, these matrilineal descent lines will be referred to as *patandrusun* bearing lines. Every individual, therefore, belongs to the male line and consequently, the gens of his father and to the *patandrusun* of his mother. But additionally he derives a peculiar status from the *patandrusun* affiliation of his father and the gentile affiliation of his mother. So an abstract statement of the kinship status of No. 7 is Av (Dy) while No. 9 the son of No. 7's father's sister is then described as Cy (Az). The letters in parenthesis (Dy) and (Az) indicate what I shall call submerged membership, indicating gens of mother and *patandrusun* of father. It is impossible to discuss functions of relation or interrelations between relatives without a full recognition of this quadruple status.

Summary of the privileges and liabilities which an individual receives from each of his four classifications:—

No. 7. Av (Dy)
   (1) Receives from his father, his gentile affiliations, A, which confers upon him:—
      1. Membership in a localized gens
      2. A gens name
      3. A gentile taboo called *nambun*
      4. Status: *luluai, lapan,* or *lau*
      5. Inheritance of some of his father's possessions
   (2) He receives from his mother membership in the *patandrusun* line v which gives him:—
      1. A matrilineally inherited taboo
      2. A position of spiritual dominance over his mother's brother's children, who belong to his mother's gens D
   (3) He receives from his mother a submerged membership in her gens, i.e., he is just one generation out of her gens D. This submerged membership combined with his active membership in *patandrusun* v gives him special privileges in gens D, chief of which is his right, which he shares with his sister, No. 8, to demand from the sons of his mother's brothers who are members of gens D but of a different *patandrusun*, a daughter to be married to his son.
   (4) He receives from his father a submerged membership in his father's *patandrusun* y, which is his worst inheritance, as it puts him in a position of spiritual dependency upon his father's sister and all her descendants in the female line. The Manus distinguish terminologically between status 1 and 3, calling the first *lom kamal*, child of the man, one who counts his relationship to a certain gens through his father. So Paliau is *lom kamal* to Peri, Nane *lom kamal* to Lo, etc. This is really only a restatement of gentile membership, but it is only used when the relationship between the children of a brother and the children of a sister is being discussed. The children of the sister, i.e., children of a woman of a gens are called *lom pein*. This term is used much more frequently, so a man will say: *Yo pati Kalat*, I belong to Kalat (gens); *Yo lom pein e Lo*, I am a child of a woman of Lo; or alternatively, *Papu pati Kalat, yay e pati Lo*, my father belongs to Kalat, my mother belongs to Lo.

Only when the relationship between cross-cousins is under discussion is the term *lom kamal* used so. *Yo lom kamal, i lom pein;* I am the son of the man (of the gens), he is the son of the woman (his mother was of the gens).

Patandrusun affiliation lacks terminology and also clarity. The lack of a name for the female descent line, the fact that it is scattered far and wide in many villages, the lack of any common feast, meeting place, ceremony, all tend to break it up into many small direct female descent lines. Not one person in ten can give the father's *patandrusun* and not one in a hundred can give *patandrusun* of someone not connected by residence or close kin. The form of the system is such that no *patandrusun* line functions as a unit; instead, it is continually split up

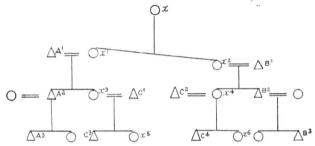

Fig. 7. Diagram illustrating the Dependence of *patandrusun* Relationship upon Residence.

into smaller divisions of three generation direct descendants from a marriage.

In the diagram (Fig. 7) a woman having the *patandrusun* x has two daughters; x^1 marries a man of gens A, x^2 a man of gens B. All the female descendants of x^1 will stand in a definite functional relationship to a male descent line in gens A, while all the female descendants of x^2 will stand in a similar relationship to a male descent line in gens B. x^2 calls x^1 "mother," in conformance with the age usage. If x^4 and x^3 are reared in the same village x^4 will call x^1 "grandmother," and x^3 "mother," but the chances are against the use of kinship terms being carried into the next generation. x^5's relationship to A^3 will be a far more active, because functioning, relationship than is her relationship to x^6, although A^3 and x^5 belong neither to the same gens nor to the same *patandrusun* line. The functioning group within the society is actually composed of the descendants of brother and sister for three generations, or, to put it more accurately, the group which carries the *patandrusun* of the mother and the group which carries the gens name of the father, from the marriage which originated the two descent lines. This important group has no name; I have designated it as a mixed descent group. The descendants of females are eliminated from the male line, the descendants of males from the female line.

When it is recognized that any effective relationship between x^5 and x^6 depends upon residence, which is a function of gentile membership

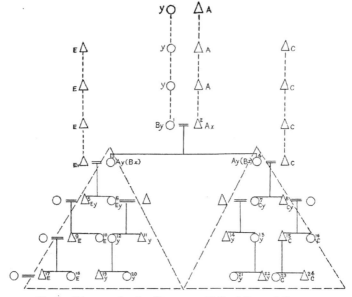

Fig. 8. Diagram showing Structure of Mixed Descent Groups.

and independent of *patandrusun* affiliation, it will be seen that x^5 and x^6 come in contact with each other, not because their mothers, like themselves, belonged to *patandrusun* x, but because their fathers belonged to a localized gens C and married within the village to which C belongs.

In the diagram (Fig. 8) which has been simplified to show only *patandrusun* membership and gens membership among the direct descendants of 3 and 4, 3 and 4 by their marriages start the smaller descent groups which are the actual functioning units in the society. So although 1, 3, 4, 6, 7, 12, 13, 20 and 21 are all female members of *patan-*

drusun y, and 5, 8, 11, 14, 19, 22 are all male members of *patandrusun* y, this group never meets, and often will not be able to trace relationship. Instead it is broken and re-formed by the marriage of 3 to a man of gens E and of 4 to a man of gens C, into two unnamed groups which I shall call for purposes of analysis mixed descent groups I and II. In group I, 3, 6, 11, 12 (and by terminological extension 19 and 20) hold a spiritual power over 9, 10. This power 3 and 6 use for good only, while 11, 12 (and by terminological extension only, 19 and 20) have power to curse as well as to bless 9 and 9's wife. The power which 6 and her descendants in the female line have over the descendants in the male line from her brother 5 is derived from her membership in the female descent line with the *patandrusun* y and gens E, which gives her the power not only to invoke the female ancestors of the female descent line of *patandrusun* y, but also the male ancestors of the gens E. 3 may invoke her female ancestral ghosts and call upon the names of her husband's male ghosts of gens E to bless 9 and 10, but only to help in blessing, not to curse. 6 holds an intermediate position; she can invoke the ghost to make barren, temporarily or permanently, 10 and the wife of 9, but she uses this power beneficently. Her children 11 and 12 exercise this same power malevolently.

Turning to group II, we find another group of *patandrusun* y women functioning towards a different gentile line, C, and when 7 wishes to bless 15 and 16 she invokes the same group of female ghosts of *patandrusun* y which 6 invoked in her relationship to gens E, but she invokes the male ancestral ghosts of her father's patrilineal line within gens C.

If the descent lines of two brothers are diagrammed, they will be found to yield converse results, that is, the descendants of one brother will be in position of spiritual dependency to a different female line and its female ghosts, from the *patandrusun* line which can curse or bless the other brothers' children, but the same male line of ghosts will be involved in each case.

But the male line, unlike the *patandrusun* line, is localized in space, even the ghosts of all the male lines of a gens are supposed to linger about the gentile island. It is to this island which a woman goes to bless her brother's child, invoking his ghosts in their proper habitat, while the matrilineal ghosts are conceived so vaguely as even to lack an abode.

If the only element in 6's ability to bless 9 and 10 was her membership in her *patandrusun* line, than 4 or 7 could replace 6 as they also are members of *patandrusun* y. Actually 6 owes her ability to being Ey and her children owe their ability to being y (E), that is, *patandrusun* y, submerged gens E. Although theoretically No. 20 may inherit the grandmother's power, this is merely an extension of terminology, and the terminology owes its existence to the membership in the *patandrusun* line alone. So a man calls all the women of his father's *patandrusun*, i.e., his father's mother and all her female descendants, *patieye*, and he calls all the women of his father's father's *patandrusun* line, including his father's father's mother, *pinpapu*, literally female father. All sons of *patieye* are *polapol*, all sons of *pinpapu* are *papu* or *mambu*.

Individuals who are members of *patandrusun* y and members or submerged members of gens E have spiritual power over members of gens E who are submerged members of *patandrusun* y. These first two memberships are expressed as yE or y(E), individuals of both memberships having all ghosts of *patandrusun* y and ghosts of gens E to command against those individuals who are E (y).

It follows that it is the relationship between cross-cousins which is the crux of the Manus system.

Holding the foregoing statement in mind, we will now consider the relations of cross-cousins. In Fig. 6, the children of 4 are members of the y *patandrusun* and submerged members (*lom pein*) of gens A. 9 and 10 can bless or curse 7. Furthermore, 9 and 10 have the right to demand from 7 one of his daughters in marriage to a son. If a son of 10 marries a daughter of 7 (a union of male Fy with female As), the child which results from this union will have the gens and *patandrusun* of the original great-grandparents submerged, i.e., the child will be Fs (Ay). Or, expressed in another way, in generation 1, *patandrusun* y gives to gens A a woman in marriage, and in generation 4, gens A gives to *patandrusun* y a woman in marriage.

The more usual marriage, and, from the Manus standpoint the most ideal marriage, is between the son of 9 and the daughter of 7. This marriage does not yield any such schematically appealing results. The child will be Cs (Aw), or, in other words, all trace of the *patandrusun* line which confers the original sanction of 9's right to ask 7 for his daughter as a wife of his, 9's, son is gone. 9 was acting as the son of his mother, not in his own right. 9 and 8 call each other *pisio*, "sibling of the opposite sex," and 4 calls 8 *asaun*, "daughter" (man speaking), although 4 calls 7 by a special term *nebonitu* and 3 calls 9 *kakali*, the same term by which he calls 10. The terminology thus reflects in two instances, i.e., terms used by father's sister, and reciprocal used between brother's daughter and sister's son,—the fact that the relationship of 8 to 9 and 10 is different from the relationship of her brother 7 to 9 and 10. Now 10 actually and 9 in native theory can wield spiritual power over 8, but the daughter of 8 may not be demanded in marriage for the sons of 9 and 10. It is this latter difference in relationship which the difference in terminology stresses. 9 and 10 can only demand a child from their mother's gens A, and the children of 8 will of course belong to another gens. The children of 8 and 9 call each other by cross-cousin terms and are forbidden to marry.

The Manus are principally concerned with the relations of cross-cousins as contracting parents-in-law. So they will say, "*Aru polapol aru, i lom pein, pe i lom kamal. Amo ki taui nat   Amo ki taui puin, nat e lom pein, i ki puti ndrakein e lom kamal.*" They two are cross cousins. He is *lom pein* and she is *lom kamal*. One will bear a son. One will bear a daughter. The son of *lom pein* will marry the daughter of *lom kamal*. But of 8 and 9 they say: "*Aru pisio aru. Nat e lom pein manbu ki puti ndrakein e lom kamal* " They two are (as) siblings of the opposite sex. The son of the *lom pein* cannot marry the daughter of the *lom kamal*.

The power of the women and first generation males of the *patieyen* line to bless the children of the male line is amplified in the case of cross-cousins by a special power of cursing. This power of cursing is contained in the powers of all the women of the *patieyen* line for they have the right to cause temporary or permanent barrenness as well as to cause fruitfulness in women. But the father's mother and father's sister are conceived of as exercising these powers only benevolently, while the father's sister's son and daughter, may exercise them malevolently also. The threat of such exercise is used by persons who are *lom pein* to enforce their wishes upon *lom kamal*. The actual exercise of this power results in a complete avoidance being set up between cursing and cursed cross-cousin.

Furthermore, between a man and his *patieyen* line, including his *polapol*, male cross-cousin, there is a ceremonial jesting relationship. This relationship is graded in response to age consideration. A man is lightly playful with his father's mother, much more playful than he would dare to be with his *ngasin*, mother's mother. Towards his father's sister, nearer to his own age, he exercises more license and to his female cross-cousin who is the daughter of his father's sister, he exercises the greatest license permitted in Manus society. This enjoined jesting, accompanying as it does a condition of spiritual dependency on *lom kamal's* part, permits a release of the strained condition which often attends the complicated spiritual and—because of marriage arrangements—economic relations of the pair of cross-cousins.

A more detailed consideration of kinship function must be postponed till a later section, but it should be said here that the mother's brother has certain definite functions to perform towards the sister's son, naming the child, piercing its ears, and important economic duties at death. Roughly, the functions of the *patieyen* are spiritual and when economic are predatory, the functions of the mother's brother are only economic and practical.

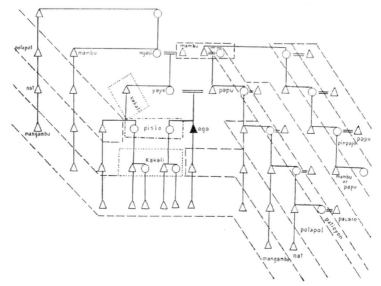

Fig. 9.   Diagram showing Terminology used between the Lines of Brother and Sister.

This concludes the general discussion of the inter-relations of brother and sister and brother's and sister's children resulting from the conjunction of a male line of ancestral spirits and a female line of ancestral spirits in the marriage of the parents. Fig. 9 illustrates the terminology with its disregard of generation, which flows from these inter-relationships.

KINSHIP WITHIN THE GENS

It now remains to consider inter-relations within the gens. As the overriding of generation outside the gens stresses the difference in status between *lom kamal* and *lom pein*, so the categories within the gens make status points also. Although outsiders speaking of two brothers or of two men whose fathers were brothers will say *aru ndriasi aru,* "They are two male siblings same sex," *ndriasi* is never used as a term of address, nor does a man say *io ndriasi,* i.e., "I am his brother." In ego's terminology and the terminology used to ego, all older brothers are classed with the father, all younger brothers with the son. Similarly, the sons of these men are addressed in terms reflecting this usage.

The father-son terminology between elder and younger brother is a very definite reflection of custom, which also accounts for the lack of confusion in the extension of the terms into the lower generations (Fig. 10). 2 calls 1 father, so technically 2 and 3 are on the same generation level, while 4 would again call 3 father in regular order, as 3 is the son of 1 whom he, 4, calls grandfather. Logically therefore 4 and 5 should call each other "brother." This situation is however solved practically, as are all situations within the gens. 1 betroths 3 while 3 is a child and makes the first marriage payments for him. Then 1 dies before 3's betrothal payments are completed and 1's younger brother, 2, takes over the duty of completing 3's payments. 2 and 3 as boys and young men have not called each other by any kinship term.

When 2 takes over the financing

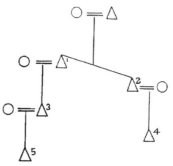

Fig. 10. Diagram illustrating Terminological Usage between Males within the Gens.

of 3's marriage, i.e., takes 3's father's place, 3 calls 2 "father." This process repeats itself until 2 dies after beginning the betrothal payments for 4, and 3 takes up the task which 2 has laid down. He takes 2's place and so becomes 4's "father."

When, however, the alternative financing of two parallel male lines does not follow this reciprocal arrangement, as is often enough the case, the Manus will argue from a given case toward a practical terminology, so:—

The father of Kemwai began the betrothal payments for Kemwai, and died (Fig. 11). Kali completed the payments for Kemwai and even though Kali did not die—as is more usual—but merely became old and decrepit, Kemwai completed the payments for Nane. Nane therefore calls Kemwai, father. Pomat is the adopted son of Kemwai's old age. Kutan is Nane's oldest son. Pomat and Kutan are within a year of each other's age. There can be no such alternative arrangement as that

described above. The chances are against either Pomat or Kutan
directly succeeding Kemwai. Instead, Kemwai will probably die before
either boy is married. In that case, Nane will continue to finance
Pomat and Kutan, and Pomat will call Nane, "father." Nane will
probably die before either Pomat or Kutan are ready to succeed him.
Some older boy whom Nane has financed may then take over Nane's
economic responsibilities and, in turn, be called father by Pomat and
Kutan. Upon which youth, Pomat or Kutan, the intermediate man's
financial mantle falls, will depend the ultimate choice of kinship
terminology used by Pomat's and Kutan's children; e.g., if Kutan
succeeds, Pomat's children will probably call Kutan, "grandfather."

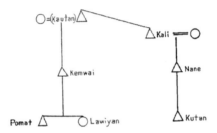

Fig. 11.   Illustrative Genealogy.

Meanwhile, the women, if asked what Kutan *should* call Pomat
will answer:—Kemwai is the "father" of Nane. Nane bore Kutan and
Kemwai bore[1] Pomat. If Nane speaks to Kemwai he says *papu*. Therefore if Kutan speaks to Kemwai he should say *mambu*. If Kutan speaks
to Pomat, he should say *papu*.

It will readily be seen that a great deal of subsequent confusion is
prevented by the fact that children use no kinship terms except *papu*,
yaye, *mambu*, and *ngasi* to members of their immediate family.

Between sisters, whose descendants are *patandrusun* kin, not gens
kin, although the same theory is operative, it is not confused by financial
operations, and the term *piloai* is used by a few female parallel cousins
of the same sex, descriptively, although not as a term of address. The
terminology used between female parallel cousins can therefore be
diagrammed in this way (Fig. 12). Only parallel cousins and very
occasionally a sister of almost exactly the same age will be spoken of as
piloai.

---

[1] Actually Kemwai only adopted Pomat.

The Manus will argue as follows in extending skewed usage (Fig. 11). So the Manus say "Kutan should call Pomat father, therefore he should call Lawian *patieyen.*" But this is merely a verbal point. In practice Kutan uses no kinship term to Pomat, and as Lawian is not the daughter of Kutan's father's mother, she does not act as a functioning *patieyen* towards Kutan. Similarly in Fig. 7 C^3 may call B^2 *kakali*, because his mother calls him *pisio*, sibling of opposite sex; and he may call x^6 *pisio*, but these also are merely terminological, nonfunctioning relationships, all of which spring from the original intra-

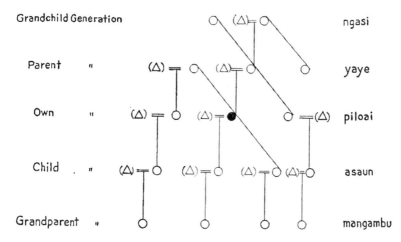

Fig. 12. Diagram showing Terminology used between Female Siblings and Female Parallel Cousins.

gentile, intra-*patandrusun* true sisterhood of x^1 and x^2. Kinship terminology within the *patandrusun* group of two gentile sisters is likely to lapse after a generation, but the Manus can always derive the proper terminology for these non-functioning relationships from antecedent functioning ones.

The distinction between elder sister and younger sister is made sharply only in affinal terms. The difference in the avoidance behavior towards these relatives prevents equal status, just as the facts of financial backing prevent any recognition of equal generation status between male members of a gens.

So a man classes all his wives' older sisters, and older female parallel cousins with his wife's mother, as *pilanasaun*, spoken of as *ala* "they," the strictest avoidance relationship in Manus. But towards all his wives' younger sisters he shares his wife's parental status, calls them *asaun* (daughter, man speaking), and observes merely nominal avoidance rules; e.g., he avoids their personal names, refers to them as *yaru*, "they two," and does not eat in their presence.

A woman must make comparable distinction between her husband's brothers, avoiding his older brothers as fathers-in-law, treating his younger brothers as sons. But here she merely follows inter-relationships already defined by the financing of her husband's marriage.

KINSHIP BEHAVIOR
MANUS MANNERS RELEVANT TO AVOIDANCE RULES

It is impossible to understand the importance or significance of avoidance and familiarity regulations within a society unless the customary norm of behavior of that society be understood. It is necessary to preface a discussion of the relationship between relatives with a consideration of Manus manners in regard to eating, sleeping, bodily contact of any sort, excretion, conversational liberties. The house in Manus is a sort of sanctuary to which only the young and the dependent and the closely related come freely. One adult will not enter another man's house without due and grave cause. Young men, when they receive the ceremonial blessing from their grandparents known as *tchani*, are instructed never to enter a house without calling out and giving the women occupants time to rise to their feet to receive them. They are further instructed never to walk on the heavy center floor board—where the footsteps would not be heard—but always to walk on the crackling side floors, in other words never to enter a house of another or move about in it except in as public a fashion as possible.

A man wishing to enter the house of another will rattle the boards of the landing platform or cough to announce his presence. One within the house will then call out: "Who is there?" to which is given the ambiguous answer "I." "And who are you?" The answer being given, the house owner then gives permission to enter, "Oh, climb up then." Children before puberty can go freely into any house with which their own household Sir Ghost is not on feud terms. To sleep in the house of another is regarded as very serious business; people go to sleep in the house of mourning, with one who has been rescued from shipwreck, and all the girls of the community sleep with a girl during her first menstruation segregation. Whenever a large number of people of both sexes are sleeping in a house, the men all sleep together in the front and the women at the back. Trade partners may sleep in the homes of their other-tribal or other-village partners, and relatives from a distant village may sleep in the houses of relatives. The only other occasion on which a man goes to spend the night in the home of another man is when he wishes to obtain from him by purchase some important piece of magic. To do this it is essential that the would-be purchaser should pass several nights in the owner's house.

There is very little communal eating in Manus. The usual arrangement for a feast is for the food to be distributed to the guests in bowls and baskets. Each guest then carries home his share, to be consumed in privacy under his own roof. On the few rare occasions when casual guests do eat in the house of another and in the presence of several other people, they turn their backs to each other and swallow their food as hastily as possible. There is no acceptable ritual by which a communal meal can be made to appear anything except embarrassing.

Excretion is always carefully guarded from the eyes of the opposite sex and from any witnesses if possible. The exposure consequent upon excretion is at a minimum. Women are forbidden to expose their bodies even in the presence of female relatives, and accidental exposure provokes both mortal and ghostly wrath. The atmosphere of prudery is so intense that it is thoroughly communicated to the children by the time they are about three.

Bodily contact except for very young children is carefully stylized. The only occasions on which I saw one person take another by the hand were ceremonial. When a boy's ears are pierced he is led down the steps of the house by his father's sisters. (This is probably true of a girl's also, but a girl's ear piercing was not witnessed). When the bride is brought to her husband's house, her mother-in-law takes her by the hand and leads her into the house. These were the only two occasions witnessed, but there are very probably others of similar nature in ceremonies which were not witnessed.

The embrace and its modifications are also purely ceremonial. When anyone is injured or extremely ill, the father's sisters ceremonially embrace him, and wail over him. They repeat this procedure for a corpse. In both these cases they are paid for their services.

When one man is teaching another magic or when he is magically immunizing another against inimical magic, he assumes a position astride the shoulders of the novice or patient. This position is a frequent theme of the carving on the handles of the lime spatulas.

For the rest, the slightest bodily contact between individuals not in special relationships is sedulously avoided. Boys are taught, about the age of twelve or fourteen, not to body handle each other, except in permitted relationships and even these do not come actively into play until later. It is significant that both in Manus, and Mr. Fortune reports, in Dobu, also, the gesture of defiance or anger is not the clenched fist, as with us, but the spear hand thrown back from the shoulder into position for throwing a spear. Physical encounters were usually avoided except when the contestants were armed with spears. There was only one physical encounter between adults during our stay in Peri, when Pokanas knocked into the sea his brother-in-law who had intervened in a fight between himself and his wife. Even here, after the two contestants had joined, they hastily separated and the struggle was not renewed.

As the Manus are shy of sleeping, eating, or exposing themselves in the presence of others, so they are equally shy of personalities in speech. One must handle the private life, the body, the affairs of another as circumspectly in speech as one must the actual body in practice. Conversation, except in the specially recognized grooves, is impersonal, formal, and never stoops to personalities except in anger.

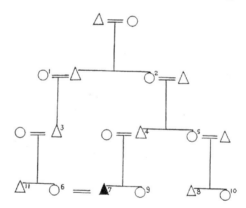

Fig. 13.   Diagram showing the Prescribed Marriage.

THE PRESCRIBED MARRIAGE AND KINSHIP BEHAVIOR

In considering affinal relationships the kinship system and prescribed marriage[1] must be borne in mind. If 6 and 7 (Fig. 13) are not betrothed, 6 calls 2 and 5, both of whom her father calls *patieyen, pinpapu,* and she calls number 4 *papu* or *mambu.* For 7 and 8 she does not use kinship terms. After 6, 7, and 8 are grown, if 6 is not betrothed to either 7 or 8,

[1] This prescribed marriage applies to first marriages only.

she will call 7 and 8 *pisio*, sibling of opposite sex. 9 she will fit into an elder or younger sister category and 10 she will call *pinpapu*, if she is asked to define her relationship to her. But if 6 and 7 marry, then 6 will call 9 *pinkayo*, sister-in-law; she will speak of 4 as *timbu*, but 2 and 5 she will continue to call *pinpapu*, but now with name avoidance. However 7 will call 3 *papu* whether he marries 6 or not. If he does marry 6, he and 11 will call each other *kaiyo*, brother-in-law.

After the betrothal, the only major avoidance relationship within this group is that between 4 and 6 and this is likewise the only type of avoidance relationship which can be ceremonially nullified in Manus. If 4 lives to see 7 married he is permitted to give a feast to 6 which she shares with her relatives and which is really an additional piece of affinal gift giving, for which, however, there is no repayment, and the stringent avoidance thereby is removed. Although men acting as fathers may do the same to their financial protégés' wives, this is not done so frequently. With the removal of this strict avoidance, the descendants of brother and sister are reunited in terms of formal household intimacy,—except for the avoidance of personal names and the use of special personal pronouns which will be discussed below.

I have arranged in a table kindred and affinal relationship categories in terms of the degree to which different types of behavior are employed. Where order is not clear the relationships are bracketed. For many years students of kinship have been discussing "jesting" or "joking" relationships, "respect relationships" and "avoidance" or "taboo" relationships. Lack of detailed day-by-day observation in primitive communities where individual relationships are known, often coupled with very inadequate discussion of the point, has led to two types of error. On the one hand, a number of relatives toward whom behavior of a certain category is used in different degrees of emphasis are loosely categorized without precise definition of difference. On the other, investigators failing to find in their own areas a definite category which has been meagerly described for other areas, but finding instead an unstylized jesting or respectful behavior between individuals will lightly discount the actual existence of the categories.[1]

---

[1]"The so-called joking relationships, at least those described by Rivers in Melanesia, appear to me to be only the exercise of the normal freedom existing between people who do not happen to be under the constraint of some bond of this type. The chaff recorded in the *History of Melanesian Society* (e.g., vol. I, 45–6) has no peculiar significance. It is of the rather crude, allusive sexual kind, and its point clearly lies not, as Rivers seems to think, in the possibility of sexual relations between the man and the woman concerned, but in their jesting mutual accusations of loose living, for their amusement and that of the bystanders. Badinage of this style is current among all the Pacific peoples and is regarded as nothing more than a display of that species of easy wit which also wins a laugh in circles higher than those of the savage."—Firth, Raymond, Marriage and the Classificatory System of Relationship (*Journal of the Royal Anthropological Institute of Great Britain and Ireland*, vol. 60, pp. 235–268, 1930), 240.

Strictly speaking, it is not possible to divide Manus behavior into grouped categories. The line which divides a man's treatment of his father from his treatment of his brother or his treatment of his sister is a hair-breadth one.

Nevertheless, the Manus themselves make three categories of behavior. Those towards whom an individual is merely *mbulen mamatche*, ashamed,[1] those with whom he may *pwotchole*, jest or play, and those whom he must *kaleani*[2] or avoid. I have therefore arranged the table in such a way as to show:—

    I. Native categories

    II. Differences in intensity of behavior toward different relatives within each . category, and

    III. If the table be read from top to bottom, for either male or female, the shading of attitudes and corresponding behavior throughout the effective kin group may be seen.

The following table of kinship attitudes is arranged so that it proceeds from the affinal relative who is most avoided through all degrees of avoidance relationships to the relative who is least avoided, between the treatment of whom and the relatives most respected there is a very slight shade of difference. Part II lists the respect relationships from the relative most respected to the relative least respected. Here again this relationship shades off into the first category of Part III, jesting or familiarity relationships, which are arranged from *slightest* to *greatest* degree of permitted familiarity and license. In Part I, Avoidance Relationships, which all occur between affinal relatives, the relationship should be understood to be reciprocal, i.e., it may be read with the addition of the word *between* and the reciprocal. So in column 1 of Part I, read the relationship between the wife's mother and the daughter's husband. But in Parts II and III reciprocity of this sort is complicated by considerations of age and sex, so that a man's relationship to his mother's mother is less familiar than a woman's relationship to her daughter's children. The genuine jesting relationships are symmetrical, however, and are so indicated in the table.

---

[1] The term for "to make ashamed" is to *tchiri mbulen*, literally, "to break his forehead." The word *mamatche* was not found in any context.

[2] *Kaleani* means literally "to go around." The substantive is *kaleal*, one whom one goes around, or avoids.

Kinship Attitudes

Ego: MALE   Ego: FEMALE

Part I—Avoidance Relationships
(Greatest to Least Avoidance)

wife's mother	daughter's husband
wife's elder sister	younger sister's husband
wife's elder female relatives	husband's father
son's wife	husband's elder brother
younger brother's wife	husband's elder male relatives
wife's brother's wife	husband's sister's husband
wife's father	husband's mother
wife's elder brother	husband's elder sister
wife's elder male relatives	husband's elder female relatives
wife's younger sister	husband's younger brother
wife's younger brother	husband's younger sister
wife's younger relatives of both sexes	husband's younger relatives of both sexes

Part II—Respect Relationships
(Greatest to Least Respect)

mother's mother	mother's father
father's father's sister	mother's brother
mother's elder sister	mother's male relatives
mother's female relatives	
mother	
mother's father	mother's mother
mother's brother	father's father's sister
mother's male relatives	mother's sister
	mother's female relatives
sister	mother
brother	
sister's sons	brother
daughter	sister
daughter's children	son
	daughter
	daughter's children
	father
	father's mother
	father's sister
	father's female relatives
	female cross-cousin
	brother's daughter

Part III—Familiarity and Jesting Relationships
(Least to Greatest Familiarity)

father's father	son's son
father's mother	husband's father's sister's husband[1]
father	husband's male cross-cousin
son's son	brother's son
son[1]	mother's brother's son
wife's brother's son's wife	
cross-cousin's wife	
wife's brother's son	
father's sister	
father's sister's husband	
father's sister's son	
father's sister's daughter	

Certain generalizations appear. Difference in age is an intensifying factor in respect and avoidance relationship and functions in the reverse way in jesting relationships. A man will treat his mother's mother with more respect than he will his mother, and towards his wife's older sister he exercises a greater degree of avoidance than towards his wife's younger sister. Difference in sex also intensifies all of these categories. In the jesting relationship a man will jest more with his father's sister's daughter than his father's sister.

Jesting between cross-cousins of opposite sex is felt to be so near the border-line of improper behavior that it is sometimes invoked by mediums to explain the anger of the spirits; and the avoidances between a man and his mother-in-law, a woman and her "father-in-law," usually actually her husband's elder brother, are the most carefully observed in Manus.

It will also be observed that there is less jesting between women than between men, so that a woman has fewer jesting relationships. Whether this should be interpreted as cause or effect of woman's isolation and lack of intimacy it is impossible to say. If female cross-cousins were on terms of intimacy comparable to the intimacy between male cross-cousins, a woman would be able to discuss her marital relations or her illicit plans with someone of her own sex. Only if a woman has a co-wife, is there a single woman who can refer intimately to her relationship to her husband, and obscenity between co-wives is always in anger, not in confidence.

Beyond the borders of defined kinship behavior lie those to whom one's relationship is too distant and tenuous for emphasis. It remains to

---

[1]Reciprocal from here on.

describe the behavior of unrelated people (by unrelated I mean those who do not speak to or of each other in kinship terms, or use special forms of speech appropriate to affinal relationship). Anyone accustomed to ethnographic problems will realize that in a village the size of Peri, in a tribe as small as the Manus, with ninety-nine per cent of the marriages within the tribe and seventy-five per cent of the marriages within the village, everyone stands in an actual genealogical relationship to everyone else,—although for the extra-village marriages it might be necessary to go back two or three more generations to find the genealogical link. I therefore use *unrelated* purely in the Manus sense. Every member of an individual's own gens will be counted as a relative although there is sometimes considerable disagreement as to the term which should be used. When the behavior of unrelated persons is observed it is found that there is a rough correlation between age and amount of respect, intensified again by difference in sex. But here the correlation is not with difference of age, but with actual age, that is, small children of both sexes are permitted the freedom accorded jesting relatives of the most intense degree. Between young men there is a mild type of free interchange, comparable to the less intense jesting behavior, and between middle-aged and old men, there is a formal etiquette-governed type of behavior comparable to respect relationship. Similarly between unrelated individuals of opposite sex, behavior becomes increasingly stylized with age. Small children have the freedom of a *patieyen* and *nebonitu*, adolescents are as circumspect as brother and sister, and persons of marriageable age and opposite sex treat each other as if they were in one of the milder forms of avoidance relationships, with the exception that personal names may be used, but because of the ubiquitousness of avoidance relatives, seldom are.

Between unrelated girls and women there is a more formal relationship than between unrelated boys and men. Although little girls play together freely, their withdrawal from the children's play group so much earlier than the boys results in greater shyness and less intimacy. (Women may never disrobe in one another's presence, except in case of illness, in child bearing, or the widow in first mourning. Men do not take quite such a drastic attitude towards accidental exposure in the presence of other men). At adolescence the relationship of unrelated girls approximates a respect relationship, which becomes in later life almost avoidance, enforced by their husbands'· disapproval of their wives' associating with unrelated women.

CHARACTERISTIC BEHAVIOR TYPES

It is now appropriate to consider in more detail the types of behavior that fall under these categories of familiarity and jesting, respect, and avoidance. The stylized jesting and intimacy has a frivolous, playful side, and a serious side. I will discuss the frivolous side first. Jesting refers primarily to sex, either in speech or body handling, and allows behavior which implies lack of respect, practical jokes, purposeful lying, etc. The type of sex reference between a man and his female cross-cousin who is his father's sister's daughter (*patieyen*) and a man and his male cross-cousin (either father's sister's son or mother's brother's son, *polapol*) differ. In jesting with a woman, the body handling is definitely sexual, a man will play with a woman's breasts, or even venture to touch her pubes. All such play is only permitted in public, and any over-indulgence is likely to be seized upon as an offense by the medium-interpreted ghosts. A distinction is made between such sex play "in the house" and out on the *arakeu* or in a large gathering. "In the house" implies too great privacy and is an approach to ghostly-disapproved license. In speech a man will accuse an unmarried *patieyen* of being married, a childless *patieyen* of having a child, or he will spread false reports that she has eloped and married while visiting in another village. With a male cross-cousin, a man may engage in horse-play, rough-house, or tusseling, which is often not of a specific sexual character, but which is nevertheless extremely intimate among a people who are taught from childhood never to lay hands upon one another.

To his cross-cousin, a man is permitted to make any number of obscene references, to his body, his marital life, his real or fancied sex behavior. Furthermore, a cross-cousin is permitted to take other types of liberties, besides sexual ones. He may interrupt a man in the middle of a solemn address to his ancestral spirits, or interpolate some frivolous comment in the midst of a cross-cousin's speech at an important economic feast.

Between young men cross-cousin jesting is body play and very broad obscenity. After both cross-cousins are married, the jesting becomes prevailingly a matter of speech, and obscene accusations more limited to references to a man's marital relations. Between man and female cross-cousins, *patieyen* and *nebonitu*, jesting becomes franker and less emotionally charged with increasing age. It is not usually practised before the cross-cousins are married. But if one or both are married, the body handling is customary. A slight difference in age—not amounting to more than five or ten years, increases the freedom of play, especially

between a man and a younger *patieyen*. For people of marriageable age
the body play is likely to be rough and scuffling, the man grabbing at the
woman's breasts, she breaking away from him and he catching her
again. But an old man will grasp his elderly female cross-cousin about
the breasts and, both of them seated on the floor, rock her back and
forth in a long embrace. It is only between such old cross-cousins that
mock handling of the woman's pubes is likely to occur. It may be remarked that women never take the initiative in bodily contacts,
although they act with less constraint in the presence of their jesting
relatives.

The non-sexual type of cross-cousin jesting emphasizes the formal
ticklish nature of personal relations between adults in Manus. In order
to appreciate it fully it is necessary to hold in mind the following facts:
mature men of equal status do not visit each other except formally to
discuss some important matter of business. Even such a matter as a
meeting between a man and his associates and subordinate financial
assistants in a forthcoming economic exchange is arranged by the
entrepreneur's catching a turtle and distributing a piece to each relative
as an invitation.   A man does not go to another man's house except on
such terms as these, or on a public occasion of festivity or calamity.
(At these latter times anyone not on such troublous terms with the house
owner as to fear ghostly punishment from the owner's Sir Ghost may go
to a house). Women are not expected to visit in unrelated houses except
upon equally formal errands—*sub rosa* dunning is one of their frequent
missions, also the collection of feast dishes, after food has been distributed
at a feast. Those adults who treat each other so formally, also are formal
in speech. Unfriendly or over-personal comment upon another's person,
ancestry, economic exploits, character or future plans are only made in
anger, in loud-voiced quarrel, when each disputant is isolated on house
veranda or canoe platform. And over and over one hears the comment
about remarks made in the jesting relationship, "His belly may not go
bad about it," i.e., he may not get angry. From this point of view the
jesting relationship may be defined as a relationship within which are
permitted words and actions which, performed in any other relationship,
would arouse the anger either of the person with whom one jested,[1] the
parents or spouse of that person, or the spirits. So the spirits will
bitterly resent personal physical contact of breast or pubes between men
and women not in a cross-cousin relationship, and women themselves

---

[1]The ceremonial form for the expression of anger in this relationship—cross-cousin cursing—is very rarely used.

indignantly refute the idea of their husband's touching their breasts. This belongs only to their mother's brother's son, *nebonitu*, they say.

To the category of acts which would anger the object of the jest belong practical jokes—sending people on fools' errands, lying to them about distance, about whether one has passed a canoe, etc., and also all disparaging comments of any type.

Cross-Cousin Jesting. The following are examples of cross-cousin jests:—

Man is addressing his Sir Ghost from a canoe in front of his house in the presence of a great concourse of people. It is about three in the afternoon. His cross-cousin shouts out: "Finish that speech. The sun is going down."

After a canoe race, in a funeral convoy when a corpse was being conveyed from one village to another, man in winning canoe says to man in losing canoe, "Your canoe is dead."

Man in the house of his cross-cousin whose wife is absent seizes drumstick and beats the tattoo with which his cousin is accustomed to call his wife and remarks, "When she comes, I will have intercourse with her."

Man in a canoe remarks to his unmarried cross-cousin, "You slept with Ngaoli last night, didn't you?" Ngaoli is merely a young girl of the village.

Man to his cross-cousin: "The widow of your older brother has eloped and re-married." The younger brother was counting on this widow's economic help and fear of her eloping was an ever-present anxiety.

Unmarried man to unmarried cross-cousin, "Copulate with your grandmother."

Man receives money payment from a white man. His cross-cousin reaches over, seizes the money, and pretends to make off with it.

Man to his cross-cousin: "When you made a *metcha* you didn't pay any *musui*," i.e., "When you made the spectacular late payment for your wife you omitted the extra gifts which are usually paid at night in secret, and for which no return is expected"; i.e., "you are stingy." This was a fact, in this case, and the remark from another would have provoked fury.

Man of his male cross-cousin in his cross-cousin's presence: "His Sir Ghost was killed in a war with the Usiai, and his skull was lost. He has only a coconut in his skull bowl."

Two cross-cousins can call each other by the names of their respective spouses.

At a *tchamoluandras* feast after twenty days of mourning the house owner was giving out tobacco to those mourners who had slept in the house. His cross-cousin called out, "You have only a little tobacco. It is nothing at all to be giving away."

Cross-cousins pass each other in canoes in the center of the village. The canoe of one is well laden with sago, the other, simulating extreme rage, calls out, "No wonder you have lots of sago, you have a woman to help you. But don't you talk to me. My wife is sick, I work hard. I work alone. You have plenty of help."

Man to his female cross-cousin, "Where is that child which you bore while you were in Mok?"

Man to his female cross-cousin, "You'll have a long trip all the way to your village. The white master of Dropal has forbidden natives to use that little island as a stopping place any longer." This was untrue, but alarming, as Dropal was the only good place to break the journey.

The following are examples of retaliatory cross-cousin jesting:—

Man returning to their common village told his male cross-cousin that his adopted son who was away working in Lorengau was very ill. His cross-cousin hurried to Lorengau, seven or eight hours of hard punting, to find it was a lie. He returned to tell his deceiving cross-cousin that his brother-in-law was dying. The first man answered angrily that this was a lie—for which the second cursed him and ended the jesting relationship forever, although later he removed the curse.

Poiyo, Paliau, Main, and others, the first two cross-cousins, the third a widow, went to a far island for a funeral feast and were wind-bound there for a long time. Paliau's canoe got back first and he said that Poiyo had married Main. In retaliation Poiyo spread the report that Sain, Paliau's wife, had borne a child when Paliau and Sain were in Mbuke.

Points which added to the jest:—

Main had had five husbands, who were reported to have died of her loose sex behavior.
Poiyo had two wives already, who were the talk of the village because of their daily fights.
Sain had been barren since the premature birth and death of her first child, six years before.

Cross-cousin jesting does not begin before adolescence. Boys of eighteen or nineteen will begin to use it frequently, and older men will jest with adolescent *patieyen.*

The climax of cross-cousin jesting has become institutionalized in a ceremony which nominally involves cross-cousins, but often involves men who are in very different and even avoidance relationships to each other. This is the athletic phallic dance performed by the chief men of each party to an important affinal exchange. This dance must again be understood against the Manus background of extreme prudery. In the dance, the G string is removed and a carved-out white ovalis shell is placed on the phallus. Old men dance quite naked, except for various ornaments, and this conspicuous phallic decoration. Today young men are required to wear cloth *lavalavas* which are, however, open in front. (This is a refinement of prudery made possible by the introduction of cloth.) The dogs' teeth and shell money of the affinal exchange are hung on lines about the *arakeu*, and on special occasions *tchinals*, dancing platform poles about eight inches wide and thirty feet long are erected on the *arakeu*. First one party dances, then the other. The men carry spears, smear their bodies with lime, advance in crouching, threatening attitudes, and then indulge in a violent phallic athleticism, to a drum accompaniment, interspersed with brief and insulting speeches to their financial partners on the other side of the affinal exchange. The women dance behind the men, when the men dance on the *arakeu;* but the women are clothed as usual, and their dance consists of hopping back and forth with feet placed close together and a spear in each hand.[1] The ceremony; which theoretically involves cross-cousins contracting for the marriage of the son of *lom pein* to the daughter of *lom kamal*, contains all the distinguishing elements of individual cross-cousin jesting: it is public; it simulates anger and hostility; and it is obscene.

There remains to discuss another type of behavior between cross-cousins which is regarded as a function of their jesting relationship—the rôle which they play to each other of confessors and confidants. The same cross-cousins are involved, mother's brother's son and father's sister's son, reciprocally, and mother's brother's son and father's sister's daughter. Within these relationships, sex affairs, past or projected, may be discussed. A man had intercourse as a boy, for two nights running with an unmarried girl in the house of his classificatory gens father. The boy was betrothed. He decided he didn't want to marry his illicit paramour, so he told his two female cross-cousins what he had done. They agreed with him that he had better adhere to the marriage plans which had been made for him. So he ran away from the village to work for the white men, and left his cross-cousin with the necessary information in case his partner in sin fell ill and confession was necessary to save her life.[2]

To a female cross-cousin a man may confess his plans for marrying a widow.

---

[1] The only time in Manus when a woman's body is ceremonially exposed is when a widow, immediately after her husband's death, walks naked and wailing in the sea, accompanied by a long line of kinswomen. But upon this occasion the men are required to stay strictly within doors.

[2] Sometimes an individual becomes unconscious or delirious before confessing. Anyone who possesses knowledge of a sin previously committed by the sick person is required to confess, thus saving the life of the sinner. Should anyone fail to reveal such a matter, and the sick person die, the ghost is believed to return and kill the one who concealed his knowledge.

In Patalian's elopement with Ngalapon, the widow of Pwanan[1] the wife of Pondramet who acted as go-between, was cross-cousin of Patalian and cross-cousin of the widow of Pwanan and therefore the perfect go-between in terms of kinship function.

When someone is suspected of a sin which is causing their own or another's illness, the duty of extracting confession devolves upon the male cross-cousin. Here there is a conjunction of two sets of Manus attitudes. The relationship between cross-cousins is prevailingly a gay and friendly one. The ordinary barriers of a puritan and formal society are down; intimacy, jesting, rough house are all permitted. In cases of voluntary confession, the relationship still retains this warmth of feeling tone. It is a cross-cousin to whom one can turn in need. But where a sinner is obdurate and refuses confession, the ferocity of the Manus religious attitude towards sexual breaches takes possession of the hitherto friendly relationship, and the cross-cousin who was a gay confidant will trick and pry, threaten and deceive, to get the necessary confession at any cost. Here anger and criticism wreck the relationship, just as in cross-cousin jesting too gross a hoax will arouse anger. In both cases, the jesting relationship is then replaced by what the Manus call a *mwere*—an "open space"—an explicit personal avoidance of all communication between the two cross-cousins involved.

As has already been noted, although a man has a male confidant, a woman has no female confidant of the same degree of intimacy. I never heard of a case, either in practice or theory, of a woman confessing to a woman. A woman can speak to her female cousin of a projected marriage, but not of projected or completed extra-marital sex adventure. And between male and female cross-cousins, confidences concerning illicit sex relations are limited to confession, sometimes voluntarily on the man's side, more often extorted from a woman. The fact that the system allows a woman no possible confidant probably acts powerfully in keeping women chaste, for without a confidant, in the crowded publicity of a Manus village, it is practically impossible to arrange clandestine meetings. To no female relative, to no female affinal relation can a woman confide what is both shameful and sinful. And husbands are careful to limit their wives' associates to women of these two categories. Nor do parents look with approval upon young girls associating with other girls who are no relation to them. Thus the rules of the kinship system wall a woman into an enjoined and confidant-less silence.

Turning to the less intense forms of jesting, the relationship between *pauaro* (man and his *patieyen's* husband) comes next in importance. Two

---

[1]Fortune, R. F., Chapter V, Subsection 43.

pauaro never jest as excessively as cross-cousins, their relationship is one of easy familiarity, as is that of men and their father's sisters and to a lesser degree their paternal grandmother and grandfather. In the relationship of a man to his *pauaro's* wife, i.e., his wife's brother's son's wife, there is a touch of mischief in the very slight license which is allowed. For instance Lalinge would tease Ngaoli, the betrothed wife of his wife's brother's son, by refusing to avoid her, although such avoidance was prescribed until after Ngaoli's marriage. This is a good instance of the way in which one type of relationship behavior may impinge upon another. Between fathers and sons the most affectionate behavior is a light teasing without obscenity, but with a strong element of personality in it. Small boys may also tease their mothers although in later life they will treat them with respect.

For example, Popoli was angry at Paliau because Paliau had refused to take him on a projected canoe trip. He therefore, in order to revenge himself on his father, went and told his mother that Paliau had sent word for her to get all dressed up and ready to go on a canoe trip. Sain spent a good hour washing and dressing, only to join Paliau and find that Popoli had been lying. As a result, a quarrel ensued between man and wife and the small boy was revenged.

The relation between father and son is one of intimacy. A small boy habitually punts his father to the latrine. Much badinage is permitted between them. But between father and daughter there is a strict barrier on such matters as excretion, although a father may caress the vulva of his infant daughter, and playfully tweak the ear, or place his hand on the shoulder of an adolescent daughter.

Respect Behavior. Between a man's treatment of his adolescent daughter and a brother's treatment of his sister comes the hair line which divides light jesting from faint respect. The Manus are quite conscious of this distinction. As one man phrased it: "A father may tell his daughter that her grass skirt is not properly adjusted, but a brother may not do it. But, if a girl is habitually careless about her clothing, a brother may formally and publicly (in a family gathering) upbraid her." The over-personal note contained in the imputation of immodest exposure on the recent occasion is eliminated from the brother-sister relationship—as is also any element of playfulness.

A brother and sister, however, observe no taboo except a respect for each other's affinal relationships. A man may not discuss his wife with his sister, nor may a sister discuss her husband with her brother. A wife fleeing her husband's house after a serious quarrel will merely say formally to her brother, in whose house she has taken refuge, "My husband scolded me about tobacco. I am come." "My husband broke my arm with a stick, I am come." The brother asks for no further details.

But a brother and his wife nurse a woman through the first month after childbirth, although no males are permitted at the actual delivery. Her husband is not permitted near her for a month after the delivery. When a woman is ill, it is her brother who sits beside her and holds her head. A woman can de-louse a brother or any other consanguineous male relative, but not a husband. This right is not reciprocal. Male relatives can de-louse each other.

Respect behavior is primarily an avoidance of personalities, trivial or casual relations, joking, and non-serious lewd body contacts. Respect behavior is the least developed type of kinship behavior in Manus. This is to be expected in a society where there is such slight respect accorded age, where primogeniture can be so easily contravened, where rich men of *lau* rank can freely insult poor men of *lapan* rank, where a boy of adolescent age can tell the aging *luluai* to "hold his noise." Actually, respect relationships are merely those close relationships in which jesting is not permitted and avoidance is not enjoined.

Avoidance Behavior. There is a general term *kaleal*, which distinguishes all avoidance relationship from merely respect relationship, but in both relationships a man is said to be *mbulen mamatche*, ashamed. In respect relationships a man is merely potentially ashamed, i.e., were he to mention anything connected with sex, he would be shy, hot, embarrassed. So a father, although he may tell his daughter that her grass skirt is awry, if he must berate her for an actual or suspected sex lapse will do so publicly and formally. Publicity in Manus condones behavior which would be embarrassing or indiscreet, or sinful, as the case may be, if done in private.

In an avoidance relationship, a man or woman is always ashamed because the relationship itself is based upon an explicit recognition that a female relative of one is engaged in an actual sex relationship with a male relative of the other. All avoidance relationships have this basis, that is, they are all between affinal relatives. Difference in sex and difference in age act intensively here also.

Only one item of avoidance behavior affects practically all affinal relatives of the same or opposite sex, including betrothed pairs and husbands and wives, that is, name avoidance. It is therefore necessary at this point to discuss somewhat extensively the problem of personal names, because they are important in Manus purely in terms of affinal relationships. Avoidance of affinal names includes an enjoined avoidance of meaningful words included in the name, e.g., if an avoidance relative's name is Kor, "place," his avoidance relative will substitute the word *kwitchal*, literally, island; sometimes actual synonyms exist which can be used, as *yap*, *nyapoke*, and *suwel*, which all mean "foreign". However, as will appear in the discussion, most personal names are not meaningful.

The names of their affinal relatives must be avoided in speaking either to a man or woman, or even when speaking in their presence. The only exceptions to the rule of name avoidance are in cross-cousin jesting and when a man has adopted and financed the marriage of his wife's younger sister or younger brother. But in these latter cases spouses' names must be avoided instead.

The personal pronouns play an important substitutive rôle in affinal relationships.

USE OF PERSONAL PRONOUNS IN AFFINAL RELATIONSHIPS

i third person singular
i aru third person dual
i ato third person trial
i ala third person plural

In affinal usage these are used optionally with the prefix *m* instead of *i;* when *m* is prefixed to *i*, *l* is suffixed. A married couple is always spoken of as *i ato* (pronounced *yato*) and addressed as *uato* (pronounced *wato*), you three.

The only affinal relations to which *i*, the singular third person pronoun, can be applied, are: wife speaking of husband, husband of wife, man of his wife's brother, woman of her brother's wife. But if one speaks to one spouse of the other, or if one spouse addresses the other, one must preserve the fiction of the trial and speak of *i aru* or *maru*. A man will say to his wife, "*yayem maru*," "your mother." A man speaking of his own brother to his wife, will use *m i*, *mil*, or *e i;* the avoidance of the name is out of courtesy to her, for he owes his brother no avoidance. Those affinal relatives of the same sex as the speaker's spouse to whom son, daughter, or grandchild terms are applied, are spoken in the dual, *iaru* or *maru*, reciprocal *iato*. *Iaru*, reciprocal *i*, is used by a man of his sister's husband and by a woman of her husband's sister. Those affinal relations of opposite sex from speaker and older than spouse, but not parents of spouse are *iato*, reciprocal *iaru*, e.g., between husband's older brother and younger brother's wife.

Those affinal relatives to whom a spouse applies terms appropriate to the generation above are called *iala* or *mala* by both sexes before marriage, and by men until the marriage payment known as *komambut* is paid. After this, only those affinal relatives of opposite sex are called *iala*, reciprocally *ialo* and those of same sex may be called *iata*, reciprocally *iaru.*

This usage is not absolute and many deviations occur. The young and the timid are likely to speak of all their affinal relations in the plural.

Reference has already been made to the formal use of *ato* to precede a collective reference to a number of relatives—so *ato ndriasi, ato papun, ato yayen, ato kakalin,* etc.

Terms of Address
Regular kinship terms used in ordinary speech[1]

MAMBU: reciprocally *mangambu*
NGASI: reciprocally *mangambu*
PAPU: reciprocally PAPU especially to small boys
kakali (mother's brother): reciprocally KAKA to sister's minor children
pisio: reciprocally *pisio*
POLAPOL: reciprocally POLAPOL
pinpolapol: reciprocally *pinpolapol*

Additionally: INA mother; reciprocally, small child, is never used except in address. It is customary for anyone to address a very small child as *ina* as a term of reassurance: e.g., "*Ina! Wiyan, Wiya, Wiya.*" "My child, it's all right."

Yaye, "my mother," is only used ceremonially by women in formal lament or as an expletive by either sex. The most usual dirge or lament over someone who is lost, ill or injured is: *Yaye Yaye Yaye—i etepe i etepe i etepe,* "My mother, my mother, my mother, why or what is the matter."

This same custom of exclaiming "my mother" is found in Dobu.[2] It is interesting to note its occurrence in both matrilineally and patrilineally stressed societies.

When the *patieyen* performs the *tandritanitani*[3] over a girl at puberty, one of the blessings uttered is:—

> "When she keens may she not say merely
>   My mother, my mother
>   May she speak the names of people
>   Then all will understand."

---

[1] Terms printed in small capitals are often used; terms in italics are less often used.
[2] Fortune, R. F., *Sorcerers of Dobu, The Social Anthropology of the Dobu Islanders of the Western Pacific* (London, 1932).
[3] Ceremonial blessing or cursing exercised by woman's line upon members of the collateral male line.

This comment probably also applies to the frequency with which women fail to learn the names of their female ascendant line whose names should be ceremonially invoked.

The word *yaye* and *papu* are also used in oaths after the death of the parents, as follows: *londrian puin e yaye!* "Inside my mother's vagina." *ku iti papu i ki ne i au!* "Copulate with my father who is dead," or merely *ku iti papu!* "Copulate with my father."

As an endorsement of truthful statement, one whose father is dead may say: *ndrangen papu i ki ne i au* "(on the faith of?) my father who is dead."

Affinal Terms used as Terms of Address

kaiyo reciprocally *kaiyo*
pinkaiyo reciprocally *pinkaiyo*
polapol (wife of *polapol* m.s.; spouse of *pinpolapol* w.s.) *polapol*
pauaro reciprocally *pauaro*

USE OF PERSONAL NAMES

Personal names may be used between all people who are not affinal relatives and between certain affinal relatives where the foster father-child relationships or foster mother-child relationship has superseded in feeling and function the original affinal relationship. Children may use personal names to their parents and habitually do so, with the exception of very small children who use the terms *ina* and *papu*. There is no feeling about children's using the names of their elders and there is no taboo upon use of the names of the dead.

A child is given a name by each of the men who assist in making the feast of sago with which its mother is returned to its father a month after its birth. All of these men act as "brothers" to its mother and are, theoretically, therefore mother's brothers or *kakalin*. A Manus will say that a child has as many names as it has *kakalin* who helped with the feast. A consideration of usage shows that sometimes the entrepreneurs of the feast will give more than one name to a child and also that neither the entrepreneur nor his assistants need be "brothers" of the woman. They may be *kakalin*, *nebonitun*, or *papun*, as this is the most flexibly organized feast in Manus.

Samples taken at random, of the chief entrepreneurs of a series of childbirth feasts yield the following results:—

Name of Mother	Order of Birth of Child	Relation of Entrepreneur
1. Indalo	1.	Adopted father: *papun*
	2.	Mother's brother: *kakalin*
	3.	Adopted father: *papun*
	4.	Mother's sister's son: who is a titular *pision*
	5.	A different mother's sister's son: *pision*
2. Kompwen	1.	Stepfather: *papun*
	2.	Mother's father's brother's son: *kakalin*
	3.	Father's father's brother's son: *papun*
	4.	Father's father's son: *pision*
	5.	same as 3
	6.	same as 3
3. Matuin	1.	Brother: *pision*
	2.	Mother's brother: *kakalin*
	3.	Same as 1
	4.	Mother's brother's son: *pision*
	5.	Same as 4

So naming cannot be said to be a function only of a *kakalin*, but only a function of any male relative of the mother who acts as her brother in providing sago for the birth feast.

The choice of names is dictated partly by consideration of inheritance, partly by whim and sentiment. In any recitation of lines of ghostly ancestors the same names recur. So, some of the acting *kakalin* will name a male for a member of the father's line, a female for a female member of the mother's line. Giving a child a name held by a living relation is avoided because of the difficulties which the name taboos would introduce. So a child could not be named after a parent or after a parent's sibling. If it were so named the other parent would be unable to use its name. The Manus are very strict in this. One must not merely avoid referring to an affinal relative by name but using a part of that name in any way.

It is, however, permissible to name a child after the recently dead, for the name taboos do not apply to the dead. Naming a child after the Sir Ghost of its household is a fairly common procedure. For example, Pokanau's youngest child, Sori, was named after Pokanau's dead brother, an acting Sir Ghost. Selan's eldest child, who was adopted by his elder brother was named Topwal after Selan's dead brother and Sir Ghost. Paliau's adopted son was named Popoli after Paliau's father's brother, who had been Paliau's Sir Ghost, antecedent to the death of Pwanau (Paliau's foster brother who was now his Sir Ghost) and the dead Popoli was now made the Sir Ghost of his small namesake. Saleiau, the name of the dead brother of Korotan, was given the eldest son of Korotan's adopted son, Tcholai.

But whim may also dictate names: so Pokanau named the baby girl of his titular sister, Ilan, after the two spirit wives of Sori, his elder brother, who was Ilan's mother's brother, and foster father. Three of the babies born while I was in the village were named after me: Piyap (woman from the west), Missus, and Makit, respectively. There was a child named *Kiap* (pidgin for district officer) and a child named Maria in Peri. The provision for many names seems to provide effectively against any hard and fast rules.

Only about a tenth of the names recorded were meaningful, the others appeared to be traditional. Examples of meaningful names are:—

>Pikawas: woman friend
>Pilapan: woman of rank
>Paliau: *bonito*
>Posangat: pigs a hundred
>Malegan: on top
>Patali: platform of a canoe

Men's names are often characteristically prefixed with *Po*, women's with *Nga* (or *Nya*)[1] or *Pi*. However, this is not a rule, only a tendency. Men's names prefixed with *Nga* occur, although I have no instance of a woman whose name began with *Po* except where the *Po* was not properly a prefix at all; e.g., *Ponyama*, liar, or *Pokila*, literally, pig he goes. Furthermore, a widow is often called after her husband with the prefix *Nya*. So the widow of Polion was called Nyapolion by everyone in the village. However, many female children are given names with a *Nya* prefix.

Analysis of names most commonly used by ninety-six women and girls shows:—

>*85 names in all*
>11 names occur twice
>24 are prefixed with *Nga* or *Nya*
>3 are prefixed with *Pi*

Analysis of names most commonly used by seventy-seven men and boys shows:—

>*77 names in all*
>6 names occur twice
>17 are prefixed with *Po*
>9 were habitually called by their father's names, prefixed with *Tali*, son of

It is interesting, however, to note that the repeated names occurred only where at least one of the persons was a child. Among grown mem-

---

[1] The pronunciation seems to vary without significance.

bers of a village, it is customary to avoid using the same name for more than one person. The reason for this is obvious; such duplication would increase the difficulties of observing the name taboos. For example, if one's sister be named Ngalowen and one's brother's mother-in-law be called Ngalowen also, one could never mention one's sister to one's brother. Another one of the sister's names which did not introduce a taboo situation would then be selected for daily use, after the brother's betrothal had made the name Ngalowen taboo. Similarly, there were two children in the village called Topal. If one were betrothed into the family of the other, one of the names would lapse at once.

This is a good example of the relationship between form and function. To single out the relationship of mother's brother for special functions is a widespread Oceanic trait. Naming a sister's child is only one of these. Its homologue is often found in matrilineal societies in the father's sister giving the name. The extension of this practice to the man who acts as a brother at the mother's birth feast and to all male relatives of the mother who contribute to the feast is characteristic of the Manus methods of extending kinship function in conformity with economic necessities. But one of the functions of the results of this Manus modification and elaboration of widespread Oceanic practice is to provide an escape from the difficulties inherent in the system of name avoidance. It would be ridiculous to claim that this multiple naming custom had its origins in a need for providing alternative names, but it does function as a way of providing such alternatives.

But the avoidance of using the same name for more than one person while it saves one from having one's tongue tied in addressing one's blood kin, still leaves the avoidance situation to be dealt with when reference must be made to affinal relations themselves.

The need for name avoidance is so omnipresent in Manus that the complete disuse of personal names would be a welcome relief. The Manus deal with persons who cannot be referred to by one of the kinship terms listed as used in address (for one does not refer e.g. to the *patieyen* of So-and-so unless her ceremonial functions are being considered) by calling them by the names of husbands, parents or grandparents, by nicknames, or by terms of bereavement.

Terms which are used with the name of another with a prefix are of two sorts.

Phrases and Prefixes used before Death	Prefixes used after Death
nat e: son of	*tali:* son of; (always used in formal ceremonial address)
ndrakein e ⎫ daughter of *asaun e* ⎭	*asali:* daughter of (this is rarely used)
pati e: wife of	*nga* or *nya:* widow of
yakamel e: husband of	

mangambu e: grandchild of (is used both before and after the death of the grandparent)

Adults particularly refer to children of other families by their parents' names. Some of this usage is taken up by the children, some not. So one little Ngalowen was almost always called *ndrakein e Pondramet* because there were two other Ngalowens in the village. Sometimes the double terminologies are heard together, e.g., *nat e Talipopwitch.* This is literally, "The son of the son of Popwitch" because Talipopwitch had become the customary name under which Ngamel was known to the community. The child in question had been called Kilipak, but as Kilipak was his cousin and titular father, the use of Kilipak had been practically abandoned. *Nat e* and *ndrakein e* are used with almost equal frequency.

Pati e, "wife of," is used with great frequency, especially by children. It will readily be seen that with wives prevailingly resident in the husband's place, it is the wife's name which must be most often avoided in the community. The comparable "*yakamal e*" is habitually only used within the family itself where all men married into it have to be referred to as husband of daughters or sisters. Where the personal name of a woman has been abandoned for many years in the village of her husband, the substitution with widowhood of the *nya* for the *pati e* comes naturally to the tongue.

When a man is resident with his wife's relatives, it is sometimes customary to refer to a man as "son" or "grandson" of his father or grandfather-in-law. This usage is not, however, as common as the use of the terms for blood or adoptive relationships.

Although a husband and wife may not use each other's names, the names of the dead parents are no longer taboo. Consequently, a woman will address her husband as Talilakolon or Talikai without embarrassment, and he can call her Asaun e Pwanau, in reply. This usage will however depend upon whether the wife's mother is living and is called by her dead husband's name. As an illustration:—

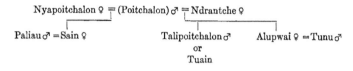

Tunu could call his wife Alupwai, Asali-Poitchalon, or Asuan-e-Poitchalon and if his brother-in-law was referred to as Talipoitchalon in his presence he need not feel offended or embarrassed. But Paliau could not use the name Poitchalon in a compound term for his wife, Sain, because it was used habitually in his mother-in-law's name and anyone referring to his brother-in-law in his presence had to speak of him as *Tuain*. When Paliau referred to his wife he always spoke of her as *Mangambun Pin Usiai* "grandchild of an Usiai woman." In this usage he was followed by his son also, while his two adopted daughters, the children of his dead adopted brother and titular father, usually referred to their foster mother as Sain, because they were seldom in their foster father's company.

But the use of these oblique kin terms does not by any means solve the problem of name avoidance. For example, a ceremony is held about fifteen days after first menstruation at which only women are present. It is held in the house where the nubile girl is confined, and it is phrased as a feast given by the women of the family to the women who have married into it. The girls who are betrothed to youths of the gens are remembered by gifts of food, but cannot be present. Guests and hostesses both provide bowls of cooked food and supplies of betel nut. Were the guests, i.e., the women married into the family not present, they would be referred to as the "pati e" (wife of) X, Y, Z, respectively. Their names are taboo to the women of the gens. But, because they are present, there is no name by which they may be addressed unless everyone knows the names of dead parents which can be employed.

Although nicknames would deal with this situation, they are not resorted to very extensively. I have a feeling that this is because personal nicknames would rapidly assume the quality of personal names and demand the same type of response. Only one type of nickname, that is, a derogatory type, is used: *mwengo*, crazy man; *pingo*, crazy woman; *paringo*, mad man; *ponyama*, liar. These names, usually employed merely as terms of abuse, sometimes become definitely attached to personalities to whom they are particularly apposite. The term *luluai* is always used, instead of a personal name, and, since the coming of government-created officialdom, (in native phrasing since the coming of the '*at*—hat) the terms *kukerai*, village constable, *tultul*, interpreter, and *dokita*, doctor boy, are used by everyone for the individuals in question.

But the most usual method of avoiding the name difficulty is through the use of mourning terms. When one refers to a taboo affinal relative by a mourning term, the appropriate pronoun must be used, but no other insistance upon avoidance is enjoined. (It will be understood that one never refers even thus obliquely to an affinal relative unless it is absolutely necessary). The following is a list of the mourning terms:—

pinyau: widow (*pi:* female prefix)
ponyau: widower (*po:* male prefix)
tamapwe: male whose father is dead (it is probable that this was originally *tamapwen* [not] now shortened to *pwe*)
potinam: male whose mother is dead
  It is notable that in many of these mourning terms the common Malay words for father and mother, *tama* and *tina* are used.
yataman: married woman whose father is dead
kutamakit: unmarried woman whose father is dead
yatinam: woman whose mother is dead
ngauwen: married woman whose brother is dead
penampwen: unmarried woman whose brother is dead
natumpwen: man whose son is dead
pilinampwen: woman whose sister is dead
ndriasimpwen: man whose brother is dead
polimpwen: man whose cross-cousin is dead ·
kaiyempwen: man whose brother-in-law is dead
ngasimpwen: one whose maternal grandmother is dead
nambumpwen: one whose grandfather is dead
kalimpwen: one whose mother's brother is dead

Technically, these terms are only used between a death and the completion of the funeral rites. Actually, if a term is convenient in solving an avoidance situation, it will be kept.[1]

---

[1]Since the introduction of pidgin English, two new terms have been added to Manus idiom: the mourning term *nufela*, one who has lost an infant child, literally, "one whose child died when it was a *new fellow*," and the term *wannem* "one name" used between or of namesakes. This should not be interpreted as the breakdown of Manus custom, but rather as proof of its flexibility and also as due to the peculiar genius of the uninflected language. The Manus can substitute the pidgin "work" for the Manus "*mangas*" or the pidgin "*gerise*" for the Manus "*kip*" without any change in sentence structure. The pronunciation of pidgin words has already been modified to meet the phonetic requirements. A fair number of pidgin words has gotten into the speech of the women and the non-pidgin-speaking men in Manus and these are not felt as foreign. *Nufela* is perhaps the most conspicuous of these, as the people argued with me at length that it was a genuine Manus word. Examples of words which have so interpenetrated Manus speech are:—
  kiki: small
  kiap: district officer
  tabac: tobacco
  massis: matches
  lice: rice
  kuta: cutter
  wok: work
  pepa: paper
  lambaran: spirit
  pilas: flash, used in the sense of to decorate, to adorn
  nuchum: newchum, tenderfoot

It was impossible to tell whether the choice of terminology in Peri was accidental or whether it represented the more usual terms. In the village of Peri there were three women called Ngauwen, two called Yametan, one boy called Tamapwe, two married couples called Nufela and a large number of widows and widowers who were all called Pinyau and Ponyau, respectively. Although informants said that all of the mourning terms should be used, investigation proved that many individuals who should have been called by various other of the terms, were not so called, and led to the conclusion that the terms are used most frequently, not as a formal act of mourning, but as devices for avoiding taboo names. This was particularly clear in those cases where a man called his wife Pinyau, a recognition of her past widowed state, or a wife called her husband Ponyau, or where these terms were used by others when referring to remarried persons.

OTHER ASPECTS OF AVOIDANCE BEHAVIOR

Between all affinal relatives (except as between husband and wife, in a marriage of many years' standing or to which several children have been born) there is a taboo against eating together.

Between affinal relatives of the same sex, who are not spouses of jesting relatives,—as, e.g., a man jests with his wife's brother's son and lightly with his cross-cousin's wife,—there is also considerable formality of behavior. All intimate discussion of any sort is barred. Nevertheless, despite this behavior brothers-in-law and sisters-in-law are expected to be friends, to coöperate with each other in all undertakings in which they are not definitely opposed to each other by the economic arrangements arising from the marriage of the sister of one to the other, or of the brother of one to the other.

Genuine avoidance is only exercised between all affinal relatives of opposite sex during the period of betrothal, and, as was remarked above, it is customary for a young person betrothed to a member of another village to avoid the entire male population of that village, as a precautionary measure. The ghosts, although supposed to take a general supervisory interest in all observances of *kaleal*, take a special interest in only two types, the *kaleal* during betrothal and the *kaleals* which are not kinship dictated,—those which arise between people who have committed or been accused of illicit sex behavior. Breaches of the former type of *kaleal* are sometimes mentioned in seances and ghosts have been known to kill for the latter. Breaches of either type are regarded as tantamount to a sex offense on the ground that no one would be foolhardy enough to risk them otherwise. Mr. Fortune has pointed out the function of the avoidance regulations during betrothal, in cases where the girl's chastity is in doubt. The angry party of the bridegroom is prevented from forcibly abducting the promised bride, by the force of the enjoined avoidance.

The rules of betrothal avoidance include a prohibition against use of names, against going to the place—gentile division of own village or other village—of the betrothed, and against looking at or being seen by any male relative of the betrothed, in the case of a girl, or by any female relative, in the case of a boy. Some children are betrothed in early childhood: in this case the adults and older children begin to enforce the avoidance before the children properly grasp what is going on. A mother will pull part of her cloak over the face of her two-year-old girl as they pass a canoe in which sits the four-year-old betrothed. If two little children who are betrothed stray into the same play group, older children will seize them and hustle them in opposite directions. Children of six and seven know enough to avoid the children to whom they are betrothed, always to stay away from their parts of the village, and not to say their name. The burden of more precise avoidance rests upon the adults, the prospective mothers-in-law and fathers-in-law. By the time girls are ten and eleven and boys are twelve or thirteen conscious avoidance of these latter relatives will be added. Girls of fourteen and fifteen are sufficiently socially conscious to avoid the youths who are betrothed to their younger "sisters," blood or classificatory. Except in the case of very small girls, and of unmarried and recently married boys, the burden of avoidances in any particular case falls upon the females.

Women are aided in their avoidance outside the home by a calico cloak which has superseded the characteristic peaked rain mat of aboriginal days. The modern cloak is simply a piece of unhemmed calico or a blanket which is bunched rudely together at one end to form a pocket for the head. It falls almost to the ground and is wide enough to wrap completely around the woman. In a canoe gathering at which her *kaleals* are present she sits huddled up on the canoe platform, her head bowed between her knees, her knees hunched, and her whole form wrapped in the cloak. The old type of rain mat could not provide as complete a shelter. Only women without *kaleals* in their own village go about freely without any head covering. Such a woman would only be free if the village contained no older male relative of her husband and no males betrothed to younger female relatives of her own. Widows who were married into distant villages are sometimes in this position in their own village, as are young girls who are betrothed to men of distant villages. Occasionally a very young or very old woman will have only one *kaleal* in the village. In this case she will habitually go without a protecting wrap, always, however, running the risk of being caught. In such plight was Piwen, the just nubile daughter of Kukun of Patusi. Piwen came to live for some weeks in Peri, with the daughter of her stepmother. Piwen herself was unbetrothed, but her younger sister·was engaged to Manawei, a Peri boy of about seventeen. Piwen wore no wrap, but spent many uncomfortable minutes crouched in the hulls of canoes, with her face flattened against the bottom, for she was Manawei's "mother-in-law."

The women who labor under the greatest disadvantage are young women in their husbands' villages, and older women whose daughters have married into their own villages. A young wife in her husband's village may have to avoid half a dozen older men. An older woman may have several sons-in-law from whom she must hide or run away. Hiding her face is only accepted in lieu of running away when running away is impossible, as in a canoe, or when a woman is surprised in a group. If a man appears on the edge of a group, the women who are his *kaleals* hastily cover their faces and drift away into the back of the house or out of the house altogether, or off the *arakeu* on to a canoe platform.

But neither men nor women may join a group in·which they know an important *kaleal* to be, i.e., a *kaleal* of the "*iala*" class. So a man will say to another, "Will you take this to X over there on the *arakeu* a *kaleal* of mine is there." Or a canoe arrives from another village for a feast which is not yet prepared. Some of the people go into a house, but two women remain outside because a *kaleal* of theirs is in the house.

Technically, for purposes of observing *kaleals*, a house is divided into two parts by one or more mats hung from the ceiling. Such a house can accommodate two households in which live a man and a woman whom he calls daughter-in-law and who must therefore avoid him, and never raise her voice so that he can hear it at the other end of a house. Nor can she ever go into his section of the house except when he is absent. This division of the house is designed to accommodate *kaleals* of the father-in-law—daughter-in-law type which are felt to be less drastic than those of the mother-in-law—son-in-law type. The occupation of a house by two brothers, in which case the younger wife must avoid the older brother, as a titular "father-in-law," is a common situation. In entering other houses, women follow the same rule. They will enter the other end of houses in which they are "daughter-in-law," but not of houses in which they are "mother-in-law" unless the titular "son-in-law" is absent. Similarly a Manus woman may attend a feast at which her husband's older brother is also present, but not one at which her young sister's husband is present.

Comment has already been made upon the way in which children are inducted into their own *kaleal* relationships. A child and a parent only share the same *kaleals* until the child marries. Before marriage, a woman and her daughter must be equally circumspect in avoiding the daughter's betrothed husband. But whereas the daughter avoids a whole group of men, all her betrothed's older male relatives, her mother will only avoid the daughter's fiancé. After marriage there is no common ground between parents and children. (Actually of course mother and daughter avoid the use of the daughter's husband's name, but the mother-in-law avoidance is of so rigid a type that it is not permissible to pair the mother-daughter behavior further).

From another angle, a parent's *kaleals* are a child's relatives. The woman whom a child calls *ngasi* is her father's most severely avoided relative, and conversely her father's older brothers are her mother's *kaleals*. Children of four or five learn not to pronounce the names of their parents' *kaleal* in their parents' presence. Most often this becomes almost automatic. There is unconscious imitation in the case of the parents' names, for young children learn to call their parents by the terms which they mutually use, "Nufelu," "Grandson of Kemwai"; "Daughter of a man of Taui"; "Pinyau," or as it so happens. *Ngasi* and *mambu* are both terms of address, so that this custom takes care of the more intimate *kaleals* of both parents, comprising as it does father's older brothers and mother's older sisters and their spouses, also. *Kakalin*, mother's brother, is seldom used; *patieyen*, father's sister, is never a term of address, but neither are these relatives important *kaleals* of the parents. Little girls of seven and eight learn, however, to avoid the names which their mothers avoid; boys are slower in making this adoption and do not show comparable quickness in adopting their father's *kaleals*. This however is partly a correlate of the fact that boys, being less with women, pay less attention to the social structure. It is also partly a result of the different response to the *kaleal* situation. Betrothed boys respond if anything more violently to the possible mention of *kaleal* than do betrothed girls. When they go through the village of the betrothed, boys, lacking protecting calicoes, must lie face down on the canoe platforms, completely covered with a mat. If the progress of the canoe is slow, broken by gossipy chats along the way, they may have to remain in this uncomfortable position for half an hour or more. Young married men whose payment for their wives has not been completed must go about circumspectly, avoiding the close proximity of their wives' elder male relatives as well as of their female relatives. Young married women do not have to exercise any comparable type of avoidance towards their husband's mother and sister. But men of thirty-five or forty, who are economically independent, can afford to take a less strict attitude towards their wives' relatives. With their wives' brothers they are on terms of near equality—the slight shade of purely technical superiority of woman's brother over woman's husband only showing with difference of the pronoun of reference: *i* for sister's husband, *iaru* for wife's brother.

If the mother-in-law of such a man is still living, she will be an old old woman, and his avoidance of her, grown habitual through ten or fifteen years, will have lost much of its emotional tone. A middle-aged man upon being asked a question which involves his mother-in-law will giggle, snicker, and tuck his head down on his shoulder, as he mutters, "I can't say her name." Meanwhile he has, of course, acquired new *kaleals* in the betrothed and husbands of young females of the household, but the onus of avoidance observation is upon them. He need fear no embarrassment if he accidentally confronts them.

For a woman it is different. As the weight of the "father-in-law" taboo drops from her shoulder, the weight of taboos based on her position as "mother-in-law" must be assumed. There is no respite for her with increasing age. She has had to avoid her "fathers-in-law" and now she must avoid her "sons-in-law." Her response to anyone naming a *kaleal*, or bringing a *kaleal* into the conversation is one of angry embarrassment. Young girls will slap small children of their households who do not observe the proper name avoidance, and women will severely rebuke their children and shout viciously at other women if they are careless. This anger is definitely of the type which is a defensive response from shame. Little girls will remark, "No, that is not a *kaleal* of mine, it is a *kaleal* of my mother's (or my sister's); I help my mother."

This difference in attitude between men and women may be more of a contributing factor to the boys' slighter attention to their parents' *kaleals* than is the boys' general lack of interest in social organization.

Kaleal relationships have special results on occasions of mourning when a large number of *kaleal* relatives are gathered in the *mwandrin*, the house of mourning, for twenty days following the death. On such occasions the women remain in the back of the house, the men all sleep together in the front, and all sex intercourse is completely interdicted.

In ordinary living, however, the back of the house, which is occupied by one brother and his wife, is felt to be sufficiently self-contained so that no such taboos are operative. The only cases in which the *kaleal* relationships are definitely relaxed are those already mentioned in which the father-in-law or husband's older brother feasts the daughter-in-law and removes the taboo. In this case she becomes like his daughter; in the case of an old man, she may prepare his food and eat in his presence. Additionally a wife's younger brothers and sisters, or a husband's younger brothers and sisters are considered as the children of the older siblings' spouse, in which case the taboo relationship to the older siblings' spouse is completely superseded.

During the period of betrothal, however, the name and food taboo will be observed between a girl and her husband's younger brother whom she will later call, "son," and for whom she may later cook.

The question of choice of relationship[1] when individuals are relatives in more than one way, is brought up in two ways in Manus, by adoption, and by marriages which set up new relationships. (The first type of choice will be discussed under adoption). It is of course an obvious point that in a small community, individuals who already trace genealogical relationships to each other will be brought into new relationships of an affinal type by either their own or their relatives' marriages. Nothing seems to be gained by elaborating a large number of individual cases on the point. But from a collection of such cases a few general tendencies emerge. In the case of important *kaleals* of the *i ala* class between members of the opposite sex, the *kaleal* relationship supersedes the genealogical. The most striking cases are those in which a woman calls her father's father's sister's son *papu* before betrothal, and must refer to him as *i ala* and avoid him thereafter. Similarly, when a woman marries her father's father's sister's daughter's son, his mother was once her *pinpapu* and now becomes her mother-in-law. In these cases, which are rare because of the infrequency of this ideal marriage, there is literally no choice. So in cases where fathers-in-law or mothers-in-law and children-in-law stood in other relationships to each other before betrothal, the new avoidance relationship supersedes the older relation-

---

[1]This point was discussed by Armstrong (Armstrong, W. E., *Rossel Island.   An Ethnological Study* (Cambridge, 1928) and elaborated in a more recent article by Raymond Firth, Marriage and the Classificatory System of Relationship (*Journal of the Royal Anthropological Institute of Great Britain and Ireland*, vol. 60, 235–268, 1930).

ship. However, in less important relationships, and, where the individuals concerned are both female, the blood or adoption category will be chosen in preference to the affinal category. Female affinal relationships are never without a certain unpleasant feeling tone and a woman will always choose against them where slighter avoidances are involved. Men have a tendency to choose almost invariably *kaleal* relationships in the case of women relatives, and usually, if the affinal relationship involved is that of "brothers-in-law," *kaiyon.* For, unlike the relationship between female affinal relatives and the shamed relationship between young men and their "fathers-in-law," the relationship of *kaiyon* is one to be sought, carrying with it a pleasant feeling tone of coöperation and interdependence.

In the one case in which a brother and sister married a brother and sister (which was felt as very aberrant in Manus) all avoidances were dropped between the four people involved. This was not a question of choice between considering a man as a wife's brother or a sister's husband, but rather a sense that the unprecedented economic balance of this alliance nullified all usual procedure.

The ubiquitousness of the *kaleal* situation in Manus is well illustrated by the behavior of a deaf mute girl of about ten. She was, of course, unbetrothed, but everywhere around her she saw women avoiding men, and she had understood the situation well enough to realize its intersexual character. The unfortunate child made one attempt after another to find out whom she should be avoiding, selecting now one male relative, then another, to flee from. The people realized what she was doing, though the non-verbal persistence which was necessary to re-educate her sometimes taxed their patience sorely and the objects of her misplaced avoidance used to remark, "I am weary of Ngalen's avoidances."

Divorced persons are under a strict *kaleal* régime, but their respective relatives need not observe the *kaleals* unless they wish. Whether they do so or not seems to be largely a matter of taste, in this case and after the death of relatives also. Between adults of opposite sex long years of shyness and habit may operate so that it seems the line of least resistance to keep up the *kaleal.* This was the case, for instance, between the widow Main and her dead younger sister's widower, Korotan. Although she had informally adopted Taliye, the daughter of Korotan and her dead sister, and although the child was with her often, Main continued to avoid Korotan as if he were her son-in-law. Conversely, in Peri there were two men who had married their dead wives' older sisters, i.e., married women who had been previously their titular "mothers-in-law." However, as all arranged marriages are prefaced by a period of the most severe avoidance this transition is not as artificial emotionally as it might seem.

AVOIDANCE SITUATIONS WHICH ARE NOT FUNCTIONS OF KINSHIP[1]

There is another type of avoidance which is not a function of kinship, the *kaleal* that follows a threat of sorcery, and *kaleals* between individuals one of whom has become involved with the other's Sir Ghosts (the results of widow-remarriage fall under this last head).

Pokanau was in a canoe with his father's sister's son up a freshwater stream in the Usiai country years ago. His cousin was stricken down in a fit and died on the spot. Thereafter, the mother of the dead man set up a strict avoidance towards Pokanau.

Pwanau was the Sir Ghost of Paliau. The widow of Pwanau and her daughter Salikon, and Sain, the wife of Paliau, were all sleeping in a *mwandrin* (house of mourning) in the house of the medium Isole and overheard Isole interpret a seance accusing Pwanau of the death of the child whose corpse they were mourning. The women of Pwanau's household slipped out of the house and reported the matter to Paliau. For some time thereafter there was a *mwere* (middle space) between the household of Paliau whose Sir Ghost had been accused, and the house of Isole, who had been the accuser.

After Tcholai had by trickery extracted from Lawian a confession of intercourse with Noan, Tcholai, and Lawian, cross-cousins, Noan and Lawian "brother" and "sister" and Tcholai and Noan were all on terms of strict avoidance.

Patalian's *kaleal* relationships to the women of Kalo gens are also interesting. Patalian was a widower of about thirty-five. He was on avoidance terms with Ndrantche, an old widow, because he had years before as a boy seduced her and had then run away to work for a white man. He was on avoidance terms with Sain, the wife of Paliau, also of Kalo gens, because he had once been accused of having sex relations with her while Paliau, her betrothed, was away at work. The charge was disproved to everyone's satisfaction, but had Sain and Patalian not avoided each other scrupulously, suspicion would have been aroused again.

He was on avoidance terms with Lawa, the daughter of Ndrantche, because he had made overtures to marry Lawa. Ndrantche had interfered and Lawa had eloped with a Patusi man. As Patalian's black magic was believed to be pursuing the Kalo gens because of Lawa's elopement after he had paid over property for her, it was necessary that Patalian should perform a series of rites over Lawa's baby. But, as Patalian and Lawa were *kaleals*, this necessitated removing the baby from its mother and putting it in charge of another woman.

Patalian avoided the widow of Pwanau (also of Kalo) because he had once been accused of wishing to marry her.

He later eloped with the widow of Pwanau, after which he was avoided by all Pwanau's relatives male and female, all of whom feared Pwanau's vengeance if they showed any friendliness to Patalian.

---

[1]Most of these instances are treated more fully in Fortune, *ibid.*, Chapter V.

SUMMARY OF AVOIDANCE RELATIONSHIP

Avoidance relationships may be summarized as follows. There are three principal classes:—

1. Affinal relatives older than one's spouse
2. Affinal relatives of one's own age and sex
3. Affinal relatives younger than one's spouse

Class 1 may then be further subdivided:—

   a. Affinal relatives of opposite sex older than spouse
   b. Affinal relatives of same sex older than spouse

Class 1, section a, are the major *kaleals*
Class 2 are affinal relatives to whom one bears a functioning relationship
Class 3 are merged with younger siblings by blood

Husband and Wife. Mr. Fortune has described the husband-wife relationship as one of disrespect, thus putting it in a fourth category of relationship behavior. There are certainly no elements of respect nor of jesting in the conventional conjugal relationship. From the standpoint of avoidance, a husband and wife have been on strictest terms of avoidance for the period of betrothal. After marriage the taboo against use of personal names still holds. Couples who have been wed only a few months and who have no children avoid each other in public and do not eat together until two or three children have been born to them or until the marriage is of several years' standing.

In Peri there were several young married couples who never appeared together in a canoe or at a public gathering. As age and number of children are easier to calculate than length of marriage, the extent of the marriage may be stated in these terms.

Husbands and Wives Who Still Shunned Each Other in Public

		Remarks
1.	Malean—*Ngalen*[1]	Married three months
2.	Polin—*Kupano*	Married two years, but childless
3.	Saot—*Ngakaton*	One child of two
4.	Topas—*Ilan*	Two children, four years and two months
5.	Nganidrai—*Patali*	One child of two
6.	Talikawa—*Pinpinyo*	Infant of three months
7.	Pomo—*Kingo*	Two children, two and a half years and infant

Of these *Patali*, Talikawa, and *Kingo* had been married before.

Also a husband is forbidden to treat his wife playfully or lightly. All sexual foreplay is regarded as "jesting" and strictly interdicted. Finally, casual conversation is considered inappropriate to the conjugal relationship.

---

[1] Italics indicates a female.

So much for the avoidance aspects of marriage. Against them must be set a man's right of access to his wife for purposes of sexual intercourse and a man's right to beat his wife. Several men in the village kept wife beaters, long flexible switches, in the house. If a husband beats his wife, custom demands that she leave him and go to her brother, real or officiating, and remain a length of time commensurate with the degree of her offended dignity. During this period her brother's house is a sanctuary which her husband and his kin cannot enter. As messengers to request his wife's return, the husband must employ women who have married into his gens, not his own female relatives.

The only exception to this behavior occurred in the household of Pokanas. The wife of Pokanas was one of the most definite characters in the village and she was admitted to rule her husband as well as her household. On one occasion Pokanas lost his temper and struck her. Contrary to custom she did not trouble to leave for her brother Ndrosal's house, but merely summoned Ndrosal, who began beating Pokanas' mother in retaliation. Pokanas then attacked Ndrosal. Ndrosal and Pokanas came to grips on the veranda of Pokanas' own house, and both fell into the lagoon, which ended the matter. The injured feelings of Pokanas' wife were assuaged.

It is customary for men to treat their wives with a maximum of avoidance and a minimum of disrespect if the men are engaged in important economic affairs in which they want their wives' help. Conversely, if the wives are deeply involved in some economic affair which concerns their own blood kin, the husbands feel themselves masters of the situation, and treat their wives high-handedly.

THE GROWING CHILD AND THE KINSHIP CATEGORIES[1]

After reviewing the types of behavior which are prescribed between different classes of blood or affinal relatives, it is now possible to consider how these various relationships affect the individual, what contributions they make to his life, economically, socially, emotionally, religiously. This can be done best, I think, by considering first the ways in which these different relationships impinge upon the growing child. Professor Malinowski[2] has made a great deal theoretically of what he calls "The Initial Situation" of kinship, that is, the immediate family situation in which the child finds itself. The initial situation may, however, be somewhat more·complex than Professor Malinowski suggests. His analysis

---

[1]For more detailed discussion of some of the aspects of child-rearing referred to in this chapter, see *Growing Up in New Guinea*, Part I.

[2]Malinowski, B., Article on Kinship, (*Encyclopedia Britannica*, fourteenth edition).

regards the child's calling its mother's sister "mother" as an extension of an already comprehended mother-child relationship. It is possible also to find the converse case in which the generalized adult-child situation is initial and from which the child later learns to particularize the "mother-child" or "father-child" relationship. This latter formulation more nearly describes the Samoan situation. I stress this here because Manus conditions do in great part bear out Professor Malinowski's conclusions. The Melanesian family, as found in Manus, Dobu, and the Trobriands, is a very close and intimate group; the walled house and the etiquette surrounding its entrance by non-residents affords a large degree of privacy. But, of course, the Melanesian family, as exemplified by these three instances, must not be regarded as a universal type— even for Melanesia.

In order to comprehend the family situation in which the Manus baby finds itself, it is necessary to understand house arrangements. The Manus house is a pile structure thirty to sixty feet long, twelve to fifteen feet wide, with dome-shaped roof sloping from ridge pole to house floor. At each end of the house is a landing platform, and a ladder, a notched log, leading from the landing platform to the house floor, some five to eight feet above the level of the platforms. The house floor is reached through a rectangular trap-opening in the floor. The sides of this opening, together with the section back of it, comprise a sort of reception room.

As a house is usually occupied by two families, the arrangement described above must be duplicated for the rear. Some indications, however, suggest that the house is designed not for two families, but for one. The person whose house it is—who is usually the man who built it, or in rare cases, the old man or woman for whom the house was built,— is known as *rametan um*, owner of the house. The front of the house is called *palan um;* the interior or central section—where there are four fireplaces, two ranged against each wall—is *lon um*, and the rear of the house is called *kuin um*. Along the center of the house floor runs a long beam which is called the *petitchol*. The pillars which support the cross beams, are stepped in the *petitchol*. The floor of the house is composed of sections of sago palm bark or betel palm wood, fastened loosely together in sections which rest in a framework superimposed on the floor structure. If the house floor is divided into three transverse sections the *palan um* and *kuin um* equal two-thirds of it, and are identical in size and construction. The central section has four fireplaces, two set opposite to each other against each wall of the house. The fireplaces are made of wood ashes on a base of old mats bordered by a square framework of hard wood. In each fireplace are two or three irregularly shaped stones about ten or eleven inches tall which furnish support for the cooking vessels. Above each fireplace is suspended a slatted shelf upon which fish are spread for smoking. Small quantities of firewood are piled against the walls, between, or beside the fireplaces. The space of two to five feet between the side fireplaces is the dividing line between the front and back of the house. Along the cross beams, long poles are ranged close together so as to form shelves for storing pots, fishing tackle, paddles, punts, masts, sails, bailers, etc. Small valuables like dogs' teeth, shell money, and tortoise shell ornaments, are kept in tightly plaited bags, the primary purpose of which is to carry betel nut; these are rolled up and put away on the shelves. The thatch shingles provide convenient places for tucking small objects, bait for drying, uncompleted beadwork, a child's bow and arrow, etc.

The house of a wealthy man usually contains a *patapat*, a carved bed, about three and a half feet high, constructed in ten or eleven pieces, which can be joined together or taken apart at will. These beds form part of the bride's dowry. Old ones are broken up for burial or placed over the corpse when it is exposed on one of the islands. The Manus dislike sitting with outstretched feet; it is notable that they have no stereotyped sitting position, as do so many peoples who habitually sit on the floor. They prefer to dangle their legs, down the hatchway, or from a canoe platform, or they sit on a *patapat* or a slit drum whenever there is one. In recent years many camphor wood boxes have been added to their equipment, and they stand on the floor in use as benches. When the Manus do sit on the floor, they lounge, get a wooden pillow, if possible, rest on their elbows, and give about as clear a picture of discomfort and lack of habituation as does a European. There are no stereotyped sitting or sleeping positions, for either men or women. When necessary they can sleep drawn up into incredibly small compass on a crowded platform or stretched along the slender canoe gunwale. Children will even sleep curved over a drum, describing a perfect arc.

In a house which contains only one family, the *palan um*, always regarded as the men's part, is its important public section, the central section is frequently screened off by one or more mats, suspended from the cross beams. These mats, called *mwetchels*, are made of transverse sections of leaf from the *laun mwetchel*, a plant which closely resembles pandanus. The skull of the house owner's Sir Ghost hangs from one of the front rafters. Skulls which have not been altogether rejected, but which have been reduced from favor, are sometimes hung in the *kuin um* among the women. In the house of rich men, there is sometimes a *ramus*, a charm, constituted of pigs' tusks and straw bound about the middle post of the house. This is a wealth-getting charm for a house, more expensive but similar in function to the wealth-getting charm worn by individuals on the betel bags, or as ornaments. Whether a house is occupied by one household or two is a question of marriage. A household is defined by a married couple, so that a widow and children, or a widower and children living with a married couple, are not considered to be a second household. (The exception to this is when the house is built for a widow.) The need of four fireplaces in houses which never, except in emergencies such as illness or death, accommodate more than two separate households, is explained by two circumstances: that each woman is supposed to cook at her own fireplace and that persons observing the taboos connected with *rites de passage* after first menstruation, ear piercing, childbirth, or widowhood, must eat food prepared at a separate fireplace. With two families regularly resident in a house the number of fireplaces only allows two extra ones for such emergencies.

The continued residence of two families in a house is formally recognized. The family of the house owner then lives in the front of the house, using the front fireplaces, the family of the secondary resident use the back door of the house for their entrances and the back fireplaces. In this case, the skull of Sir Ghost of the younger or dependent man is hung at the back of the house, the place otherwise reserved for slightly superseded ghosts of the house owner. Men who are not of sufficient importance to have houses of their own do not have *ramus*. When two men resident in the same house quarrel, the dispute is phrased in terms of the two Sir Ghosts, who could not live amicably under one roof.

Within a two-family house there are usually avoidances. If the two men are brothers, the elder must avoid the younger brother's wife. When the younger man is resident in his wife's place, the wife of the elder may have to avoid the younger man. A mat is hung on at least one side of the *lon um* to form a partition, and the younger person resident in the *kuin um* must never raise the voice when the prescribed elder is in the house. Early in the morning all men and boys leave the house and repair to the rear of one of the small islands which is used as a latrine. This gives the women an opportunity to make their morning toilet. The men usually go to market, so that in the early hours of the morning the women are alone in the houses. Later, when the men return the women go for firewood and water. There is a tendency for men and women to spend as little time together as possible. Within a two-family house the small children roam freely while the men are away, the mats are lowered for greater coolness, and the women gossip together, with some formality as they are usually affinal relatives, but nevertheless with an appearance of friendliness which binds them somewhat together in the feeling of the child. Both women address the little children as *ina* and sometimes as *papu*, the children reply *ina* to them. Similarly, both men address the little boys as *papu* and the little girls as *ina*, and the small children reply *papu* to them. Men, however, do not as a rule pay a great deal of attention to children who are not their own or adopted children. When two women in a house, or two related women in neighboring houses are both suckling children, the child of one is frequently left with the other. As it is customary to give a child the breast whenever it asks for it, children are very often suckled by other women besides their own mothers. The other women will repulse a child at an earlier age than will the own or adopted mother, however, and give it a piece of taro to chew instead. But for the first two years of its life, the child is accustomed to being suckled, oftenest by its real or adopted mother, and frequently by other women. Professor Malinowski[1] questioned the possibility of such behavior, on the grounds, apparently, that he did not observe it in the Trobriands. It may be that the reserves incident to a sorcery society render its occurrence less likely there.

The argument that there would not be enough women with milk is based upon a complete disregard of the long duration of suckling in many primitive societies—a point which Professor Malinowski has himself stressed for the Trobriands.[2]

Let us take as a sample the group of houses at the seaward end of Peri village in March 1929:—

House No.	No. of Women	State of Nurture	Age of Children
1	1	Suckling (also suckling child of parallel cousin)	2 months
2	1	Suckling	3 months
	2	Barren	
3	1	Suckling	1 year
4	1	Suckling adopted child (own child has been at breast two years before)	3 years
	2	Suckling	2 years
5	1	7 months pregnant	

[1] "And this is the point at which we have to deal with the unprofitable assumption of communal lactation. In the relatively small savage communities where there occur perhaps one or two childbirths in a year within reach of each other the idea of mothers synchronizing conception and pregnancy and clubbing together to carry out lactatory group-motherhood, at the greatest inconvenience to themselves, the babies and the whole community, is so preposterous that even now I cannot think how it could ever have been promulgated by Doctor Rivers and upheld by Mr. Briffault."—Malinowski, B., *The New Generation, Parenthood—The Basis of Social Structure.* New York, 1930. (p. 136).

[2] Malinowski, B. *The Sexual Life of Savages in Northwestern Melanesia. An Ethnographic Account of Courtship, Marriage, and Family Life among the Natives of the Trobriand Islands, British New Guinea.* (New York, 1929); also, *Sex and Repression in Savage Society* (London, 1927).

These are five adjacent houses in one end of the village. A glance at the age distribution will demonstrate the way in which well-spaced births will nevertheless permit of groups of women who will be able simultaneously to suckle each other's children.

The case of Ngamasu (house No. 1) who was suckling two children is worthy of mention. It has already been touched upon under the discussion of Patalian's avoidances. The child which Ngamasu was suckling was the infant of Lawa. Patalian was the former suitor of Lawa and his magic was suspected of having caused pre-natal illness for the child, therefore he was now treating it to an extensive course of exorcism. For this purpose the child had been removed entirely from its mother and given to its mother's father's brother's daughter to suckle during the charming period. Lawa meanwhile suckled the year-old infant of another woman who lived in the house next to her own, so that her breasts would not become dry.

Although little children play freely about the house, and are given the breast by the other woman who lives in it, when the fathers enter there is a definite rift between the two households. Women will endeavor to keep their children in their own end of the houses, so that there will be no embarrassing necessity to call them. So the entrance of the father serves to re-crystallize for the child the intimate family group which had been slightly generalized by the care and attention given the child by more than one woman. In Manus the tie between father and young child is much more definite and special than the tie between mother and child.

Into the maternal grandmother-grandchild situation the avoidance rules enter long before the child has any understanding of them. So Popoli's maternal grandmother, Nyapotchalon, lived in a tiny house next door to the house of Popoli's foster father. Popoli could go freely to her house and demand food there, but it was a place set apart to which his father could not go, where his father could not be mentioned. In the house of a paternal grandmother, on the other hand, the child's mother is on formal terms, ill at ease, careful of her words.

It will be remembered that suckling the child at birth is the duty of a woman towards her "brother's" wife. The formal attempts to cement appearance of friendship between a woman and her affinal woman kin, if they live in the same village, sometimes take the form of giving a child from the bridegroom's kindred into the temporary charge of the engaged girl. So Lawian, the betrothed of Ndroi, would be called "mother" by the infant son of Tuain, Ndroi's elder "brother." Tuain and Kemwai, the father of Lawian, lived next door to each other, and the wife of Tuain frequently entrusted her baby to Lawian's care. Similarly Ngaoli was engaged to Manui of Kalat. Manui's "father's" wife, Konambo, on her way to some distant errand, often brought her five-year old son or her two-year old baby and left them with Ngaoli at the other end of the village. This was a request which an engaged girl would be too shy to refuse when made to her by her fiancé's female relatives. But the engaged girl was made doubly embarrassed by the situation, fearful lest the young child should pronounce a taboo name or see his father—a most rigid avoidance relative—pass and call out to him. The child acquired a new mother, temporarily, but the strain between his own mother and the temporary mother was very strong. So into all of a child's first contact with women, other than his mother, an element of strain enters— because of his father's strain with his mother's relatives, because of his mother's strain with his father's relatives, because of the couple's strain with affianced women of the next generation. The women who care for him are not a group to which the child can turn with singleness of feeling and lack of restraint.

His relationship to his own mother is complicated by the relationship which exists between his mother and his father. It is the mother's task to discipline the young child, to inculcate respect for property, physical proficiency and sphincter control, but she does this disciplining in continual fear of her husband, for a man always takes part with the child against his wife, and will often strike his wife if she strikes the child. So, between mother and child, the shadow of the father also falls.

To the father alone is a child's relationship perfectly clear. If he has, as is sometimes the case, two or three acting fathers, they do not impinge on each other, because there is one father, own or adopted, who is almost invariably most important.

Sibling relationships among young children are somewhat obscured by the paramount importance of the relationship of each child to the father and by the lack of any custom by which older children are expected to foster younger brothers or sisters. Child siblings do play together, but their relationship is not a deciding element in play choices, as all the children play in a group in which other factors enter more importantly.

Children are taught kinship terms very gradually, as the relationships become functionally important in their lives. I give below, in outline form, a statement of the approximate ages at which different terms are used correctly.

Ages at which Children Use Kinship Terms

(This table is presented for boys after the age of five. Girls learn the later acquired terminologies from two to three years younger.)

Up to three to four years a child calls its father and mother by the terms which they call each other, and uses *ina* and *papu* in address. (Uses *mambu* and *ngasi* if those relatives are resident close by.)

At six to eight years a child can describe siblings correctly, as *pisio, piloan*, or *ndriasin.*

At eight to ten years a child can describe his mother's brother as *kakali* and will substitute *kakali* for mother's brother's wife instead of former *ina* or *ngasi.*

At twelve to fourteen a child can describe a father's sister as *patieyen*, and can describe cross-cousins. He does not use any of these terms. He observes his parents' and his own name avoidances and can return *pauaro* and *polapol* jesting, but does not initiate it.

The *pinpapu* relationships, to father's father's sister and her female descendants, and the proper distinction between father's sister's daughter and mother's brother's daughter, and the relationship between a man and his father's sister's daughter's son, who are also called *polapol*, are the last to be properly comprehended. Most people are very uncertain about the terminology for a father's father's sister's son. Asked formally, they will say that a father's male cross-cousin is called *papu;* they will reply with equal assurance that the son of a *pinpapu* should be called *mambu*, and when instances are cited their replies will vary, with the exception that the son of a *pinpapu* who is one's father's cross-cousin and one's own father-in-law will always be described as *papu*. Unless there is a strong active cross-cousinship between the son of a *pinpapu* and the father of an individual, or a marriage contract which has this aspect, *mambu* will prevail.

The reason why a child distinguishes his *kakali* so much earlier than his *patieyen* seems to be a matter of terminological usage rather than of relationship function. *Kakali* is used as a term of address with the reciprocal diminutive *kaka* while the terms *patieyen, nebonitu*, and *asaun* are never so used except ceremonially. It does not mean a closer relationship between child and mother's brother than between child and father's sister. On the other hand, the *kakali* relationship is actually more formal. Both relationships become ceremonially important to the child at the same time, at ear piercing, when the father's sister leads him by the hand, and the mother's brother pierces his ears.[1]

With patrilocal marriage, the father's sisters and mother's brother might both be expected to be resident elsewhere, but because of the

---

[1] A possible exception to this statement may be the functions of one or both of these relatives at the feast of child hair cutting, which is, however, only held for a small number of male children.

presence of several gentes in a village and the lack of village exogamy, this is not the case. Three fourths of the existing marriages in Peri were intra-village. When a marriage is temporarily disrupted, very small children may live for several weeks in their mother's brother's house, but after their mother's successive pregnancies, they as often live in their father's sister's house during their mother's segregation for the month following delivery. The jesting relationship between a woman and her brother's son, or her mother's brother's son is effective upon his initiative, but not upon hers, so that it is not until he is past adolescence that a youth enters into any special relationship with his *patieyen*. A girl's relationship to her *patieyen* is always ceremonial only. I have stressed this point at some length because recent discussion of kinship has relied upon explaining terminology in terms of childhood usage.

Children do not use kinship terms among themselves. The first terms used between children are the affinal terms, *kaiyo* and *pinkaiyo*, which may occur as early as ten or eleven for girls, and thirteen or fourteen for boys. Adults will comment upon two children's relationships: "He is the mother's brother of this one." "They are cross-cousins." But the children do not imitate this usage. The only terms which the parents actually teach the child are *mambu, ngasi, papu*, and *yaye (ina)*, especially as applied to siblings of the parents.

EFFECTIVE INTER-RELATIONSHIPS IN ADULT LIFE

In Manus the relationships which function most definitely in adult life are, for males: sister, wife, brother, brothers-in-law, male cross-cousin; for females: brother, husband, sister-in-law. For females, sisters are usually of less importance, and the cross-cousin relationship only important ceremonially and for occasional jesting. We may discuss the relationships in turn. I have omitted here any discussion of relationships between adults and their parents, because owing to the early age of death, an adult of thirty with a living father is atypical. Widows typically return to their own kin.

BROTHER AND SISTER

Children will say of this relationship, "He is my brother. He hits me and I hit him." "She is my sister. I take her canoe (play canoe) and she takes mine." Later in life an adult will say, "She is my sister. Her *metcha* became my *metcha*." (i.e., the great late marriage payment for her marriage was paid to me, and with it I made a similar payment for my wife). "She is my sister, when I die she will weep for me." "A man likes to marry a woman who has wept long for her brothers.

She is a good woman." "He is my brother. He gives me sago. I give him beadwork.[1] When he dies I will weep for him."

The home of the brother is a refuge for the sister during a temporary disagreement with her husband and also after divorce, or during widowhood. The privilege of returning to her brother's house can be phrased more accurately as claiming the exercise of a kinship function, than as an economic right. (Among the agricultural Samoans, a woman retains a claim upon the land of her paternal descent line, and at any time she may return, take up residence in the family house built on village land, and cultivate part of the family garden. She inherits an economic claim upon her father's property whether her father was the *matai* (head man and administrator) or merely a subordinate member of the descent group. It is possible to phrase a woman's return to share in the life of the hereditary household in this way as a claim upon her own group in which she has never relinquished membership—even though in Manus there is no question of family owned land.

Idealogically, an unmarried girl has no special relationships to her brother. If her brother, or any male relative of her own generation whom she would normally call brother, arranges a betrothal or gives the *mwelamwel* for her marriage, she calls him, thereafter, "father," i.e., he is regarded as having played a "father" rôle. The wife of such a man is called "mother"; e.g., Molong in the genealogy given on p. 322 calls Ngandaliu her father's step-son "father," because he financed her marriage. Similarly Melin calls her sister Sain, "mother"; Sain's husband, Paliau, financed her marriage. When, however, a woman becomes pregnant for the first time there is a shift in kinship function. Henceforth the responsibility for her part of the affinal exchange is assumed by her "brother." Her husband, whose economic obligations have hitherto been discharged by his "father" must now discharge his own. That is, with the first conception and the first pregnancy payment, the economic responsibility passes from one generation to the next. (The fact that concluding economic payments for any individual marriage are usually not made by members of the present generation, but by an intermediate generation above has been discussed on p. 237.) Appropriately the payments involved in these birth feasts are not of the greatest valuables, but involve principally sago and belts. In the birth feast for a first child, the young mother wears a complete bridal outfit, but this is merely a gesture. The bridal outfit is returned to the elder

---

[1] This translation, beadwork, is used to cover the old type of handicraft with shell ornament and seeds as well as the new with varicolored beads.

of her own kindred who has lent it to her. It is not paid to the husband's kindred as is the bridal outfit at marriage and in the late marriage payment (*metcha*). The collection of sago involves either working sago amid sago swamps wrested in war from the Usiai or arduous fishing to obtain fish which can be exchanged for sago. Both are primarily young men's work.

In addition to making a series of birth feasts, beginning as soon as pregnancy is known and culminating in the large feast when the mother is returned to her husband, the brother assumes the care of his sister from a few days before delivery until thirty days after the birth of the child. The method of carrying out this charge rests in the brother's discretion. He divines as to whether the spirits prefer that his sister be moved to his house, or that she remain in her husband's house. If the latter reply is given, the husband vacates his own house and the brother and his wife and children move into it. The husband and his children go to live with the husband's sister. When it is remembered that the house is owned by the husband or his kindred, this latter move is all the more peculiar. In four of the ten births which took place while we were in Peri, the husband was thus evicted from his own house. During this month the brother provides food for his sister and her children.

This economic relationship is repeated for each childbirth. There is no slackening with later births, although the first birth ceremony itself is considerably more complicated ritually than the feasts for later born children. But the mother of a tenth child is cared for by her brother and the father lives through thirty days of ceremonial leisure as punctiliously as for the first.

When a boy or girl has the ears pierced, the mother's brother is again responsible. The mother's brother and the mother's brothers' wives come to live in the house, but in this case the father is not excluded.[1]

There are then these periods of ceremonial dependence of a woman upon her brother; her residence in his house during recovery from delivery; when she has left her husband; and in widowhood (after the initial ten months' mourning among her dead husband's kin); his residence in her house during his exclusion from his wife, either ceremonially or because of a quarrel in the course of which his wife has left him; and his residence in her house during the ear piercing of her children.

Furthermore there are certain other economic contacts between brothers and sisters. A man keeps his ceremonial property—charms, war charms, the skull and bones of his Sir Ghost, in his own house, but

---

[1]See also, *Growing up in New Guinea*, 55–56.

his most valuable secular property, shell money and dogs' teeth, is kept for him by his sisters. It is their task to keep the shell money aprons in repair, to work strands of shell money into belts, and new aprons, and to string dogs' teeth in distinctive ways so that one string will be known from another. As a man accumulates small amounts of currency towards a large payment, such as a marriage payment for a son, he takes them to his sisters who put them away for him.

There is some confusion here between sister's functions, for it is through her that shell money comes to the man, and it is she who cares for shell money which he obtains in other ways. In ordinary phrasing, women will say, "It is through us, his sisters, that our brother made his *metcha.*" Both her rôles, that of a pawn in a scheme of affinal exchange and that of the careful treasurer of her brother's wealth, are included in this statement. Also when a man wishes to get new contributions to his collection of wealth, he goes and waits upon (*kaka*) his sister's veranda until she, or her husband in her name, contributes. These contributions are re-paid later. The relationship between brother and sister is economically reciprocal, as he provides sago for her birth feasts and cares for her dur-ing childbirth, so she fashions shell money and beadwork for him, and cooks and cares for him and his children whenever he and his wife are separated. This part of the relationship is conceived of economically rather than affectionately. There is no pretense of free and casual giving to relatives, such as is frequent among the Samoans.

In addition to the ceremonial and the economic contacts, there are many slight day-by-day contacts between brother and sisters. Although the peaceful coöperation of husband and wife is often threatened by a brother's economic demands on his sister and her demands on him, it is the small intimacies between brother and sister (the mood of complete reciprocity and understanding which the little girl described in the phrase, "He is my brother, he hits me and I hit him") which interfere most with marriage. It is the only completely reciprocal relationship un-complicated by age, as is the relationship of father and son, or by one-sided initiative, as between man and female cross-cousin, or by possibili-ties of one-sided cursing, as between male cross-cousins. The same attitude of utter trust is expressed by young girls who, after they have discussed their fear of young men with imported love magic, will add of A and B and C. "They are my brothers, I can talk to them. I am not afraid of them."

Between brother and sister there is no taboo, only an enjoined reserve in matters pertaining in any way to the body. This reserve acts as a guarantee of safety, of pleasant confidence, to a people as puritanical and shame-faced as the Manus. It must be regarded in Manus, as making for better relations rather than detracting from them. Mr. Fortune has discussed[1] the functioning of the brother and sister taboo as one way in which the solidarity of marriage is protected against kin solidarity, contrasting Dobuan lack of taboo, with its accompaniment of village incest and broken-up marriages, with marriage conditions in the Trobriands. In a society which values sex experience, even such slight reserve as obtains in Manus might stand to protect the marriage relation against the too great claims of the kin group. But this is not the case in Manus. Between brothers and sisters there is also an enjoined seriousness. The gravity of the relationship may even sanction otherwise interdicted intimacy as when a brother may mention his sister's immodest dress in serious rebuke. Throughout, it is a relationship concerned with property, with obligations, with material and ceremonial interdependence. The Manus are not over given to laughter, and the segregation of the play element to the cross-cousin relationship does not detract from the pleasantness of the brother and sister relationship. In his sister's house a man can be sure of a welcome. She will not indulge in unseemly jests, she will never embarrass him by any reference to sex, she will listen gravely to his requests, and carry them out with becoming seriousness.

So, day after day, a man seeks out his sister in his free hours, he takes his baby to his sister's house to play, he goes to his sister's after successful fishing and leaves some of his choicest fish for her cooking. His sister sees him in his best mood, and often gets first choice of his fishing catch. When he eats in his sister's house, his sister eats with him, an intimate family meal, while her husband sits apart or leaves the house altogether, for brothers-in-law may not eat in each other's presence. And when a woman is sick it is her brother who sits and holds her head, while her husband sits at a distance, unwanted.

The brother-sister relationship is extended in various ways to include practically any contemporary male relative of the woman, either matrilineal or patrilineal. A woman does not necessarily depend on her own brother; she may live instead with a parallel cousin, or a mother's brother, in fact with any male relative. The tabulation which I used to illustrate the choice of "brother" on p. 259 applies here also. Below I give a sample of the refuge taken by ten runaway wives during a period

---

[1]Fortune, *Sorcerers of Dobu, The Social Anthropology of the Dobu Islanders of the Western Pacific* (London, 1932), 9–10.

SAMPLE OF TEN RUNAWAY WIVES IN PERI

Village of Wife	Name of Husband	Village of Refuge	Took Refuge With	Kinship Term used by Runaway Woman to her Host
Taui	Selan	Husband's	Father's mother's sister's son	papan
Patusi	Pwisieu	Brother's wife's	Brother who was resident in wife's village	pision
Tchalalo	Pokanau	Husband's	Father's brother's daughter's son	nebonitun
Peri	A Loitcha village man	Own	Brother	pision
Peri	Tchaumutchin	Own	Adopted father's classificatory sister	patieyen
Peri	Tchauan	Own	Father's brother's son	pision
Patusi	Talikai	Husband's	Mother's son	pision
Peri	Topas	Own	Mother's classificatory younger brother	pision
Patusi	Ndrosal	Husband's	Father's brother's daughter	piloan
Peri	Pokanas	Own	Called in own brother to settle fight	pision
Tchalalo	Ngamel	Own	Own brother	pision

of as many weeks. So that in adult life, the actual choice of a "brother" to whom a distressed wife may turn for refuge is very widely interpreted. Residence during temporary widowhood, i.e., widowhood while a woman is still young and out of which she may be expected to remarry, is as variously arranged. In Peri there were only two young widows and one divorced woman during our stay. They lived with several different male relatives in turn. As women ordinarily outlive men in Manus, old widows live sometimes with their sons, more often with their brother's sons, or sister's sons, all of these terms being understood in the widest sense.

Nevertheless, the Manus conceive the brother and sister relationship very formally as one of mutual aid and interdependence, and when true sibling-ship exists it will be recognized first. The women who run away to other relatives either have no own brothers living, or else they live so far away that it is not practical to go to them for a short time—if one is suffering from a broken arm or a cut head. There were twenty-six Peri women married in Peri, nine had full gentile brothers in the village to whom they could turn in emergencies, the remaining fifteen had to put up with various types of classificatory brothers, or other male kindred.

HUSBAND AND WIFE

The relationship between husband and wife is conditioned by two things, children and common economic interests. The marriage begins without either of these ties. If a married couple have no children, real or adopted, they have no genuine grounds for any type of coöperation. It is the man's duty to provide food for his wife; it is her duty to cook it. It is a woman's duty to help her husband's kinswomen in household tasks. But these are regarded as exactions from one person upon another. Meanwhile, all of the man's economic interests are with his own kin group. He has to work for the male kindred who have financed his marriage. Pregnancy and birth serve to break into the husband and wife relationship by separating them,[1] and also, while the children are little, they tend to separate their parents. The man plays for the child's affection and beats his wife for neglecting it. Children however do tend to help bind women to their marriages, for unless the child is an infant at the breast a father will keep a child when his wife leaves him.

That this is not a mere reflection of patriliny, but rather a special father-child attitude, is shown by the fact that when a man dies the widow is often permitted to keep the children, to take them away with

---

[1]For further details see *Growing up in New Guinea*, Chapter IV.

her to her own village, where they are ultimately adopted by some male of of the mother's kindred or by a subsequent husband of the woman. This is most likely to be the case if children have not yet been betrothed. If one or more members of the father's gens, or maternal relatives of the father who are resident in the father's village, have made betrothal payments for the children, they are likely to claim the children. But even here, if the widow is a member of the same village, girls will be permitted to go with their mothers, only returning to their paternal kin for ceremonial occasions upon which expenditures of property are necessary. There is not the sense that children belong to their own gens which in so many parts of the world accompanies strict unilateral organization and also often accompanies the institutions of wife indemnity. Rather, children belong to their parents, but more importantly to the father than to the mother. The mother's claim is always subsidiary.

With the advent of children then, women are bound more firmly to their marriages, and men take a more continuous interest in their wives, scrutinizing the care which they give their children, and seeing to it that the mother does not monopolize the children's affections. When a woman has borne several children who have lived, the marriage begins to assume an appearance of permanency. Barrenness and death of children are both likely to precipitate divorce, although divorce is phrased on grounds of lack of intelligence and inefficiency, initiated by the kin group involved or by the husband himself.

The only incompatibility which the Manus men recognize is one of relative efficiency and intelligence. This is in keeping with the low estimation in which the emotional life, and especially sex, are held. Every man and woman in the village is judged in terms of "ability to make affinal exchanges," "ability to talk." The particular type of intelligence involved is a combination of shrewdness, good memory, ability to plan, ability to manipulate the kinship categories to desired ends—and this mental make-up, to be effective, must be combined with energy, aggressiveness, industry, and initiative. An intelligent Manus not only estimates the degree to which everyone in the village possesses these qualities, but is also conscious of the relative status of husband and wife. It is possible to find people who will designate the wives who are known to "instruct their husbands"—these women are usually wives of many years standing. But the observations are made almost from the beginning of the marriage. So Mbosai brings his son's bride home, while his son is still away from home. Watching her day by day he decides that she is unintelligent and remarks to one of his brothers that he won't be at all sorry if she runs away or gives some other cause for offense, because she is stupid.

As original betrothals are all made on the basis of the economic status of the contracting entrepreneurs, no consideration at all is given to the intelligence of the two children concerned. In Peri village two of the most brilliant boys from the dominant gens were betrothed to stupid little girls, who came from a long line of stupid and definitely unstable people. It is pure chance if the economically dictated marriages unite two children of compatible mentalities.

Laziness and carelessness are regarded as inefficient and hence unintelligent. Occasionally, after a man has demonstrated his stupidity, older relatives will attempt to find him an intelligent second wife who can manage his affairs for him.

Women do not give the same reason for leaving their husbands. Instead they instance: husband's taking another wife—almost certain to arouse the first wife's ire and therefore a definite obstruction to polygamy in Manus; death of children from the anger of the husband's ghosts; active distaste for intercourse; weariness with the husband's attentions to his sisters; general boredom and annoyance with the marital situation; that is, all the reasons they give are in the field of the emotional life, while the men's conventional explanations all deal with economics.

During the period before the children are betrothed, husband and wife continue in a sparring attitude towards each other, quarrels are frequent; then the wife runs away to her "brother" taking the youngest children with her. Both husband and wife wait anxiously to see what the older children will do. If older children fall ill during such a period, they are likely to go to their mothers. The right of a mother to care for a sick child is one of her few privileges; the most devoted and self-confident father will call loudly for his wife if a child is taken ill, or involved in an accident. Adolescent boys will evade the issue by going and sleeping with a comrade. The tie between father and son has already been weakened by this time; the house is dreary without a woman to cook in it, and an adolescent boy would be too self-conscious to follow his mother.

Economic coöperation between husband and wife beyond the mere day-by-day routine of living begins with the betrothal of a child. Until then the principal economic activities of the household have been between the kin group of the wife and the kin group of the husband. Each conferred apart with his or her kindred in planning the exchanges which hinged upon their marriage relationship. With the child's betrothal the division by which the wife and her kin are concerned with one type of property, the husband and his kin with the other, vanishes. ' If the child is a girl, the husband and his kin as well as the wife's kindred must provide dowry property, sago, pigs, and oil. If the child is a boy, both groups collect dogs' teeth and shell money to make the bride-price payment.

For the first time husband and wife plan together. Because of the system of entrepreneurship described below (p. 190) such coöperation is very rare. It is only the wealthy men and their wives who become effective partners in this way. Dependents cannot make their own plans; their economic arrangements are made for them. The poor independents on the other hand, do not betroth their children early; the time of economic partnership between husband and wife is therefore postponed until the children are adolescent. The chances of both parents living to see their children adolescent are not high. Of the fourteen young people at or just past adolescence in Peri, only seven had both real or principal foster parents living. The betrothal of very young children is only done by very wealthy men, whether the children concerned are their own or offspring of their dependents. Among the wealthy, where there was ample chance for economic coöperation in planning a whole system of betrothal and marriage exchanges, were found a number of reasonably satisfactory marriages. Husband and wife treat each other like hard-bitten but trusted business partners. The irritation born of a badly adjusted sexual situation is dimmed.[1] The most intimately involved affinal relatives, brothers-in-law or sisters-in-law, have become business partners also. Women have given up the fight for their children's or the husbands' affection and settled down to the economic prestige game of middle age. After their husbands' deaths, women turn again to the personal life and make bids for the affection of pre-adolescent and adolescent girls.

Here they have no competition. The girls' fathers have given them up because the avoidance situations render their company embarrassing. The girls have rejected their mothers in favor of their fathers and they attach themselves to some old widow in their kinship groups. Widowers continue to enjoy the society of smaller children especially.

---

[1]For discussion of sex attitudes in Manus see Chapter IX of *Growing Up in New Guinea*.

BROTHER AND BROTHER

The essence of the brother-to-brother relationship is summed up in the statement that the simple word "brother" is sometimes used in a descriptive or general sense, but never, except by children, when referring precisely to a given sibling relationship. The father-son terminology is the effective one. Theoretically, the Manus system favors primogeniture. Failure to obey an older brother was twice invoked by Manus mediums as cause of ghost-sent illness during a six month period. But in both these instances the elder defied by his junior was also definitely the dominating personality. Actually, in any group of brothers, the most aggressive and intelligent dominates the situation.

I have discussed elsewhere in detail[1] the importance of the close association between men and their own or foster children as an element in personality development, and pointed out that Manus children can be divided into three groups, according to whether their fathers, during the first two to six years of their lives were aggressive, dominating entrepreneurs, young men with aggressive temperaments which were not yet allowed full play, or meek, compliant men, economically unambitious, or economic failures.

If all children were reared by their own fathers in Manus and all men passed through a period of social unimportance and dependence and a period of economic dominance, it is obvious that eldest sons would receive less stimulus to aggressive behavior than would the children of the father's middle age. It would, under these circumstances, need a very strong social insistence upon primogeniture and a lack of social premium upon personality traits, to discount the differential impact of the father's personality upon a group of sons.

In Manus, however, where primogeniture is little more than a fiction, and where direct father to son inheritance practically never occurs, owing to the short life span of the men, personality, acquired in early childhood by association with dominant men, either fathers, foster fathers, grandparents, or other male relatives is permitted to show itself.[2] Power and leadership within a group of brothers goes to the most efficient. Efficiency in Manus demands intelligence plus aggressiveness.

Primogeniture may of course lead to some hard feeling and it would be reasonable to expect dominance of one brother over another without any such formal sanction to be even more resented. Actually, although I saw many relationships in which the younger dominated the elder, I

---

[1]For further discussion see *Growing Up in New Guinea*, Chapter VIII.
[2]See *Growing Up in New Guinea*, Chapter XII.

did not see active rivalry between brothers. There was great sulkiness and resentment on the part of the very young men who had just married and who had to work for their economic backers, who were sometimes elder brothers, oftener elder parallel cousins, or young uncles. But this is essentially a parent-child situation without the tenderness of the true father-son relationship which the young men have known in childhood. It is a spoiled child rebelling against authority to which he is unaccustomed. After five or six years of married life and its consequent economic servitude, a man is sufficiently mature to take stock of himself, and the economic rôle which he will play during the next few years of his life. Such a stock-taking is usually precipitated by a death, the death of the elder male relative whose leadership the young man has been following. Every such death leaves two to five men of different ages leaderless, because a Manus village represents a series of constellations—groups of men who coöperate economically with one dominant relative. For example:—

Leader: Korotan—Pere Gens

Dependents	Age	Relationship to Korotan	Gens
1. Talikai	Middle-aged	Father's son	Pere
2. Ndrosal	Middle-aged	Father's son (same mother as Talikai)	Pere
3. Pwoitchon	Middle-aged	Father's son (different mother from 1 and 2)	Pere
4. Saot	Youth	Mother's sister's son (by a gentile brother)	Pere
5. Tcholai	Youth	Brother's son	Pere
6. Polin	Youth	Gentile sister's son	Rambutchon

Korotan went blind, and was unable to maintain his economic leadership. The control of affairs is passing to Talikai. Pwoitchon remains Talikai's dependent, but Ndrosal is vacillating between Talikai and Pokanas, his sister's husband. The wife of Pokanas is a very dominating person, ruling both husband and brother, and she seized this opportunity to attach her brother more firmly to her economic organization which was, of course, nominally her husband's.

Saot's services were requisitioned by Ngamel also of Pere, but by another economic group. Ngamel had helped finance Saot's marriage as an independent entrepreneur with Korotan and he now succeeded in attaching Saot to his own ménage. Tcholai who lived in Korotan's house coöperated with his uncle as did Polin. Talikai, through his sister Isole, could also count upon close coöperation from Isole's husband, Kemwai of Lo gens.

To take another instance:—

Leader: Paliau—Pere Gens

	Dependents	Age	Relationship to Paliau	Gens
1.	Tunu	Middle-aged	Adopted father's son	Pere
2.	Luwil	Young	Adopted father's son	Matchupal
3.	Tchamutchin	Middle-aged	Own brother adopted into another gens	Matchupal
4.	Pomele	Young	Wife's younger sister's husband	Lo
5.	(Pomalit)	Young	Fostering elder brother's son (away at work)	Pere (away at work)
6.	Bonyalo	Young	Wife's mother's sister's son	Kalat
7.	Mumbupoapil	Middle-aged	Foster father's gentile brother's son	Pere

Paliau is at present the leader of these men, all of whom are younger than he except Tchamutchin. If he dies soon, Luwil is the only person who can take his place, and he is less gifted than Paliau and would not be able to organize very large exchanges. Neither Tchamutchin nor Tunu are capable of economic leadership. Tchamutchin and Tunu would probably continue to coöperate with Luwil in this case and some of the younger ones might fall away. But if Paliau lives to see Pomalit married for four or five years, Pomalit the child of Pwanau's successful middle age will probably succeed him. In this case Tchamutchin, Luwil, and Tunu will probably become unimportant independents, virtually withdrawing from the affinal exchange scene, while Bonyalo's and Tchamutchin's son Nyesa, now adopted by Paliau and Paliau's son Popoli would form a nucleus of youth under Pomalit. Pomele will have to decide whether to return to Lo; it is just possible that he may have become important enough to strike out for himself. Mumbupoapil, who is stupider than any of the others, will probably remain as a dependent of Pomalit, despite his great seniority.

Sometimes residence and economic dependence fail to coincide accurately. Polin had lived for some years with Ngamel, an important Pere man who coöperated with Korotan, but was not strictly speaking a dependent of his. Polin, after his marriage, moved into Talikai's house and worked in close coöperation with Talikai in overseas trade. (Talikai owned the largest canoe in the village). Later, Talikai became involved in violent domestic altercations, and Polin and his Rambutchon wife moved into the house of Kemwai, whose wife, Isole, also belonged to Pere gens.

In the back of Pwoitchin's house lived Kala, an unimportant man of Kamatatchau, a practically extinct gens. Kala did some fishing for

Pwoitchon, but was really too humble a man to extend his relationship to Pwoitchon's older brother and economic leader, Talikai.

On the other hand, Saot, although he was Ngamel's dependent and a member of Pere gens, lived in Matchupal in the back of Luwil's house. Luwil and he were sons of Potik of Pere, by different mothers.

It is a comment on the Manus recognition of personality and the fluidity of the system that men of different gifts fall so readily into the leader-led relationship within the sibling groups. The tendency to take the place for which one is fitted by temperament and ability is encouraged all through childhood by the absence of age groupings.[1] Children's personalities are fixed by six or seven and they are then allowed some ten to fifteen years of practice in finding their peculiar niches within the play group. As no two niches are regarded as identical in childhood, and with the exception of the position of *luluai*, each position in adult life is also unique in each new generation, individuals can take their places with a minimum of friction.

In a society with fixed positions which only a few individuals may attain and towards which a large group of candidates aspire, rivalry between siblings should be more prone to occur. Primogeniture represses active rivalry into social impotence and resentment. Societies which offer several types of occupation provide for a kind of differentiated rivalry in terms of varying special gifts. In Manus, however, neither of these conditions occur. The *luluai* alone is a hereditary position within a family line. Heredity seems definitely recognized and not subject to contravention here. With the small families and short-livedness of the Manus, keen rivalry within a sibling group would only occur occasionally. Outside this one position of *luluai* which it was not possible to study in detail because of the abolition of war in the last fifteen years, status in the village is a matter of economic powers, resulting from enterprise, industry, and shrewd manipulation. Every one succeeds or fails in economics alone, and not according to any ideal scheme, but merely in relation to the other men of his age group. Because of the simplicity of the situation, a man will stand in relatively the same position towards the members of his own generation throughout life. Adult status is merely a prolongation of childhood status. The fierce rivalries in the village are between age mates, not siblings, even as such personal antagonisms occasionally occur between two aggressive children.

---

[1]See Mead, Margaret, Two South Sea Educational Experiments and their American Implications (*Proceedings of the Eighteenth Annual Schoolmen's Weekly*, vol. 18, 493–497, 1932).

The general brother-to-brother picture is thus one of coöperation under the leadership of the most aggressive, an attitude of mutual interdependence and common work. Mediums will mention in seances brother's failure to assist brother as a sin for which the ghosts have sent punishment.

BROTHERS-IN-LAW

To understand the relationship between brothers-in-law two aspects of Manus culture must be borne in mind: the avoidance situation between affinal relatives, and the economic relationship between *tchelingen*

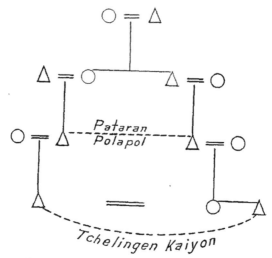

Fig. 14.   Diagram showing the Relationships between Brothers-in-Law where the Ideal Marriage Arrangements are made.

or formal partners in affinal exchange. If the ideal marriage plans were followed out, and true cross-cousins were *pataran*, economic partners who initiate a marriage, their sons would inherit their father's relationship to one another (Fig. 14.)   The Manus say, "If the sons of cross-cousins are not brothers-in-law, then they call each other 'brother'." Actually unless they are brothers-in-law the relationship usually lapses altogether.

So in the ideal scheme the brothers-in-law would take up the economic obligations which their respective fathers had initiated. The Manus use three terms for the type of economic *vis-à-vis* in which an individual on one side of an affinal exchange regularly exchanges with an individual on the other side. *Pataran* is used of the two contracting parents, or chief entrepreneurs in initiating a marriage; *tchelingen* are important pairs of *vis-à-vis*, while *ndrengen* are any pair. Although this relationship is superficially one of opposition and exchanges between men in a *tchelingen* relationship are accompanied with manifestations of war-like hostility, open derision, and insults, it is nevertheless a very real bond. As each individual entrepreneur in Manus is the center of many economic ventures he has a whole series of *tchelingen*, some of them more important than others. The success of his economic activities really depends upon speed. The more quickly his creditors pay him, the more speedily he can initiate new affinal exchanges, or repay outstanding debts. A man's prestige depends primarily upon the number of major affinal exchanges which he has organized and carried through. Upon the solvency and promptness of his principal economic *vis-à-vis* depends the rate of turnover of his investments. As the exchanges are reciprocal, the *tchelingen* depend equally upon each other, and through many years of exchange a relationship of great trust and confidence grows up. A man will speak of another as "my *drengen*" or "my *tchelingen*," with the same feeling of a fixed relationship involved in the use of a kinship term.

I will give two instances to illustrate the feeling involved here. In the public speeches on the village platform in which two foster parents were reproaching their adolescent ward for having gone aboard a white man's schooner with a native crew,[1] the phrase "Was there a brother of yours aboard? Was there a *tchelingen*?" occurred again and again. The implication was that although the girls would have been outraging the avoidance rules, by going among their betrothed's relatives—for *tchelingen* here means merely one of the contracting relatives on the future husband's side—still such affinal relatives were involved in the protection of the betrothed girl's honor. Their presence would have been a guarantee that no immoral liberties had been taken.

The second case occurred during the furor over the elopement of the widow of Pwanau.[2] Paliau, the widow's dead husband's heir, had made a pact with the widow that she would not remarry until the extensive economic preparations for the final mourning feast for Pwanau had been carried out. When the widow violated this promise, Paliau felt vengeful towards all of her kin. Now Salikon, the widow's daughter, was old enough to have her ears pierced. This is a ceremonial privilege of the mother's brother, and the occasion of an affinal exchange of

---

[1]For fuller account of this incident see *Growing Up in New Guinea*, 185–187.
[2]For an account of this episode see, Fortune, R. Chap. V.

property. Paliau was so angry at the remarriage of Salikon's mother that, in revenge, he himself, and without ceremony, pierced Salikon's ears. This was a directly inimical attack on Pokanas, the "brother" of the widow. There was no way in which Pokanas could undertake direct reprisals against Paliau. But Pokanas' daughter was betrothed to a Kalat boy whose gentile sister was betrothed to Pwanau's son. Sanau of Kalat was the principal financier of both of these marriages, but he was a *pataran* of Pokanas' and only a *tchelingen* of Paliau's—that is, Pokanas and Sanau had been the originators of the marriage contract in one case, while in the other, Paliau had merely inherited Pwanau's position. Pokanas persuaded Sanau to threaten Paliau with breaking off the betrothal between the son of Pwanau and the "daughter" of Sanau, as a reprisal. So a *pataran* relationship was invoked in a quarrel just as a kinship relationship would be invoked.

Men come to trust each other and prefer each other so that they will be *ndrengen* to one another in a number of different affinal group exchanges.

Now although *pataran* are usually not true cross-cousins, brothers-in-law are almost always *tchelingen*. It is true that the principal "brother" rôle in a birth feast may be taken by another male relative of the woman, but nevertheless the own brother will always contribute fairly heavily. And if there is no own brother, and some other male relative habitually acts towards a woman as a brother, his relationship to her husband will be correspondingly particular.

The economic exchanges centering about the birth feasts in which all men participate to some degree, develop for wealthy men into the final great exchange, the *metcha*, which is always made between titular brothers-in-law. A rich man could not make a *metcha* if his wife's kindred were all too poor to coöperate in making the proper returns for it. So a rich man is dependent upon the economic caliber of his brother-in-law. (It should be noted here that these economic relationships are really important only for the leading members of the community).

Brothers-in-law also coöperate on a smaller scale. As they are always members of different gentes they possess hereditary rights to different types of fishing apparatus. Yet most types of Manus fishing require two men, either actually to handle the net as in the use of the *kau* (the two-man net), or for the arduous labor of manufacture, as in making the long bamboo fence for a *kalo* (a large fish trap), or merely for companionship in the early morning hours on the reef. On p. 216 I discuss the extreme flexibility of these fishing rights. Owing to the negligent way in which these rights are defended, there seems little real need for brother-in-law coöperation as a device for obtaining the use of other gentile fishing gear, but as this aspect of the situation is recognized, it may have once been a consideration.

However this may be, it is true that among the older fishermen brothers-in-law fish together more often than brothers. It is possible that this may also be related to the fact that many older fishermen are not entrepreneurs and they substitute this day-by-day simple coöperative activity for the more elaborate economic activities of the financiers of the village. As all social relations in Manus are regulated along strictly economic lines, these fishing partnerships are practically the only social relationship permitted the economically negligible members of the community.

A situation analogous to the fishing coöperation which legalizes a man's use of a fishing device of another gens occurs when Manus natives own sago swamps, as some families do in Peri. A woman may take her husband with her to work sago on her brother's sago land and a woman may likewise bring her brother to work sago on her husband's land. In both cases it is regarded as a privilege; it is not often done, and it does, to a certain extent, upset the rationale of the affinal exchanges in which sago is an element. As Manus ownership of sago is comparatively new, recent spoils of war now protected by the government, it is possible that the sago working privileges of brothers-in-law are merely an extension of the fishing privileges which involved no such contradiction of the order of affinal exchange.

So much for the economic bonds between brothers-in-law after the birth of children to a marriage. (If no children are born for several years, the marriage is assumed to be barren, and the first and most important birth feast is as the native idiom puts it, "just made, that's all." A childless couple will usually adopt children; the exchanges incident to ear piercing, adolescence, etc., then follows the usual kinship pattern. It is deemed essential to the continuity of the marriage that the affinal exchanges nominally depending upon the birth of the first child should be made in any event.

With the betrothal of the children, brothers-in-law are more closely united, just as are husband and wife, both by the partial obliteration of opposing economic activities, and in common economic endeavor in the name of the child. However, the economic opposition also continues throughout a marriage, until the conclusion of the mourning ceremonies after the death of one spouse.

In addition to this economic interdependence, brothers-in-law have one common interest which binds them very closely together—their mutual stake in the chastity of the same woman—who is wife of one and sister of the other. Mr. Fortune has discussed this point in relation to the Sir Ghost cult,[1] and I shall merely summarize here. The Manus Sir Ghost cult punishes for the sex offenses of a relative or a co-resident in a house. The punishment in the form of sickness or death falls not necessarily upon the guilty person, but upon any of the other persons involved with the sinner. A woman who sins will endanger her own kin, that is, both her brother and his children, and also her own children. As long as a woman is virtuous, her brother will give her sanctuary against her husband, but should she sin, all houses, that of her husband and that of her brother, are closed against her. When the relationship between brothers-in-law is discussed in Manus, the older men almost invariably add, "If a woman committed adultery, the husband would call his brother-in-law and if they decided not to accept *kano* (indemnity payment) the husband and the brother-in-law would summon the adulterer, and both groups, the husband and his brother-in-law, the adulterer and his kin would fight." This reply is so stereotyped that, coupled with the very small record of adultery, one is inclined to put it down as another one of the Manus ideal forms. Actually women hardly ever risk adultery; if they wish to change marriage partners they run away first for a period to their brothers' houses. But this solidarity between brothers-in-law on the subject of women's chastity is one of the great forces making for stability of marriage and moral coercion of women in Manus.[2]

Theoretically, a man might well be jealous of his wife's close affectional ties to her brother, but actually this is not the case. The men do not expect affection from their wives. They are content with the affection of their children. The economic coöperation and common demands on the woman's virtue are much stronger than any genuine jealousy over the wife's affection, although the husband does grudge his wife's work for her brother, on economic grounds.

I have discussed first the coöperative aspects of the brother-in-law relationship. There are other elements in it, however. One is the constraint arising from the enjoined affinal avoidance, the other is a slight attitude of disparity of status between brother and sister. The affinal avoidance between brothers-in-law is strongest when the marriage is new, especially strong if there has been any default in marriage payments on the part of the man's kin. Names are always avoided, as are also sexual reference and jesting. But despite these handicaps to

---

[1]Fortune, *Manus Religion, ibid.*, 97–99.
[2]Contrast the way a woman's kin take part with her against an accusing husband in Dobu, Fortune, *Sorcerers of Dobu*, 48–49.

intimacy, brothers-in-law are essentially contemporaries, which contributes an element of give and take to the relationship. A great disparity in age between them is immediately re-read into the father—son-in-law or son—father-in-law pattern.

The second difference is reflected in the fact that a man calls his sister's husband *iaru* (dual), while the sister's husband may speak of his wife's brother as *i* (singular). This is the only trace in Manus terminology of a sister outranking a brother, that tendency which has reached such a conspicuous development in Tongan social organization.[1]

The position of slight superiority which the pronominal usage implies for the sister's husband over the wife's brother is also shown in other almost inconspicuous ways. The husband can borrow the brother's canoe, or demand that he go fishing with him, with just a shade more dominance. This is one of those unformalized aspects of kinship behavior which so often go unnoticed and are so difficult to record in objective terms. Taken together with the usage of father-son terminology between the children of brother and sister in the Pak system, and the comparable but more developed usages in Samoa[2] and Tonga, it assumes more significance. The Manus are perfectly conscious of the importance of the pronominal distinction. A man will say, "He must speak of me as *ei aru* but I just call him *e i*".

CROSS-COUSINS[3]

We come now to the other strictly contemporary relationship of Manus male adults, that of cross-cousins. Much of the formalized behavior of cross-cousins will be discussed under the head of the *tandri-tanitani* cult, and I shall confine myself here to remarks on the social aspects of the relationship. Obviously a man has many *polapol* if he includes all those to whom the terminology can be applied. It would include all the men whom his mother calls *nebonitu*, who may be either in the generation above or the generation below him—(relationships further removed than this, although theoretically possible, are only reckoned under pressure of tracing relationship). But for practical purposes his *polapol* may be classified into three groups, on the basis of his behavior towards them: 1, cross-cousins who are also *patarans*, the ideal but statistically unusual situation; 2, cross-cousins who are contemporaries

---

[1]Gifford, E. W., Tonga Society (*Bulletin 61, Bernice P. Bishop Museum,* Honolulu, 1929). In Tonga a man has to treat his sister's husband with the same type of respect which he accords his sister.
[2]In Samoa the child of the sister, *tama fafine*, outranks the child of the brother, *tama tane*, and within a household the boys honor the sisters by permitting them to eat first.
[3]The reader will remember that the relationship between mother's brother's daughter and father's sister's son, which the Manus classify as sibling of opposite sex, has been, by definition, excluded from the term "cross-cousin" throughout this discussion.

and between whom a continuous jesting relationship is maintained; 3, cross-cousins who are known to be persons toward whom the jesting relationship can be invoked, but where this is not habitually done.

1. The remarks which have previously been made in regard to *tchelingen* apply here and the difficult situations which arise from the attempt to keep the betrothed pair of young people chaste tend to complicate this relationship.

2. The relationship between cross-cousins who are contemporaries is one of the most friendly relationships in Manus. If such cross-cousins live in different villages, one will use the other's home as a base for activities in the other village. Cross-cousins are also often fishing partners, overseas traveling partners, etc. The seniority situation between brothers, the constraint and avoidance between brothers-in-law are both lacking, and also importantly neither man must avoid the wife of the other. They are included in the jesting relationship sufficiently to permit almost casualness of contact. Such pairs of cross-cousins will make an institution of their special inter-relationship, depending upon it for companionship, coöperation and ease.

3. The third category, known but seldom invoked cross-cousin relationships, is usually between people of disparate age. If a boy wishes to be particularly impudent to an older man, he will preface his speech with *polapol*, using the kinship sanction for his liberties. But between individuals of disparate age continuous jesting or coöperation was not observed.

The relationship of a man and his female cross-cousin is largely ceremonial and has already been treated. It is not a relationship upon which an individual relies in day-by-day living.

The possibility that *lom pein* can curse *lom kamal* if the jesting goes too far or if *lom kamal* shows anger or resentment is not a very potent factor in day-by-day relationships. This power to make children of one's mother's brother's son sicken and die is so fierce a sanction that it is seldom invoked. In the village of Peri it had only been invoked three times within recent years, twice in economic quarrels, and once in the case cited on p. 251 as a result of too great license in the jesting relationship. A light sanction might have been more effective as a check upon too great liberties in the cross-cousin relationship, but the Manus have too strong a sentiment about fatherhood to be willing to deal out death lightly in this way. So actually, while the jesting is a daily occurrence, the cursing is only an infrequent and deprecated possibility.

SISTER TO SISTER—PILOAN

As the problem of seniority in Manus is so heavily bound up with economics, it does not intrude itself upon relationships between female siblings to anything like the same extent as among men. Sisterhood as a status of near contemporaries is much stronger. It begins to function earlier in a woman's life and is also more subject to disruption from residence arrangements than that of brotherhood. Girls are withdrawn from the play groups at puberty or sometimes a little before puberty.[1] By this time they are all betrothed. The exigencies of avoidance and the demand for surveillance both militate against the continuation of childhood comradeship between non-related female age mates. Adolescent girls are thrown back upon sisters and female parallel cousins for companionship. The girl, at first menstruation has, as her closest group of companions, her sisters, real or classificatory. Elder-younger sister relationships are reinterpreted into the mother-daughter situation, without however the element of strain which arises from the rivalry for the father's allegiance which is encouraged in the young child. If sisters live near each other, they continue to see a good deal of each other, subject to the demands for avoidance between the elder sister and the younger sister's husband. These avoidances do, however, prevent full intimacy.

SISTERS-IN-LAW—PINKAIYON

The chief relationship of strain between adults in Manus society is between husband and wife, second to that comes the strain between sisters-in-law, which is as definitely a strained relationship as that of brothers-in-law is a prevailingly friendly relationship. Superficially the dictated behavior is similar—name avoidance, and an avoidance of all intimacy, especially any allusion to sex. However, often, except in the case of a bride in her sister-in-law's house, eating avoidance is not enjoined. But here the analogy ends. Manus is a patrilineally organized community. The males in the community with three or four exceptions, grew up together. Furthermore, a husband and a brother have a common stake in a woman's chastity, which theoretically a sister and wife should share over a man's chastity, but which actually they do not, as a man's relationship with a men's house prostitute[2] or with any wives of another tribe, does not come under the supervision of the Sir Ghost cult. A sister is therefore indifferent to such activities. They do not endanger her health or life, nor the health or life of her children.

---

[1] For a more detailed discussion see *Growing Up in New Guinea*, Chapter X.
[2] The institution in which a woman of a hostile tribe was taken as a captive and kept in the men's house as a village prostitute until she died or was superseded by a newer captive.

But a wife is bitterly resentful of both. A Manus woman cannot commit any extra-marital sex act without the Sir Ghost cult of both patrilineal lines, that of her husband and that of her father and brother, taking cognizance of it. Furthermore, a woman is dependent upon either her husband or her brother for food and shelter, while a man, having his own house, is usually independent, except during his wife's confinement. Then a disagreement with one sister would merely send him to another sister—but a woman ejected from her husband's house for non-chastity would find all doors equally barred against her.

But whereas the men of a community are united by ties of life-long association and by common stakes in the behavior of their women kind, a woman comes into her husband's gens as a stranger. Even in intra-village marriage the long years of virtual segregation between puberty and marriage make girls of the same village shy and ill at ease with one another. The wife entering as a stranger immediately encounters the ill-will and hostility of the man's sisters upon whom he has depended for female companionship. It is a definite fact of Manus culture that the women show more jealousy of an affectional type, that they more active-ly resent their spouses' lack of attention to themselves or greater atten-tion to others, than do the men. The most usual form which a wife's resentment takes against the uncherished position in which she finds herself is in a definite act known as *sobalabalate*, accusation of incest be-tween the husband and one of his female relatives.

This is an insult, and at the same time a desperate attempt on the part of the wife to assert her position, desperate because it is an act which is punishable by the Sir Ghost cult. A woman who says to her husband "Your 'mother' or your 'sister' is my co-wife, I see," or "I see you have two wives now" is not making a serious accusation. She does not believe for one moment that her husband has had or ever would have sexual relations with his sister. It is simply an institutionalized way in which she can complain about her husband's emotional allegiance to his kin. For *sobalabalate* is a sin on two counts, it is an outrage against the solidarity of the kin group, and also an offense against the puritan code. There is no comparable behavior, formalized or unformalized, between brothers-in-law. If this pattern of wifely accusation be regarded from a strictly cultural point of view, it may be said that it is a Sir Ghost en-forced patrilineal system intimidating a woman from making trouble within her husband's kin group.

But all women do not use *sobalabalate*. It is not comparable to the institutionalized bad language between co-wives of one man, for instance, which is regarded as an inevitable correlate of an intolerable situation. Elders of the village may beat a drum to "shame" the quarreling women, but the spirits take infrequent cognizance of behavior which actually offends every dictate of Manus sense of decency. The expressed jealousy between sisters-in-law which is, usually, one-sided—wife to husband's sister,—although culturally recognized is simultaneously condemned. Only women goaded to frenzy by their husbands' pronounced and continuing preference for sisters take the risk of indulging in it. When only a small proportion of individuals makes use of a cultural form, especially, as in this case, when the form is specifically interdicted, it is permissible to seek a psychological explanation of the behavior of those individuals. Such an explanation must, of course, stem from the facts of the culture. This *sobalabalate* situation seems to occur in the case of women who are unusually anxious to make their marriages into important relationships, when this desire on the part of the wife coincides with an extra affection for a female relative on the part of the husband. In other words, a situation which the culture defines as spiritual delinquency[1] arises from aberrant temperament—for most Manus women make slight bid for happiness in marriage—coinciding with an over-emphasis on the usual brother-sister relationship.

Another aspect of the sister-in-law situation is the obligation of the wife to care for her husband's sister during late pregnancy, delivery, and the first month after delivery. The wife often has to move out of her own house, into the house of her husband's sister's husband. This involves endless inconveniences, both practical and spiritual. The Manus do not go about from house to house lightly. Around houses other than their own clings the aura of other ghosts. Furthermore, the Sir Ghost of one's own house may resent the prolonged absence and make one of the children sick as a reminder that it is time his ward returned to keep a fire burning in the house which shelters his skull. In addition to the spiritual danger which her children may be encountering there is the practical burden of caring for the convalescent woman, preparing her special food on a special fire. Whether the first weeks or so are spent in her own house, or in the house of her sister-in-law they are weeks of extra work, much coming and going of relatives, irksome observance. At the same period, her husband is harried by the necessity to provide the sago for the birth feast. This means that all the fish which can be spared from the household must be traded for sago—and this at

---

[1]For a discussion of delinquency from an analogous combination of aberrant temperament and aberrant cultural situation see *Coming of Age in Samoa* (New York, 1928), 173–180.

the very time when there is an extra mouth to feed. Nor can she supplement the household fare by shellfish because she must remain in constant attendance on the new mother. Altogether it is a wearisome nonreciprocal obligation, because when she bears a child the same obligation will be discharged by her brother's wife in much the same spirit.

So it will be seen that while brothers-in-law stand in a relationship of mutual interdependence, mutual helpfulness, with common stakes, sisters-in-law are institutionally opposed to each other. The society insists that sisters-in-law should preserve an appearance of friendliness,[1] but it is usually merely a surface matter. Nor can women go to their brothers' houses with the same freedom that their brothers come to theirs. For the women are the cooks; a woman can feed her brother in her husband's house, where her position as mistress of the hearth is undisputed, but she may refuse to cook for her husband's sisters. Her husband has no redress, except an open quarrel which would send her off to her brother's house. Here again she exercises a formal right of entry and residence which her brother's wife cannot dispute.

FEMALE CROSS-COUSINS—PINPOLAPOL

The relationship between female cross-cousins is characterized by lack of strain rather than by any pointed behavior. There is most infrequent jesting, which the spirits are likely to punish as unseemly, for in Manus theory a woman should have no intimates, no one single person in whose presence she may disrobe, actually or figuratively.

CO-WIVES—PALU

This is an unusual situation permitted by Manus custom, but rendered difficult by the very precise balances of the affinal exchange system. In Peri, in 1929, there were two men who had two wives, one of them had been a legalization of an illicit relationship, the others were the two wives of the acting *luluai*. One other man had quarreled with his two wives and evicted them both about eighteen months before. One recently married young woman had been a co-wife in Patusi. Two of the twenty widows had been co-wives to each other. This from a population of two hundred and ten, forty-four married couples and twenty widows, will give some impression of the relative frequency of plural wives. As was remarked above, all the ordinary restraint upon speech is removed in the relationship between two wives. They are permitted to shout obscenities at each other, each is privileged to refer publicly to

---

[1] Compare the Dobuan insistence upon cross-cousins, institutionally opposed to each other by the cultural arrangements, presenting an appearance of friendliness.

the sexual life of the other with the common spouse. A man may attempt to keep two wives in one house, but this is likely to cause even further dissention. Polygamy is distinctly an institution which is at the present time incongruous with Manus economic arrangements and Manus standards of behavior. It only exists in a state of open breach of the dictated decencies of the community.

TRADE FRIENDSHIPS

The economic relations centering about affinal exchanges have already been discussed. There is one other category of personal relationship in Manus which is outside of the kinship-affinal-relative patterns, and yet is in some degree assimilated to them. This is the trade friendship obtaining between men of different tribes. This relationship is non-ceremonial in character; it carries with it neither rites nor observances which would make it directly comparable to the *kula*[1] partnership. Sometimes kinship bonds, established by an intermarriage three or four generations ago and grown tenuous, are slightly perpetuated in a trade friendship. Nowadays the circle is widening in two ways; first, work boys from different parts of the Admiralties make friends while away at work and continue this relationship afterwards; and second, the natives appointed to local official positions by white government tend to regard each other as united by peculiar bonds, so that one "doctor boy" will set up trade relationships with the "doctor boy" of a village of a different tribe.

These trade relationships—a trade friend is known as *moen kawas e io*—literally, "sir trading partner of mine"—are more important than the daily market contacts in which nearby settlements barter foodstuffs and daily necessities. In a *kawas* relationship some credit is given between partners, and a man of one tribe will count upon his partner in another tribe to provide him with large objects, such as a tree for a canoe, or a large amount of fish or sago needed for a special feast. A trade partner is one to whom one may give notice of one's needs and expect to have them met—for a price of course—but the element of coöperation is present.

Trade partners may go to each other's houses, expect to receive food there and sleep there. Marriage is forbidden between a man and any woman of his trade partner's household—the relationship is assimilated to the usages of incest relationships, and so the wife and daughters of the host are protected from the guest whom, among the Manus at

---

[1]Malinonski, B., *Argonauts of the Western Pacific.* London, 1922.

least, they may treat with easy friendliness. A trade partnership may follow intermarriage, but it cannot initiate it. For the first two generations after an inter-tribal marriage the trade relationship is, of course, couched in affinal terms.

A man will also resent any injury done to a trade partner of his kin. So the village of Peri was split into two divisions, Peri and Pontchal, because the young men of the side of the village which is now Pontchal carried off a daughter of the Usiai trade partner of the *luluai* of Peri.

Religious Ramifications of the Kinship System

Mr. Fortune has devoted an entire section of his book to this subject and I shall merely recapitulate here briefly in the interests of completeness.

Two religious cults may be distinguished in Manus, the Sir Ghost cult, that is, the cult of the immediate dead male relative whose duty it is to protect and chasten all the members of the patrilineal household, and the *tandritanitani* cult of the conjoined lines of ancestral male and female ghosts which may be invoked by descendants of the female line in the interests of or against the descendants in the male line. These latter ghostly lines are invoked at all the crisis rites; it is through them that individuals are endowed with health, wealth, and power, that women are dowered with domestic virtues and men with warlike prowess. Most importantly, on these ghostly lines, as invoked by their female descendants, rests the power of giving or withholding conception to the women of the male line and, to a less extent, to the wives of men of the male line also. By this arrangement the control of offspring in the inheriting line is in the power of the disinherited line. In the hands of the women of the female line also rests the power of determining the sex of the child. If the *tandritanitani* cult alone were present, a balance between the interests of the descendants of brother and sister, based upon the power of the female ghostly ancestors of the mother and the male ghostly ancestors of the father—of that brother and sister—would obtain for the next generation. The *tandritanitani* cult is then the sanction behind the prescribed marriage. In the second generation, if the ideal plan were followed, marriage between a male descendant of the sister and a female descendant of the brother would establish a new and reciprocal relationship, the descendants of which, for the next two generations, would be under a new conjunction of ghostly lines.

This three-generation group is neither a gens nor a *patandrusun* group, but a combination of descent lines, unique with each marriage, which is somewhat like a sib. Each marriage establishes such a group (if there are offspring). The group consists of the parents, the children, the two opposed lines of children of brother and children of sister, who are subject to the same set of ghosts. As a pair of brothers can never marry a pair of sisters, no two of these groups are ever identical; that is, individuals with the same gentile taboo—and the same *patandrusun*—will occur, but they will not be subject to the same conjoined ghostly lines. There is no Manus word for this group of descendants from a marriage; I have used for descriptive purposes the term *mixed descent group* which implies the opposition in sex between the brother and sister progenitors, and also the idea of descent. This mixed descent group is one of the two most formally important groups in Manus, controlling as it theoretically does, pregnancy in one generation and marriage in the next.

The other effective group in Manus is the patrilineal household, using household here to include a man's economic dependents as well as the immediate residents of his own house. This use is permissible because the Sir Ghost of an economic leader presides, in a general way, over the behavior of all his economic dependents and they must take care not to anger him in any way. This patrilineal household must be distinguished from the gens with which it is never synonymous unless the gens has shrunk to only one or two adult members. (When this last condition occurs the gens may scatter and the survivors become identified economically and residentially, and therefore religiously, with a household within another gens.) In the interests of these patrilineal constellations within the gens, the Sir Ghost punishes all infractions of the moral code by members of this group or their wives. This patrilineal group which is centered about a leader in the case of important men—in the case of humble independents it will be limited to those resident in the house—is the most important in Manus, controlling as it does, residence, all sorts of economic endeavor both in supplying daily wants and in the large affinal exchanges, and also moral conduct. Women are detached from their own households and placed under the jurisdiction of their husbands' Sir Ghosts, thus enormously strengthening the powers of patrilineal morality. A woman ill has no Sir Ghost who will assume all the responsibility; a woman sinning has directed against her the anger of her husband's Sir Ghost, and, should she try to take refuge in his household, her brother's Sir Ghost, also.

The *tandritanitani* cult is only concerned with showering blessings upon the young of the brother's line, and with occasional curses. By making marriage a highly flexible matter, the power of the *tandritanitani* cult has been further emasculated. Actual day by day maintenance of a sober, moral, industrious régime, the arrangement of economics, the payment of debts, the maintenance of virtue, are all under the Sir Ghost cult.

Should, however, the members of the *Lom Pein* group actually use the power of the *tandritanitani* curse against the *Lom Kamal* group, frequently and effectively, it would alter the entire complexion of Manus society, and considerably reduce the patrilineal emphasis. As it is, at present, the line of the father's sister is ceremonially important, but the supernatural sanctions which individuals of this line can invoke are only rarely invoked, in personal quarrels. The *tandritanitani* curse is used almost as infrequently as the *sobalabalate* accusation of incest.

JUSTIFICATION OF ENSUING COMPARISONS

It is appropriate here to give some brief explanation of why Manus will be compared in subsequent pages with Western Polynesia, especially with Tonga, Samoa, and Fiji. This selection is not made because of the accident of my having worked in Samoa; rather is the choice made on strictly sociological grounds. Although the Manus are much darker than the Samoans and in many ways are characteristically Melanesian, nevertheless they share many cultural forms with western Polynesia—just those forms, be it remarked, which distinguish western Polynesia very sharply from central and eastern Polynesia. The most striking of these likenesses, center about the kinship system, the recognition of the two lines of descent, the ceremonial recognition of the father's sister in a patrilineal system, cross-cousin relationships, etc. Professor A. R. Radcliffe-Brown has outlined as an essential method the comparison of different varieties of a type within a related geographical area. Although distant by so many miles from western Polynesia, it seems that Manus can be profitably regarded as one variety of a general type, a type complicated in its western Polynesia form by the peculiarly Polynesian elements of rank, taboo, cosmogony, and cult of high Gods, etc. In my paper on Manu'a I expressed the opinion that Samoa, Tonga, and Fiji must be discussed together if an understanding of the cultural forms of any one of them was to be reached. Manus presents the kinship forms of western Polynesia in a far sharper and clearer outline and contributes considerable illumination to the understanding of these forms as they occur in combination elsewhere.

In the discussion of Samoan social organization[1] I pointed out that there are two principles at work in Samoan society, the intricate balances

---

[1] Mead, Margaret, *ibid.*

of the mixed descent group and the principle of locality. Throughout Samoa, Tonga, and Fiji, different compromises have been made with these two principles, always with rank as an institution which could be combined with the other two. In Samoa the compromise was made in terms of each individual village and the autonomy and common interests of the mixed descent group, resident in several villages, was superseded by the joint household, all resident in one village and subject to one head man—the *matai*. The sanction behind the power of the *matai* was the power of the *fono*, the village council.

In Tonga, the power of the father's sister was enlisted to preserve the integrity of the patrilineal household, with its basis in primogeniture, by permitting her intervention whenever disagreements were threatened between brothers. In parts of Tonga, and extensively in Fiji, cross-cousin marriage also served to solve the conflict of the two separately resident parts of the mixed descent group, by binding them into one unit again. The more spectacular political institutionalizations of the kinship pattern in the royal households of Tonga and the inter-tribal *Vasu* of Fiji do not concern us so much here, where we are considering a compromise between a formal grouping with interests often antithetical and a practical local grouping which could work effectively towards local and immediate ends.

In Manus, for all practical purposes, the element of rank is lacking, but a new element enters in: organized, named, localized gentes. The supernatural sanctions lying behind the internal balances of the mixed descent group were antithetical to the gens principle, lodging, as they do, power over members of the gens, in the hands of members of other gentes. A solution of this conflict is found in the patrilineal constellations in Manus, which act as units, and even have virtual jurisdiction over the female members of other gentes resident within them, and the way in which marriages are made to follow the arbitrary and formal dictates of the mixed descent group. Whereas the sanction for the organized joint household in Samoa was the village council which possessed well-defined penal powers, the sanction for the patrilineal household in Manus is the Sir Ghost cult, the Sir Ghost being conceived as exercising supernatural penal powers over all the members of his economic constellation.

When we consider the functioning of the kinship system, so much of which is contravened or rewritten in the interests of the patrilineal constellations, we shall find again analogy between the development of social forms in Manus and in western Polynesia. In western Polynesia the kinship system has provided social forms upon which the society has elaborated, as already remarked, in village terms in Samoa. There the village acts as the family of the high chief, with the two orders of talking chiefs discharging the functions of the male and female descent lines (*tamatane* and *tamafafine*) respectively. The development has been in tribal terms in Fiji, where if an individual is *vasu* to a chief he is therefore *vasu* to the chief's tribe also, and where two tribes come to stand in an institutionalized cross-cousin relationship, *tauvu*, to each other.[1] In Tonga the inter-relations of the mixed descent group may be said to have provided a national pattern.[2]

In all of these instances the kinship system is dynamic, and the tendencies within the society making for village, tribal, or national solidarity have utilized the kinship system as a form through which these respective solidarities could be elaborated consonantly with the genius of the culture.

In Manus there is a trend towards individualism, towards the recognition of individual differences and opportunities for individual initiative which is incompatible with a rigid kinship system by which a man's rôle in life is inextricably combined with that of his cross-cousins; i.e., in which all his important associations are fixed by birth. Samoan society, with its concept of rank, has dissociated the individual from the position, disregarded primogeniture, and so developed a system by which the most able person can be placed in a fixed position. Manus, lacking any such concept of rank, has developed differently. Fixed positions, defined by birth within the confines of an unyielding kinship system, have been practically eliminated, and instead, the able individual is permitted to define his own position in relation to other individuals of varying caliber. In Samoa, if the idea of rank had not been modified the chieftainship would go to the eldest son, regardless of his fitness for the position. In Manus, conversely, without the modifications which will be discussed in the chapter on the Contravention of the System, the most able man would be held to a cramped position, regardless of his potentialities. Both these undesirable results have been avoided, in Samoa by emphasizing the position as independent of the man, in Manus by emphasizing the man as independent of the position.

---

[1]Hocart has also suggested that the institution of heralds and envoys in Fiji originated in the relationship between elder and younger brother. An equally plausible case can be made out for its origin in the *tamafafine* relationship in Samoa, while in Tonga the herald is called by a word which also means man's sister's husband and husband's sister.

Sources for the above discussion: Gifford, *Tongan Society*, 29 and 140; Hocart, A. M., Chieftainship and the Sister's Son in the Pacific (*American Anthropologist*, n.s., vol. 17, 631–646, 1915); The Fijian Custom of Tauvu (*Journal of the Royal Anthropological Institute of Great Britain and Ireland*, vol. 43, 101–108, 1913); Heralds and Envoys in Fiji (*Journal of the Royal Anthropological Institute of Great Britain and Ireland*, vol. 43, 109–118, 1913); More about Tauvu (*Man*, vol. 14, no. 96, 1914).

[2]Gifford, *op. cit.*, 19.

The Manus kinship system is simply regarded as a system of legal devices, of possible categories in terms of which an individual may act. The intelligent and the enterprising invoke these categories to suit their own economic ends. "To understand *kawas*" (trade) in Manus means actually to understand the manipulation of the kinship categories, to exploit one's possible relationship claims to the full and to be able to find ways of rewriting any relationship should it seem desirable. Samoan society presents the picture of a fixed hierarchy into which the able climb. Manus presents each individual with a set of possibilities which the most able will recognize and use.

CEREMONIAL PLUNDER

Plunder, by the sister and her descendants of the brother and his descendants, is characteristic of that area of western Polynesian culture with which the Manus kinship system has so much in common. It may be very slight and attenuated—as in eastern Samoa when the *ilamutu* (titular father's sister) takes the best fine mat from the dowry of her brother's son's wife, or it may be elaborated to a major cultural institution as in the *vasu* of the sister's son in Fiji.

The system of ceremonial plunder in Manus is rather anomalous and contradictory. The *patieyen* group plucks the finery from the bride of their *nebonitu* in a manner strongly suggestive of the Samoan marriage customs, in which the bride's fine mat clothes are taken off and shared with the father's sisters of the groom. Theoretically, in Manus, a man who is child-of-sister (*lom pein*) may plunder his cross-cousin who is child-of-brother (*lom kamal*), and the child-of-brother will not venture to demand redress or repayment because of the possibility of incurring the cross-cousin curse. But, actually, this form of plunder does not occur. Child-of-brother and child-of-sister live on very friendly reciprocal terms, although the possibility of using the curse as a sanction for outright plunder, undue borrowing, or injury to the property of child-of-brother, is verbally recognized. It is possibly indirectly invoked when the child-of-brother requests the assistance of his mother's relatives in making feasts, but this is only to ensure assistance which will be repaid in full later. There is no plunder of the mother's brother; this is a respect relationship. The mother's brother does, however, have to make a feast for his sister's son if he escapes from illness or danger. Although this duty is not now so interpreted, it may possibly have once belonged in a near-plunder category.

But the really institutionalized plunder in Manus goes against the curse instead of with it and is the exact reverse of the *tauvu* situation in Fiji. When a man who is child-of-sister dies, the men of his mother's brother's male line, i.e., those men who were children-of-brother to him, may tear down the house of the deceased, plunder its contents and throw the skull of his Sir Ghost into the sea. The kin of the dead usually anticipate this visitation by secreting as much of the movable property as possible. This institution is known as a *ngang*. The Manus rationalize it as follows: "A woman of A gens has married into a strange house of B gens, a house which is presided over by strange ghosts. There she bore a child to the ghosts of B gens. The ghosts of the B gens house have now wantonly permitted that child, grown to be a man, to die. Therefore, the outraged men of A gens, the gens of the dead man's mother, come to destroy the house and skull bowls of these ghosts who have permitted their kinsman, a child of a woman of their gens, to die."

I have deferred discussion of this institution until this point because of its relevance to the religious ramifications of the kinship system. It will be recalled that the cult of the conjoined lines of ancestors, the males of the male line and the females of the female line—the *tandri-tanitani* cult—supports the powers of the children-of-sister, while the Sir Ghost cult supports the patrilineal household. The *ngang* is a formalized, institutionalized expression of the clash between these two cults. The woman of gens A, mother of the deceased *lom pein* (child-of-sister) has had to forego the protection of her long line of ancestral ghosts, for although she may invoke them in the interests of her brother's children, she and her own children are subject to her husband's Sir Ghosts. This aggressive patrilineal emphasis of the Sir Ghost cult contradicts the balance between *lom kamal* and *lom pein*, by which one receives the temporal, the other the spiritual benefits of their common inheritance. The *ngang* may therefore be interpreted as a ceremonial expression of the fundamental conflict between the two cults.

INHERITANCE

The question of inheritance has been dealt with in other contexts throughout this study, but it seems advisable to summarize here for the convenience of comparative students. The most important legacy in Manus is the skull of the legator, bequeathed by spoken testament when there is sufficient warning of approaching death. The skull is the pledge that the dead man will become the Sir Ghost of his heir. With the skull goes the nominal economic status of the dead man, his house site, and such parts of the house as remain after the ceremonial destruction. (Sometimes a house is burned, more often it is only hacked about in places and the thatch torn away, leaving the posts and principal parts of the framework intact.) After a death the patrilineal kin of a man secrete such parts of his movable property as they can, in the shape of small canoes, tools, nets, drums, pots, etc. All of these are theoretically the spoil of the plundering group, their seizure by the patrilineal kin is extra-legal and not regulated by hard and fast rules. Such dogs' teeth and shell money as a man may have collected are still in the possession of his "sisters" who are the usual custodians of such property, and are used to pay the debts or initiate the exchanges for which they were collected. For example, Pwanau died just before making his *metcha* (the large late marriage payment) and Paliau, his heir, made this for him with the property which Pwanau had left and some additional contributions of his own.

The major inheritance is simply status—as a ward of the dead man, as his nominal heir. The heir takes over the economic assets and liabilities of the dead man very much as a tradesman purchases the good will of a trade site. Similarly, unless the heir can maintain the status, inspire confidence in his kin, plan wisely and trade shrewdly, and muster the necessary property to carry on the affairs in which he has inherited a major position, they are taken over by others. The inheritance of rank is similarly dependent upon ability. A man inherits *lapan* blood; he must be rich and energetic if he would openly parade the privilege of a *lapan*.

As has already been indicated, the heir may be brother, brother's son, father's younger brother, father's brother's son; less often, own son, sister's son, or even wife's younger brother, all of these own or adopted. With the average age of death for males between thirty-five and forty, a man's own son is seldom old enough to succeed him. The effective generations in Manus may be said to be ten year periods, as is recognized in their own term *aiyo*, rather than twenty or twenty-five year periods. Effective leadership seldom lasts over ten years.

CONTRAVENTION OF THE KINSHIP SYSTEM
IMPLICATIONS OF THE AFFINAL EXCHANGE SYSTEM

Societies differ tremendously in their attitudes towards their social forms. It is of course a truism that theory and practice never agree exactly, that in any department of social life there will be found deviating individuals who refuse or fail to conform to the accepted practices of the society. But some societies, despite the variability of the individuals of which they are composed, remain fundamentalistic, firmly adhering to their prescribed code, and branding, while they tolerate, its breach. Such a society is Dobu which recognizes hard and fast rules of marriage, forbids marriage into one's own clan, father's clan, and into a village into which another member of one's own village has already married. These interdicted marriages do occur, but they are recognized for what they are, breaches of a code which is not modified to give the aberrant individuals comforting quarter.

In Manus and Samoa the difference between theory and practice is not such a mere individual matter, but a definitely cultural one. In Dobu, aberrant marriages, of which the community disapproves, are merely tolerated because the community is so organized that it is unable to prevent them. But in Manus, the society itself bends its traditional forms to accommodate aberrant practice. This socially recognized contravention is a result of a flexible pragmatic attitude towards social forms which contrasts sharply with the fundamentalist attitude. Forms which interfere with the essential trends or emphases in a society are contravened, evaded beneath a plentiful verbal recognition, and by doing so the society accomplishes ends more appropriate to itself.

The Manus kinship system with its prescribed marriage forms, if followed carefully, would at best prevent the Manus from the exercise of discretion in forming marital alliances. Furthermore, it assumes a democratic equality between individuals which is foreign to the Manus individualism, an individualism which has successfully eliminated the kind of descent-group common action which in many parts of Oceania permits the weak to shelter behind the strong. The Manus have made the affinal exchange system a pivotal point in their culture; in order to do this, it has been necessary to eliminate the binding forms of purely blood ties.

Affinal exchanges in which the relatives of the bride exchange property with the relatives of the bridegroom are a common feature of Oceanic society, and occur in many other parts of the world also. The Oceanic system is distinguished from wife indemnity by the fact that the relatives of the bride are obligated to make a return strictly commensurate with the value of the gifts which they have initially received.[1]

---

[1]Mr. Williams in Orokaiva Society (*Anthropological Reports, Government of Papua,* No. 10, London, 1930) gives an interesting case in which what he believes was once brother and sister exchange is combined with payment in such a way that if the second bride is not demanded or forthcoming then an exchange tantamount to the familiar Samoan, Manus type of affinal exchange takes place instead, i.e., formerly an Orokaiva descent group A paid a bride price for a woman of descent group B. A few years later, group B pays a bride price of a similar kind for a woman of group A. Under these conditions group A and group B over a series of years have exchanged two women and two sets of gifts of similar composition. It cannot be said that there has been wife purchase. This ideal form has broken down among the Orokaiva. Often an acceptable woman is not found among the bridegroom's group, and then, sometimes but not always, the group of the bride makes a return gift which Mr. Williams calls the "husband price." If this "husband price" were always paid and the exchange of brides fell completely into disuse, the result would be a system of validating economic exchanges in which bride-price is exactly matched by dowry. Whether this later development among the Orokaiva is, as Mr. Williams very plausibly suggests, a breakdown of the old bride exchange system, or merely a widely diffused Oceanic pattern to which current Orokaiva practice is approximating more exactly, can only be ascertained by a distribution study, if at all. But this Orokaiva usage throws an interesting sidelight upon the more general affinal exchange system.

In the Manus system, marriage, all events which concern the principals to the marriage, or the children of the marriage, set in motion an exchange of property. The Manus call the two parties to the exchange "The side of the man" and "The side of the woman."[1]

The "side of the man" contains the people who were the "side of his father" and the "side of his mother" in the marriage of his parents,[2] so that each side is a bilateral kin group. Each of these groups is originally organized by an economic entrepreneur, the father, or acting father, of the bride or of the groom. Although the large payments by one side to the other are made all at once, the contribution which each individual makes is carefully noted and later returned by his or her partner, *ndrengen*, of the other side of the exchange. Theoretically kin groups are so balanced that a relative of the groom exchanges with someone similarly related to the bride, e.g., mother's brother of groom with mother's brother of bride, etc. In practice, economic sufficiency, not kinship status, is the criterion in choice of *ndrengen*.

The man's side always pays dogs' teeth, shell money, and shell or bead belts; the women's side, pigs, oil, sago, pots, grass skirts, cooked food, and, on special occasions, an elaborate bridal costume of shell money aprons and dogs' teeth ornaments, a carved wooden bed, and sometimes obsidian spears. (In modern times cloth has been added to the contributions appropriate to the bride's side of the exchange. All initiative in paying dogs' teeth and shell money lies with the man's side, the pigs and oil are repaid over a period by individuals to their *ndrengen*. The initiative in the smaller exchanges where sago is repaid in belts, is taken by the woman's side.)

Because of the short span of life in Manus—only two men in the village had lived to see their sons married—the leadership in these economic transactions shifts. A father may make the initial payments for his son, but in the normal course of events will die before his son is married. The father's place is then taken by one of his younger brothers or by his father's young brother's son who will continue to make the necessary exchanges up to the young man's marriage. Later, the husband is expected to take over his own economic exchanges which he now conducts with his brother-in-law. Late in life, after a couple have been

---

[1] The word for side is *soal* which is translated in pidgin as "half" so the full pidgin is "half belong man" and "half belong mary." It is used for the other part of a house, the other end of the village, the other side of an island, etc., being literally one part of a whole. So one part of the descent group concerned in a marriage exchanges with the other part of the descent group concerned in the same marriage.

[2] The Manus are careless in their terminology and it is not always clear whether they are speaking of the halves concerned in an individual's own life or of those of his parents. The Samoans who use the term *itu* for the Manus *soal* will say there were several *itu* represented in one exchange, preserving a recognition of the groupings which centered about parental and collateral marriages.

married ten or fifteen years, the brother-in-law may die, so that in the final event a man may be exchanging with his wife's brother's heir. This is merely the theoretical scheme.

The principal exchanges are as follows:—

Betrothal payment by the bridegroom's kin: *komambut*

Minor exchanges at the first menstruation of a betrothed girl

Large pre-marriage payment by bridegroom's kin: *mamandra*

Payment by bride's kin at the actual marriage: *mwelamwel*

Post marriage payment by bridegroom's kin: *matiruai*

Exchange at birth of first child

Minor exchanges for birth of each child, ear piercing of each child, and first menstruation of unbetrothed girls, and at the death of any child born to the marriage.

Last marriage payment made after children are half grown: *metcha*.

Series of mourning exchanges made at the death of either spouse. Sometimes before this series of exchanges is completed, the exchanging kin groups become merged in financing the prospective marriage of the children born to the marriage which originally connected them.

In the system of affinal exchanges and the arranged marriages about which these exchanges center there are certain assumptions. If the prescribed marriages were followed the initiators of a marriage contract would be cross-cousin *patarans: lom pein* the father of the prospective bridegroom, *lom kamal* the father of the prospective bride. At the same time the father of the bride would stand in a *pataran* relationship to *his* mother's brother's son from whom he would be demanding a daughter in marriage to his son. When his cross-cousin on his father's side paid him the betrothal payment for his daughter, he would take this same betrothal payment and pass it on to his cross-cousin on his mother's side. The return payment on the part of the bride's relatives would move in a reverse direction. If bride-price and dowry both consisted of imperishable valuables this might be conceived of as an endless chain in which no one won or lost, but merely for a brief moment held the validating property. The system implies furthermore that all exchanges be of the same size, a man would only pay for his son's marriage what he received for his daughter's marriage.

Furthermore, the system demands an equal number of boys and girls within descent groups, although not within one family, if coöperation between brothers were granted. For a group of brothers who were sons of the same mother would all be subject to approaches from the same cross-cousins who were their mother's brother's sons. However it should be noted that the *lom-pein*ship which gives a man or woman a right to demand a mother's brother's son's daughter in marriage applies strictly to a family line not to a gens, so, of many individuals in Manus it is said "He has no *lom pein,*" that is, his mother's brother's line has died out. This is a neat example of the kind of social compulsion which may lead from a simple kinship system to the classificatory system. A frank acceptance of the principle of extension of kinship terminology with a commensurate extension of kinship function would have been one way in which the Manus could have met this problem. It has already been shown that the Manus derive a theoretically classificatory system from the effective system by extension, e.g., when they call the children of a female *lom kamal* and a male *lom pein,* who are "brother" and "sister" to each other, *polapol.* They had only to go one step farther and permit all *polapol* to contract their children in marriage to solve one difficulty of the disparity of the sexes. But this they did not do; the type of extension of function with extension of terminology simply does not occur.

One clue, although not a complete clue to the lack of this development must be found in the peculiar configuration which invests *lom pein* with his power because of his mother's *patandrusun* affiliation plus her gentile affiliations. The specificity of this relationship cannot be generalized to cover an extended group of relatives; mother's sisters who were classificatory mothers would lack the same gens connection as the mothers, the sons of father's classificatory brothers would owe no spiritual dependence to their classificatory father's wives' *patandrusun.* In expanding the range of relationship so as to make it more flexible, the Manus have resorted to a different expedient, viz., adoption of a special type. Theoretically, the *patieyen* line determines magically the sex of *lom kamal's* children, but the Manus do not rely upon this doubtful expedient to correct disparity between the sexes in a given family.

ADOPTION

Child adoption is one of the fundamental kinship reliances of Manus society. Adoption of children under six or seven is regarded as so final, as establishing so close a bond between the adult and the child, that there is no term to distinguish between an adopted or foster child and an own child. When pressed for definition, a Manus will finally answer "He took him as his child." And the customary request to adopt a child is couched in similar terms. One man simply says to another, "I will take this child to be my child." Adopted children are deemed to have the full benefits of the spirits of the foster father's line and of the spirits of the foster mother's line. The blood tie is not regarded as essential in either case.

There is no way in which a man need be concerned as to whether a child is his own or adopted; in either instance, the child belongs to his house, to his gens, to his spirits, to his rank. But there is one respect in which the tie between mother and child is insisted upon, for a woman cannot become a medium unless she has borne and lost a male child. There were, however, a few dissentors to this theory, who claimed that if a woman had suckled a male child who subsequently died, he might serve as a control, even as her own child would have done. I found no case of this in practice. From the above requirement may come the custom of women's lying about motherhood, although there is no comparable custom among men of claiming false paternity. Another reason for the women's lying insistence upon maternity may rest in the fact that adoption is into the foster father's gens, and the adopting mother in case of divorce may have to relinquish all claims to the child. This is a matter where the right of the child to claim son-ship and the right of his mother to claim motherhood are rendered disparate by the operation of the patrilineal emphasis within the society. A father's rights are not threatened by his adopted son's claiming *lom-pein*ship to his divorced wife's brother's children, but a father's rights over his adopted child would be threatened if the mother attempted to take the child away with her, as a woman sometimes does with young children of her own.

In contrast to the adoption of young children there is another type of adoption which is financial, when a man assumes the responsibilities of a father in promoting a young person's affinal exchanges. Such an older person will be said to *pwokeani* the younger person, literally "to strengthen him." The children of the younger will call the elder, grandfather, as the theoretical but not often effective terminology for the elder from the younger is "father." Financial help of this type establishes socio-economic bonds between elder and younger kinsmen, but the adoption lacks the finality of earlier adoption.

Adoption in early childhood may take many different paths. The commonest forms are the adoption of a child of a dependent younger relative by a financial elder. This is the most definitely planned type of adoption in Manus and the place where there is a definite effort made to arrange sex ratio. However, there is also a strong sentiment of compassion for childless people and sometimes a man will permit a financial dependent who desires a child, but has had none, to adopt one of his children. Adoption of a child by its mother's brother is also fairly common, although usually associated with the death of the father during the child's infancy, and the return of the mother and child to the mother's place. If children of living mothers are adopted before they are weaned, they are left with their own mothers until weaned, spending part of their time with their new parents.

Often children are adopted so early that they never know who their real parents are until they are grown. The distinction between real and adopted is so flimsy that a discovery of real parents is no shock to a child and merely provides him with an extra *lom pein*ship if he so desires. At other times children are adopted after they have learned to use kinship terms to their real parents, and will be able to explain their double relationship quite clearly. There is also a type of nominal adoption by which a man or woman does not actually assume charge of the child, but nevertheless the child uses "parent" terms and may exercise a son's privilege freely in the house of this titular type of parent.

THE MODIFICATION OF THE KINSHIP TERMINOLOGY

Both early adoption and financing affect the kinship terminology, the one the individual's own terminology, the other, to less degree, the individual's own terminology, but more importantly, the terminology used by the children of the financed person. Revisions of terminology in case of adoption show up clearly the Manus tendency to count each distant relationship through its derivatory lines and the lack of generalizations of a classificatory type.

As examples:—

1. Pwasa, a girl of about ten is the youngest daughter of Ndrantche and Poitchalon. She has been adopted by Alupwai, her older sister, so she now calls her sister "mother" and her own mother "grandmother."

2. Ngakakes and Taliye are the daughters of Korotan, but Ngakakes has been adopted by Korotan's female ortho-cousin. So Ngakakes and Taliye call each other *pinpolapol*, female cross-cousin, and Ngakakes calls her own father "mother's brother."

3. Ngapating, a girl of about eight has been adopted by her father's elder "brother" (ortho-cousin) so she calls her father *"pisio"*, "sibling of opposite sex."

4. Kali and Moendras were brothers. Moendras bore Kemwai, a man, and Pwekaro, a woman. Kali married Pinkas, who bore him a son, Nane, and died. At his second marriage Kali married Kiteni, a widow, who had a son, Ngandaliu by a dead husband. Kali and Kiteni bore Molung, a girl. Molung was adopted twice, as a child by Pwekaro, and later her marriage was financed by Ngandaliu, who had been adopted by Kali. Molung is now a woman of thirty. She calls Kali, her own father,

"grandfather" because she calls Ngandaliu "father" because he financed her. And she calls Nane "brother" although she calls Kali grandfather and although Ngandaliu calls Nane father because Nane is his elder adopted brother. But she calls Kemwai, whom Nane calls father, "mother's brother" because of her childhood adoption by Pwekaro, Kemwai's sister.

Expressed in summary form:—

Name of Relative	Genealogical Relationship to Molung	Terms used by Molung
Kali	father	"grandfather"
Ngandaliu	father's stepson	"father"
Nane	elder half brother-father's son	"brother"
Kemwai	father's father's brother's son	"mother's brother"

Molung is typical here in that she makes no attempt to make the terms which she uses consistent, but merely argues from one particular case to a terminology which, when it is considered alone, flows from it.

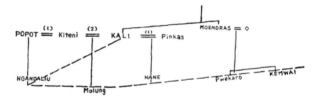

Fig. 15.   Genealogy to illustrate Terminology used by Molung of Lo Gens.

But the result is that she calls one male member of her father's gens "mother's brother."

Numerous examples exist in my notes and could be multiplied, but without advantage. The Manus attitude towards kinship usage is fluid. Adoption and financing may modify any given relationship without necessitating comparable revisions in other relationships.

This is a highly individualistic attitude to take towards kinship. It differs markedly from the situation in which adoption is final in that an individual moves bodily from one kinship category to another and counts all his relationships consistently from his new status. Many adoptions in Manus do not involve a change in status, but only a re-arrangement of some terms of relationship.

Complete revision of terminology is not made, very probably, because of the desire to remember as many adoptive mothers as possible. Adoptive fathers are not useful on the same scale, and, a man's final gens affiliation usually determines which fatherhood he will remember. But to the brother's children of an adopted mother a man is *lom pein,* and has the right to demand a girl in marriage for his son. *Lom pein* rights are the charter to the exercise of economic volition.

A man or woman can count a *lom pein*ship through any woman who has stood in a fostering relationship. These include own mother, father's other wife if the marriage were polygamous, stepmother, adoptive mother. Adoptive mothers may be older sisters, older brother's wives, grandmothers, mother's brother's wives, etc. A father's sister cannot be counted unless all relationship to the father is superseded by some later fatherhood, as a man cannot be *lom pein* and *lom kamal* simultaneously to and in one male line.

ILLUSTRATIVE CASES

An example is the case of Pwasa who was adopted by her sister Alupwai. Ndrantche, the mother of Pwasa and Alupwai, belonged to the gens of Lopwer. The father, Poitchalon, was a man of Kalo. Pwasa was therefore born *lom kamal* in her father's line of Kalo, *lom pein* to her mother's line in Lopwer. But she has been adopted by Alupwai and Alupwai's husband, Tunu, who belongs to a powerful line in Pere gens. So Pwasa now belongs to Pere, the gens of her adopted father, and is *lom pein* to Lopwer line and *lom pein* also, through Alupwai, to a Kalo line, the children of her blood brothers.

The reverse situation is found in the case of Pokenau. His grandfather was Gizikau who had a wife from a Tchalalo line. Pokenau was the son of Gizikau's son, Tano, and a Patusi mother. Tano and his wife both died, and Pokenau was adopted by his paternal grandfather, Gizikau. Pokenau called Gizikau "father" and took over terminology appropriate to Tano in most instances. For example, he calls Gizikau's sister's daughter's daughter, *patieyen*, "female descendant of father's sister," when by actual genealogical relationship she is "female descendant of father's father's sister," *pinpapu*. But Pokenau counts himself as *lom pein* to a Patusi line and *lom pein* to a Tchalalo line.

Furthermore, a man may count himself as *lom pein* to more than one line through the same real or adoptive mother. If his adoptive mother had been adopted, she may have foster brothers in two different male lines in two different gentes. In that case her adopted son will claim two sets of cross-cousins for purposes of initiating marriage arrangements.

A man does not, however, call himself *lom pein* to the brother's line of all the women whom he calls *yaye*, mother, because of the kinship system, e.g., his mother's younger sister's foster brother, for instance. He can only claim as "mother" the woman who bore him and women who have actually fostered him as a child. It is not a legal matter so much as a question of closeness of tie to the woman through whom he must approach the line of female ghosts upon whom formally his power of *lom pein* depends.

An adult views his genealogy from a strictly practical point of view, not of what blood runs in his veins, but of what kin connections he has upon which it will be profitable to act. He keeps track of his claim to his gens affiliations and to his house site, and of his *lom pein* claims, that is of all women he can call "mother" in a functioning sense, all

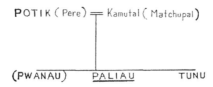

Fig. 16.   Paliau's Genealogy as he Originally gave it.

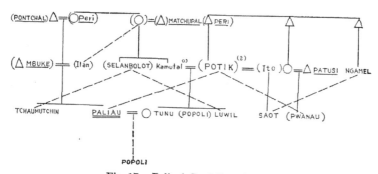

Fig. 17.   Paliau's Real Genealogy.

the men whom he calls "mother's brother" through such "mothers," and all the sons of such "mother's brothers." He has a tendency to drop out of consideration all relatives of "fathers" except the one through whom he counts his effective gentile affiliations. If, however, he has a real father's sister, or father's sister's daughter in a position where she can be useful to him, e.g., in a distant village, or married into another tribe with which trade is desirable, then the memory quickens.

As an example of the way in which an intelligent Manus adult views his genealogy, I shall present the salient facts in Paliau's genealogy in sequence as they were obtained (Figs. 16 and 17).

1. On first being questioned about his genealogy, Paliau said he was the son of Potik and Kamutal. Potik belonged to Pere and Kamutal belonged to Matchupal. Pwanau who was dead, and Tunu, were his two brothers, the sons of Potik and Kamutal.

2. A week or so later, I took the genealogy of Tchaumutchin of Matchupal, who informed me that he was the blood brother of Paliau and that he and Paliau were the sons of a Mbuke father by Kamutal of Matchupal, who had subsequently married Potik of Pere who had adopted Paliau. Tchaumutchin, on the other hand, had been adopted by Selanbolot of Matchupal, the brother of Kamutal. So Paliau and Tchaumutchin, full brothers, belonged to different gentes.

3. Some time later, I took the genealogy of Luwil, of Matchupal, the heir of Selanbolot above-mentioned. In the back of Luwil's house lived Saot. Luwil said Saot was his brother. Furthermore, he said that he and Saot were both brothers to Paliau as they were both sons of Potik, but he and Saot were sons of different mothers. Potik having married twice, Saot's mother, Ito, belonged to Kalo and through her Luwil claimed *lom pein*ship to Kalo. Luwil added the information that he was the son of Kamutal, but that Paliau was not, Paliau and Tchaumutchin were sons of the dead sister of Kamutal who had also belonged to Matchupal. Furthermore, Pwanau, the brother whom Paliau had mentioned was not the son of Potik and Kamutal, but an adopted son.

So far then, Potik was not Paliau's father; Kamutal was not his mother. Pwanau was not his brother. He had a full brother in another gens whom he hadn't mentioned.

Then I interviewed Kamutal, to discover that the mother of Paliau, Ilan, had not been Kamutal's sister but Kamutal's mother's sister's daughter and had belonged to Pere, but had been subsequently adopted by Kamutal's mother. Paliau's real mother was this Pere mother, Ilan, who had been adopted by a Matchupal man, husband of her mother's sister, married a Mbuke man, and gone to live in Mbuke. She bore Paliau and Tchaumutchin. Her Mbuke husband died and she returned to Pere when Paliau was an infant. Then she died and the two children were adopted by Kamutal, an unmarried girl living in the house of her brother, Selanbolot. Kamutal then married Potik. The infant Paliau was adopted by Potik while Tchaumutchin remained with Selanbolot, Potik and Kamutal bore Tunu and Luwil, and Potik by another wife fathered Saot. While Paliau was still a child, Potik adopted Pwanau. Pwanau was Potik's father's brother's daughter's son.

Tchaumutchin had always remained in Matchupal, Luwil was later adopted by Selanbolot, his mother's brother, and became his heir when he died. Saot was adopted by Potik's father's brother's son and became identified with another descent line in Pere. This left the effective kinship as Paliau saw it, Potik and Kamutal, parents of Pwanau, Paliau, and Tunu:

The question now arises, Was Paliau's original account of his genealogy mere stupidity? But Paliau was one of the most intelligent men in Pere. At the same time there were others who took more of an interest in cultural form than he. He might be considered as typical of the middle range of formal cultural interest, but in the upper range of intelligence. When confronted with the statement that neither he nor Tchaumutchin were Kamutal's sons he agreed, yes; it was true Kamutal had adopted them, they were really Kamutal's sister's sons. Both Paliau and Tchaumutchin had white Sir Ghosts which were the heritage of a Mbuke family. When asked where he got this ghost, Paliau said his father had been a Mbuke man. Also, when Paliau needed pots for a feast, he imported a *patieyen* (father's sister) from Mbuke, the pot making center, to make them for him. When asked to explain the kinship path along which the marriage of Salikon, the daughter of the dead Pwanau, had been arranged, he explained it in terms of Pwanau's original Patusi parentage. When asked about Luwil and Saot's relationship to himself, he gave their parentage correctly and reverted to stating that Potik was his father. There was only one point in the genealogy which he actually did not know: that his own mother was not Kamutal's true sister and had not belonged to Matchupal. The reason why he did not know this was obvious, it would have no use to him. He could not claim *lom pein*ship in a Pere gens where he already claimed gens membership, so Kamutal had never troubled to impart this piece of useless information to him. In contrast to his lack of knowledge about his mother's original gens membership stood out his knowledge that Kamutal's older sister had married in Mbunei and taken Kamutal to live with her. The Mbunei man was a widower and already had a son about Kamutal's age named Gizikuk. Kamutal called her sister's husband "father"; Gizikuk called Kamutal's sister "mother" so Gizikuk and Kamutal were *pisio*, sibling of opposite sex, to one another. Paliau as the son of Kamutal is therefore *kakalin* of Gizikuk and *lom pein* to Gizikuk's children. As Gizikuk is a very powerful person, Paliau takes pains to remember the relationship.

It is also interesting to note with which *patieyen* group, the father's sisters and descendants of his real or adopted father, Paliau jests. He claims relationship to his Mbuke *patieyen* for economic reasons, but it is to Isole, Potik's ortho-cousin's children that he turns for cross-cousin jesting and blessing.

But there is another kinship function, the duty of a man's sister to keep and arrange the dogs' teeth and shell money of her brother, for which Paliau turns not to a distant relative of Pere gens, but to Kamutal's brother's daughter, Saundran, whom Kamutal adopted. Paliau calls Saundran "sister" and she keeps his valuables for him.

Paliau also failed to mention Popoli, the dead son of Potik and Kamutal. Popoli had been Paliau's Sir Ghost until the death of Pwanau, when he was deposed and made the Sir Ghost of Paliau's son, Popoli's namesake. The ghost Popoli had taken his deposition rather badly and had made Paliau's wife and Paliau's pig sick, until Paliau had built a separate house for his mother-in-law in which the skull of Popoli could hang safely. Paliau does not feel very friendly towards his deposed Sir Ghost. The metamorphosis from younger brother to powerful Sir Ghost had long since obliterated all memory of Popoli as a brother.

Although Tchaumutchin and Luwil both belong to Matchupal, not to Peri, they both coöperate economically with Paliau, far more closely than does Saot, who had a different mother and was adopted into a different Peri descent line.

I have discussed this case in some detail because it illustrates well the way useful and effective ties tend to supersede ineffective ones.[1]

We have now considered the way in which the kinship system may be expanded "within the law." A man may correct disparity in the sexes of his children by adoption, a man may claim *lom pein*ship through any one of the women who have been his foster mothers. But this merely extends the range of family lines into which he may marry his sons by birth or adoption. It permits choice, but not enough choice for Manus preference for economic freedom.

The dictates of the kinship system are legally expanded in two other ways—the category of a man's children is expanded to include any younger person in his own, his mother's, his wife's or other related family line for whom he cares to become responsible in terms of the affinal exchange system, and second, the actual requisitioning of the "daughter"

---

[1]Incidentally it also illustrates vividly the small value of genealogical work of the casual sort in Manus. This one genealogy is the result of approximately fifteen or twenty hours of work, interviewing, re-checking, interrogating. Obviously, to obtain the genealogies of the tribe in such connected detail would take many months. Needless to say, there is no way in which the possibility of this type of memory for useful (and disregard of useless) relationships can be allowed for statistically.

in this greatly extended sense of *lom kamal* by *lom pein* has been dissociated from subsequent process of financing the marriage so initiated. This requisitioning process is termed "making a road." Under the rigid rules of the system, a boy child could properly be married to his father's mother's brother's son's daughter or to his mother's mother's brother's son's daughter, that is, his mother could "make the road." This permission dissociated the financier father from the act of making the road, so that the father's *pataran* was not his own cross-cousin but his wife's cross-cousin, or his *pauaro*, also a joking relative, however. So within the system itself there was legal provision for the dissociation of financier and road maker. This dissociation has been carried to the most extreme lengths. Actually, in practice, anyone can make a road for anyone else. Roads can be made nominally by small children for anyone else. A man may get a distant connection on his mother's side to make a road, along which he finances the marriage of a young distant connection on his father's side. They still cling to the letter of the law, however. The "road" must be made by a *lom pein* through an own or foster mother to a *lom kamal*.

The result is that a few aggressive initiating men finance half the marriages in the community which splits up into three distinct classes which have very little to do with the *lapan, lau* distinctions. These classes are rich and powerful economic entrepreneurs, the dependent relatives of these men, and men who are poor and obscure, but who are not dependent upon others. The entrepreneurs finance the marriages of their dependents and their dependents' children, and in return their dependents fish for them.

Upon the skeletons provided by the kinship system rich and enterprising men are thus able to build up a dependency who will fish for them and serve them in their middle years. As an illustration of this I will present a list of the marriages which Paliau, whom we have already discussed in this chapter, is financing.

Men who lack the initiative to climb to a place of importance may choose to remain humble, but independent, and conduct their own marriages and their children's on a very small scale or they may attach themselves to some wealthy man, fish, trade, and navigate for him. In return, the rich man will finance the birth feasts and the marriages of their children. There are, however, certain prestige feasts which the rich men only give for themselves, notably, *metcha*, which is a great marriage payment made after many years of marriage, and the *kan tchinitchini poenpolan*, the feast of hair cutting for a boy (only the sons

MARRIAGES WHICH PALIAU IS FINANCING

Name	Relation to Paliau	Relation of Roadmaker to Paliau	Why Roadmaker claims his *Lom Peinship*	Relation of Roadmaker to Marriage Principal
Tunu[1]	Mother's mother's sister's daughter's son; son of foster father	Wife	Through father's co-wife	Foster brother's wife
Luwil[1]	Mother's mother's sister's daughter's son; son of foster father	Foster mother	Through father's co-wife	Own mother
Bonyalo[1]	Foster father's brother's son	Father's brother's wife	Through stepmother	Paternal grandmother
Palimat[1]	Foster father's foster son's son	Wife	Through mother	Father's foster brother's wife, called "mother"
Melin[2]	Wife's younger sister	Foster father's sister's son	Through mother	Made it himself
Ponyama[2]	Wife's younger sister	Mother-in-law	Through own mother previous to adoption	Mother's brother's adopted son
Salikon[2]	Foster brother's daughter	Foster brother	Through own mother, previous to adoption	Father's brother
Topas[1]	Wife's mother's sister's son	None	Through own mother	Mother's brother's son
Popoli[1]	Adopted son, half Usiai	Himself	Through foster mother's elder sister	Foster father
Pindropal[2]	Brother's daughter	Himself	Through foster mother	Father's brother

[1] Male.
[2] Female.

of the rich have their hair grown and matted in preparation for this feast), and the more elaborate death ceremonial including the destruction of the house by a *ngang*. The complete cycle of economic exchanges which are arranged on the underlying structure of the kinship organization is therefore only completed for the rich, although the economic exigencies of the poor are used by the rich to keep their wealth in circulation, to balance the sexes of the principals, in whose name the exchanges are made, and to obtain economic dependents.

To illustrate further the practical working of Manus social forms, I shall now present an account of one gens, the gens of Lo. I have chosen this gens because it presents special points of interest and because many of the personalities have already been mentioned, as this gens through a death, an illicit sex affair, a house moving, a betrothal payment, a *metcha* and a birth was very much in the limelight during our residence in Peri.

ANALYSIS OF THE GENS LO

Four generations ago there was a split in this gens, and all of the *lapan* left Peri and went to live about three miles away in the village which they founded and which is now called Tchalalo. Only the *lau* remained. The *arakeu* of Tchalalo was abandoned, as far as house sites were concerned, although it was still used in invoking ancestral spirits. The present male members and partial members of the gens of Lo are: Kemwai, Nane, Ngandiliu, Pomele, Pope, and Kali. Kali, one of the four old men of Peri, is a widower who has become too old to exercise any real influence in his gens or in the village.[1] He lived in the house of Nane, had as his Sir Ghost his dead son Malaut, and played a very slight rôle. Kemwai was Kali's father's older brother's son, so that he outranked Nane as a member of the elder line. Pomele was the son of a more remote member of the Lo *lau* whose father had been dead since he was a child. His mother had belonged to the gens Pere and he had been reared by his mother's people. He had married the younger sister of the wife of Paliau, to whom Paliau had acted as titular father, and he was habitually known in the village as "*nat e* Paliau," "son of Paliau." So, although he was a full member of Lo, he acted more often with his mother's people than with his father's. He was a young man; his house had been built by Paliau for his titular daughter and Pomele was therefore of little use to the gens Lo. Ngandiliu did not really belong to

---

[1]See Fortune, *ibid.*, Chapter V, subsection 13, for an account of the way in which he, too old to cling to life, jeopardized not only his own safety, but that of his descendants by catching and marketing the tabooed *Pwitch* fish.

Lo at all. His own father had belonged to Taui, but after the death of his father his mother had married Kali, who reared Ngandiliu. Ngandiliu's younger brother, Selan, had been adopted by Tchokal, a *lapan* of Pontchal. Ngandiliu sometimes acted with his younger brother and sometimes with the gens Lo. Pope was the son of Kali's older sister, Ngamean, who had married into Matchupal. His marriage payments had been made by Lo and he was said to belong to Lo, although he was a doubtful asset to any gens, as he was an economic waster and subject to cataleptic seizures. He was popularly known as Mwengo, literally Sir Crazy.

As the women of a gens are also important, it will be necessary to deal next with the Lo women in Peri. The old widow Ngamean, lived now with Nane, now with Pope. She was slightly silly and no longer to be reckoned with. Nane had a younger sister, Molung, who had been adopted and financed by Ngandiliu. She had married Luwil, the sister's son and heir of Selanbolot, a *lapan* of Matchupal, who was likewise the titular brother of Paliau. Luwil was one of Paliau's dependents. A third Lo woman was Pwailep, the sister of Pope, a stupid barren woman, who was married to Engdrangen, an inferior unimportant childless member of Matchupal, who acted as dependent of his younger brother, Topas. A fourth Lo woman was Tino, daughter of the dead brother of Kali. She was a young woman who had married Bonyalo, a *lau*, a very minor member of Pere gens, also a dependent of Paliau. The fifth Lo woman was Tchomole, wife of Kalowin, who was himself the son of a Pontchal father. On his father's death he had been adopted by his father's brother. His paternal grandmother was a member of Tchalalo and his father's brother was married to a Lo woman and had obtained for him Tchomole as a wife. Kalowin was a most undistinguished man; his son was married to Pope's daughter, and lived in Pope's house. He was subject to crazed fits, and also to curious compulsions when he used to go out and build up a piece of the reef as if it were an *arakeu*. Isole, the wife of Kemwai, had used a communication from the ghosts to induce Kalowin to move into Nane's house and work for Nane. The sixth Lo woman was Main, Kemwai's widowed sister, a woman of very weak brain and uncontrolled and easy impulses, who in a puritan society like Manus where every sexual lapse was a public danger, was a very heavy liability for any gens to carry. Main had been five times married, once as a *palu*, i.e., co-wife, and three of her husbands had been of so little account that no one had troubled to save their skulls and enlist them as Sir Ghosts. Main lived at present in the house of Kemwai, dividing her time between Kemwai's household affairs and those of Nane.

Turning from the Lo women, to the wives of the Lo men, there is a better story. Kemwai had married Isole, the most brilliant medium in Peri, the true sister of Talikai, who was now supplanting Korotan, the blind *luluai*, as *luluai*—Korotan's adopted son being too young, Kemwai's sister, now dead, had married Korotan, the present *luluai*, so that Kemwai's immediate family had made two excellent matches, into the leading family in Pere.[1] Kemwai had built his house near the Pere *arakeu*, next to the house of Talikai, whose house abutted on one *arakeu*, while Korotan's house abutted on the other Pere *arakeu*. Also Kemwai lived principally under the tutelage of a group of Pere spirits who were no longer represented by skulls, but whom the resourceful Isole had resurrected to preside over their joint household. Kemwai was a very conservative, docile, upright man, who followed where Isole led and was therefore able to work in harmony with the rich and enterprising Talikai, his brother-in-law, and to profit thereby.

Nane had made an equally good marriage with Isapwe of Kalat. Kalat was a small but very powerful gens, and this marriage provided Nane with three of the chief men of Pere, Mbosai who was living in the place of a Matchupal *lapan* mother's brother but who also acted with Kalat, and Sanau and Tchanan of Kalat. As we have seen, Nat-e Paliau had married the ward of Paliau, and she also belonged, on her mother's side, to Kalat which ensured some backing from the powerful Kalat trio as well as from Paliau. Meanwhile both Molung and Tino were married to the financial dependents of Paliau. Furthermore Nane was the son of a woman who came of a powerful Mbunei family.

So much for the present situation of Lo. It numbered two powerful men, although Kemwai's power was only a reflection of close association with his wife's people, and one reasonably well placed man, Ngandiliu, who through his wife was a financial partner of Paliau. But all were *lau*, and furthermore the gens carried a heavy load of the unfit in the persons of Pope, Pwailep, Kalowin, and the poor marriages of Tino and Pwailep. But Kemwai, through the help of Nane who was the most enterprising man in the gens, and one of the most enterprising men in Peri, had made his *metcha* for Isole which placed him at the pinnacle of achievement in Peri. Nane made his *metcha*, meeting his three powerful "brothers-in-law," if not quite on equal terms—for he did not give the customary secret extra-payment known as *musui*—still on creditable terms. At Nane's *metcha*, he and Kemwai both preserved their unpretentious *lau*

---

[1]See Fortune, *ibid.*, Chapter V, subsection 42, for an account of the way in which Selan insulted Korotan with the behavior of his affinal relatives of Lo, whom Selan implied did not believe that Korotan's credit was good, but who actually were not able to meet their obligations to the *luluai*.

status, hanging only fifty dogs' teeth on a string. Any attempt to
assume higher status is more complicated for them by the fact that their
lapans, although they have left them, are nearby. Between them and
the *lapans* of Tchalalo there is a curious relationship. The men of Tchalalo
did not help with Nane's *metcha*, but Kemwai and Isole went to live for a
month in Tchalalo before making the final death feast for the deceased
Kuckerai[1] of Tchalalo; their express purpose in going was to fish and
trade for sago for the feast. The relationship between the *lau* group
of Lo and the *lapan* group of Tchalalo is therefore still partly functioning, although of course, pretentious *lau* like Nane and Kemwai could not
ask their *lapan* relatives to help them make a feast to which they were
not really entitled. But there was one slight indication that Kemwai
and Nane were working towards an assumption of greater dignity,
towards consolidating the results of good marriages and Nane's excep-
tional skill as a turtle fisherman, from which he had amassed much of the
wealth for his *metcha*. When Nane's son Popwitch died,[2] Nane, as is
customary, moved his house, and Kemwai was planning to do likewise.
Nane moved his house to the other end of the village, near, although not
absolutely abutting on the old *arakeu* which had belonged to the Tchalalo
lapans.

But the fortunes of a gens are always shifting, depending upon the
births and deaths and marriages of each generation. Pere is the only
gens the prosperity of which can be definitely prophesied for the
next generation because if one line fails, there are others to survive.

It is now necessary to consider the next generation in Lo, the growing boys. Kemwai had five daughters and only one son; this son and
two of his daughters are dead; one daughter is married in Mok to a
man of slight importance, a second is married fairly well in Mbunei, and
a third had just eloped from her Patusi husband (where she was a
younger co-wife) with a young ne'er-do-well, who had been cast off by his
dead father's younger brother who should have been financially responsible for him. He is the only one of the three sons-in-law who may
possibly throw in their lot with Kemwai. Because Isole and Talikai
play such a dominant part in Kemwai's affairs, there is always the danger
that any dependent of Kemwai may become automatically a dependent
of Talikai and pass over into a Pere allegiance.

His only son dead, Kemwai had adopted Pomat, the orphaned son
of Isole's dead sister. This adoption had taken place in infancy, and

---

[1]Government appointed headman.
[2]For full account see Fortune, *ibid.*, Chapter V, subsection 13 et seq.

Pomat's personality closely approximated to that of Kemwai. He was slow, cautious, unimaginative, only mildly aggressive, but persistent and definite. He was practically the same age as Kutan, Nane's eldest son, a none too intelligent, exceedingly aggressive youth. Nane had three younger living sons, one of whom, Posuman, had been informally adopted by Kalowin, who now lived, as seen above, under Nane's roof as a virtual, and not too useful dependent. But Pomat was the adopted child of Kemwai's middle age and Kutan was Nane's fifth son, the four eldest having died. Neither father could hope to live another ten years until Kutan and Pomat were old enough to assume leadership in the gens. Turning now to the less integrated members of the gens, Ngandiliu had one adopted child, Topal, who was only eight. Pope had a son of twenty-odd, Noan, an idle, untruthful thieving lad of low mentality, unbetrothed, and already the cause of much scandal in the village, including responsibility for the death of Popwitch, Nane's second son. Noan would never be an asset, any more than his father had been. Noan's younger brother, Tchokal, was undersized and sly, but shrewd. He was two or three years younger than Kutan, however. Kalowin's son, Ngangidrai had married Pope's daughter, Patali, but both of them were stupid and shiftless. Nat-e-Paliau belonged half to Lo and half to Pere as he was working for Paliau, his wife's sister's husband; it was very doubtful whether he would throw his lot in with Lo. He was about twenty-seven, the only member of the age group between Kemwai and Nane and Pomat and Kutan.

There was then, one son of Kemwai, four of Nane, one of Ngandiliu, two of Pope, in the young generation, but there was no link in between except Nat-e-Paliau. It has already been remarked that effective generations in Manus are ten year periods. Two strong men of forty cannot hope to hand their economic affairs over to their sons under twenty. There must be a man of intermediate age to carry on when the older men die. It is very probable, therefore, that although Kemwai and Nane by advantageous marriages and hard work had succeeded in putting their truncated gens into a much better position than they had found it, and although the generation of their children contained seven males, that nevertheless Lo would sink into a position of insignificance, if not of extinction, with the next generation.

By way of completing the picture, it may be permissible to prophesy the probable course of events. It will be remembered that Ngandiliu only coöperated partially with Lo, the gens of his stepfather, and as often acted with his younger brother, Selan, who was the heir of an important man. It will also be remembered that both Kemwai and Nane had very important brothers-in-law, Talikai of Pere gens, and Mbosai of Matchupal and Kalat. Now should Kemwai and Nane die without any younger men to take their places, and barring some very improbable turn of fate, such younger men will not be forthcoming, Talikai would assume responsibility for Pomat's future, and Mbosai for the children of Nane. Even though Talikai and Mbosai should die before Kemwai and Nane, Talikai and Mbosai both have efficient heirs, who are now young men in the late twenties. These heirs could assume responsibility for the boys of Lo. If Lo showed signs of complete social extinction in this fashion, then Ngandiliu would act only with Selan, Nat-e-Paliau would continue to act with Paliau or possibly with some of his Matchupal relatives, and Pope dead, Kalowin, Ngangidrai and Noan would sink to the level of very poor and very insignificant men.

It will be seen that such a future would alter the gentile complexion of the village only, but would not materially alter the future hope of prosperity of Kutan and Pomat, who would be well off; financed by the heirs of the prominent and provident Talikai and Mbosai. Kutan and Pomat might well in their turn, become heirs of these men, and assume positions of importance in the economic leadership of the village. But the gens of Lo, originally depleted by the departure of all its *lapans* to form the village of Tchalalo, would have disappeared because of the age distribution of its members, the accidents of its affinal relationships, and the personalities of some of its members. Gentes the size of Manus gentes have a most uncertain life, owing to the small numbers and to the fluid social arrangements which offer no real objection to the adoption or financing of a boy by his mother's brother or by his father-in-law, although this arrangement almost inevitably tends to take him out of his gens and so impoverish the gens.

SUMMARY

To summarize: The original ideal structure of Manus society provides for two classes in society, *lapan* and *lau*, with a preference for a *lapan* marrying a *pilapan* (female *lapan*). The kinship system provided for the intermarriage of the children of cross-cousins the son of *lom pein* to the daughter of *lom kamal*, and for the validation, by a series of prescribed exchanges of property, of this marriage and subsequent events of pregnancy, birth, hair-cutting, ear-piercing, menstruation, etc., which occur in the lives of the individuals involved in that marriage. Between *lapan* and *lau* there is a type of mutual helpfulness expected, not unlike a slight version of the feudal relationship—the *lapan* takes care of the economic needs of the *lau* and the *lau* works for the *lapan*.

This formal and fundamentalist social structure based upon concepts of blood relationship, and noble birth, has been revamped by the Manus into a type of capitalism. The prescribed marriage requirement has been stretched until it is only a legal fiction, a form of etiquette. By expanding the marriage requirement it has been possible for aggressive and enterprising men to obtain position regardless of their rank by birth. So *lapan*ship has shrunk in importance and the situation occurs in which a rich *lau* can command the services of a poor *lapan* whom he has financed. The relationship of interdependency between financier and one financed has replaced, in large measure, the theoretical relationship between *lapan* and *lau*.

It may be questioned why I consider it legitimate to speak of a structure which is so flagrantly disregarded and reorganized. I do this because the Manus themselves conceive their system formally, ideologically, without making explicit allowance for the continual contravention. Although *lapan* works for *lau*, it is still commented upon in each individual case, e.g., "His father was a *lapan*, but he is no account and just works for Mbosai." I may refer again to the case of Selan and Ngandaliu, whose own father was a *lapan* of Taui. When he died, Ngandaliu was adopted by his stepfather who was a *lau* of Lo, but Selan was adopted by a *lapan* of Pontchal. The children of Selan wear dogs' teeth transversely across their breasts, the sign of a *lapan*, but the son of Selan who was adopted by his brother Ngandaliu wears no such ornament, for Ngandaliu was adopted by a *lau*. When Selan quarrels with a *lapan* he boasts of his *lapan* blood, but Ngandaliu keeps silent.

Similarly with the kinship system which the Manus treat so highhandedly in practice, if two cross-cousins stand side by side, the bystander will remark, "These two are cross-cousins. When they grow up and marry the son of one will marry the daughter of the other."

And in the adjustments to adoption, although the terms used are inconsistent within themselves, nevertheless, the individual acts in each case whether it be towards a putative sister or cross-cousin or brother-in-law along the lines prescribed by the kinship system. The whole blood relationship pattern provides a grand plan, an ideology upon which the pragmatic expedient customary behavior of the Manus is built. In this respect Manus bears the strongest resemblance to Samoa, where a system of a blood inheritance and blood kinship has been similarly contravened in practice, but is nevertheless present in ideology.

Professor Radcliffe-Brown[1] has shown that the social forms of certain areas contain within themselves certain tendencies; viz., the reoccurrence of identical kinship developments in different parts of Australia. Hocart[2] in a series of brief articles suggested ways in which Fijian political organization had modeled itself upon kinship form, notably the rights of the sister's son-*vasu*, the cross-cousin relationship, *tauvu*, and the elder brother, younger brother relationship. Mr. Gifford[3] made the same observation in Tonga where intrafamilial organization provides the political groundplan. In my study of Manuan[4] (Samoan) social organization, I attempted to demonstrate that the political pattern of the tribe in Fiji or of the state in Tonga was partly based upon the form of the kinship system.

It is impossible to speak of the Manus scheme as political. The contravened structure with its insistence upon *lapans* and the rôle of the *luluai* presents more of a picture of political organization than does the effective form of present day Manus society. It is nevertheless a system by which power is wielded in terms of a kinship system which is no longer dominant in practice, but only in thought.

The kinship system has important elements in common with Samoa, Tonga, and Fiji, and it therefore is not surprising that this tendency of translating kinship form into a basis for extra-kinship activity which is so markedly developed in western Polynesia should appear in Manus also.

---

[1]Radcliffe-Brown, A. R., The Social Organization of Australian Tribes (*The Oceania Monographs*, no. 1, [1930]; also published in *Oceania*, nos. 1–4, 1930).
[2]Hocart, *ibid*.
[3]Gifford, *ibid*, 49.
[4]Mead, *i bid*.

NOTES ON OTHER ADMIRALTY ISLAND SYSTEMS
Conditions of Collection

Experience in Manus revealed the unreliability of kinship systems in the Admiralties derived from one informant. The use of genealogies, while providing a valuable check, is usually not a sufficient one, because of the small size of families. When a certain relative does not occur in a genealogy and the investigator has to introduce, "But if so and so had a son, what would X call him," the possibility of error becomes very high indeed. On the other hand, dealing with abstract genealogies constructed of cans of peas and beans to symbolize males and females required a higher degree of conceptualization than the average native was accustomed to. When the investigator remains for a long time in one village, it is possible to find actual cases for every kinship term and finally to report a complete kinship system, including a record of the divergence between theory and practice. But where it is necessary to deal with only one or two informants, in pidgin English or through the medium of a different dialect which they only imperfectly comprehend; where all the individuals in a genealogy are strange and the ramifications of the social organization are not known, only the most fragmentary results can be obtained. If no kinship system were thoroughly known from the Admiralties, I should not present these scattered notes at all, as I believe that the presentation of such imperfect material can often be far more misleading than useful. It will be noted that none of these systems are complete, nor have I attempted to make any full analysis of categories. The nature of the material is such that in no case would such analysis have been justified, as the range of usage is unknown and actual checking within the community was impossible.

But within an area as compact and in many respects as homogeneous as the Admiralties, notes upon surrounding systems become meaningful in the light of one complete system. All of these systems show the tremendous emphasis upon the two lines descended from brother and sister; many of them reflect clearly the typical marriage between the children of cross-cousins. Even these scattered notes show clearly that these other systems all belong to the same general type as does the Manus.

The Balowan Kinship System

The Balowan kinship system was investigated twice; once with a group of young Balowan men in Peri for trading purposes and later with a group of Balowan natives, during a stay of two days on the island of Balowan. Both investigations were conducted in a mixture of pidgin and Manus, as several of the Balowan men spoke Manus quite well. While the informants in the first instance were young men and rather badly informed, the later group included two village head men, and several intelligent older women.

CONSANGUINITY

aupong: great grandparents b.s. and their siblings
tubun: grandparents b.s. and their siblings except father's mother's brother
tamang: father, father's brother
sain: father's sister
nukunung: mother's brother, and father's mother's brother (?)
pwai: brother, male parallel cousin and male cross-cousin, when elder and younger
         are not distinguished
toung: older sibling of the same sex, b.s., includes cross and parallel cousins; son to
         father's brother-in-law (*polangtong*)
naing: younger sibling of the same sex, b.s., includes cross and parallel cousins
patingen or *pindai:* female sibling, m.s., includes cross and parallel cousins
mowang: brother, w.s.
wuliong: brother's son or daughter, w.s.; sister's son or daughter, m.s.
narung: child of either sex, b.s.
maiwen: grandchild, reciprocal of *tubun.*
aupong: great-grandchild

AFFINAL TERMS

atong: husband
patong: wife
polang tong: brother-in-law, m.s.
ipong: sister-in-law, w.s.
katingen: son's wife
sain: mother's brother's wife
nukunung: father's sister's husband

These five terms are the only affinal terms in the language; otherwise terms of consanguinity are used.

A man calls his wife's relatives, with the exception of her brother and the special terms flowing from the marriage of children of cross-cousins which will be discussed below, by the same terms which she uses, and a wife similarly uses her husband's terms except for her sister-in-law, her brother's wife, and the same exceptions.

SPECIAL TERMINOLOGY

Certain special terminology flows from, or is at least correlated with the marriage of children of cross-cousins. As this system can only be read with comprehension after the Manus system has been mastered, I shall use here the Manus terminology of *lom pein*, child of the woman, and *lom kamal*, child of the man.

Between cross-cousins themselves there is no special terminology, the sibling terms are used throughout. But the wife of *lom pein* calls *lom kamal, narung,* "son," and he calls her *tinang,* "mother," and she calls *lom kamal,* male's son, "grandchild." *Lom kamal's* wife is included in this terminology. It is only in the second generation from the brother and sister progenitors that the interesting terms appear.

The son of *lom pein,* male, calls *lom kamal,* male, his father's male maternal cross-cousin, "brother," that is the male sibling, same generation, male speaking term.

The son of *lom pein,* male, calls the son of *lom kamal,* male, *narung,* "son."

The daughter of *lom pein,* male, calls the son of *lom kamal,* male, *wulian,* "brother's son."

The daughter of *lom pein,* male, calls *lom kamal,* male, *manong,* "male sibling, same generation" w.s.

These terms reveal the expression of seniority given to *lom pein* by the attribution of a generation difference between his children and *lom kamal's* children, a tendency which will be found in much more marked degree in other Admiralty systems.

THE EXPRESSION OF SENIORITY

Balowan is one of the two recorded systems in the Admiralties with special terms for elder and younger sibling of the same sex, b.s. The Manus system, it will be remembered, lacked such terms and used the terms for father and son, mother and daughter in substitution.

Balowan stress the importance of order of birth in another way,— by a system of order-of-birth names which are given to both boys and girls within a family. So male children are named, in order of birth, excluding female births from all consideration: *mime, ni, nga, awai, kual, yip, silio, ngawen.* Female children are named, in order of birth, and excluding male births from consideration, *alup, asap, nino, neasol, non, nauwon.* The terms for elder and younger siblings of the same sex are preserved in the next generation, so the children of *awai* (fourth son) would call the children of *ni* (second son) *tung,* reciprocal *nain.*

The Balowan is the simplest system which has been recorded for the Admiralties. A few facts stand out at once, the paucity of the affinal terms; the excessive use of consanguineous terms in affinal relationships; the lack of distinction between cross and parallel cousins; the application of the term for mother's brother to father's sister's husband, and of father's sister, to mother's brother's wife; the use of one term, *wulian* for child of brother w.s. and child of sister, m.s., and the emphasis upon order of birth.

In the social organization of the Balowan islanders, some correlated facts also stand out, in contrast to the surrounding peoples. Although the Balowan people have child betrothal and follow the customary Admiralty island pattern by which the son of *lom pein* marries the daughter of *lom kamal*,[1] yet there are no avoidances, not even between the betrothed pair. There is no type of affinal avoidance whatsoever and there are no jesting relationships. Marriage is consummated publicly in the presence of the relatives of both bride and groom, who are said to "praise" the new couple.

The comparative Oceanic student will immediately realize where all these aspects of Balowan organization which differ so strikingly from the rest of the Admiralties point, to Polynesia. The absence of distinction between parallel and cross-cousins is a conspicuous characteristic of Polynesian systems, as is the term for elder and younger sibling of the same sex, and a specialization of the term "sibling of opposite sex" into two terms. One term for sister's child, m.s., and brother's child, w.s., is reported for one Maori system. The perpetuation of order of birth differences between the children of male siblings is also Polynesian,— especially developed in Tahiti. Were it not for the special terms used between the children of cross-cousins and the terms used between the *lom pein* and *lom kamal*, and the extension of the term, *sain*, to mother's brother's wife and the term *nukunung* to father's sister's husband, the system might be easily pronounced a Polynesian one.

When all these facts are considered together with the use of *kava* on Balowan, the presence of the *ifoga* ceremony (Samoan), the presence of the Polynesian form of possession, the use of sennit, stone walls, and the absence of a men's house, they assume extra significance. This is especially so when the likenesses between the Admiralties and Western Polynesia as a whole are considered.[2]

Comment should also be made upon the linguistic aspect of the terms themselves. These show marked affiliations with other Admiralty

---

[1]Satisfactory results were not obtained in the attempt to find out whether the son of the male *lom pein* could marry the daughter of the female *lom kamal* (the Manus forbidden marriage). The terminology gives no clue and no genealogy which adequately tested the matter was gathered in the short time at our disposal.

[2]I hesitate to record here, even in a footnote, one of those intangible impressions which can never be accepted as scientific proof, but which every ethnologist will recognize as having validity of its own. When I landed on Balowan, after six months spent among the Manus, I felt as if I had stepped into the midst of a Samoan group. The whole attitude toward life, the casual gestures, snatches of song, casual attitudes towards sex and other bodily processes which the Manus veil in such prudery, to the way in which the women carried their babies on their hips, instead of on the back of their necks, like the Manus, or in bags like the Usiai,—all doubtless contributed to the very strong impression—which was not based upon any preconceptions—that I was among Polynesians. Yet the Balowan people although lighter and better looking than the Manus, are far smaller than any Polynesian group, and their hair is only slightly less frizzly than is the hair of the Manus.

Island terms, the strongest similarity being to the terms used by the Matankor people of Lou, the nearest neighbors of the Balowan folk except for the Manus village of Mok.

THE LOU SYSTEM

The kinship system of the Lou islanders was obtained under great difficulties, but fortunately it is one of the neatest of the systems recorded so it is not necessary to report as many discrepancies as a more inconsistent system would probably have offered. We spent only one night on Lou, arriving by native canoe at dusk and leaving as soon as the wind was favorable in the morning as our Mok crew were unduly restive and unwilling to remain longer. We had no native contacts of any sort and the people were sulky and suspicious; after crowding around the government barracks while we settled in, they all departed to their village, about a quarter of a mile distant, and announced that they did not intend to return that night. Mr. Fortune went into the village and collected a group of men, who returned with none too good grace and were fairly restive during the interview. We worked together, using the entire group of informants, taking a genealogy first, and then I recorded the terms abstractly and Mr. Fortune recorded them concretely, so as to have a double check.

TERMS OF CONSANGUINITY

tubung: grandparent
tamong: father, father's brothers
tinong: mother, mother's sisters
sareng: father's sister
tuknong: mother's brother
tering: older sibling of same sex, includes parallel cousins
tiong: younger sibling of the same sex, includes parallel cousins
patingen: sister m.s., includes parallel cousins
maneng: brother w.s., includes parallel cousins
moma: cross-cousin of opposite sex
teing: male cross-cousin m.s., children whose mothers were cross-cousins and children of *lom kamal*, female, and *lom pein*, male
pware: female cross-cousin w.s.
iliung: brother's child w.s.; sister's child m.s.
narung: son
pindang: daughter
nanong: used between a man and his paternal cross-cousin's son, i.e., between *lom kamal* male and the son of *lom pein*
marguing: grandchild
nomarue: used between daughter of *lom pein* and the son of *lom kamal*, that is, between a woman whose father is child of the woman and a man whose father is child of the man, reciprocal

pariong: daughter of *lom kamal* to son of *lom pein*, that is, used between the man
whose father is child of the woman and the woman whose father is
child of the man. Reciprocal is *asong*. These are the terms for husband
and wife.

ANALYSIS OF CROSS-COUSIN TERMS

Male *lom pein* to male *lom kamal:* *tering*, reciprocal *tering*
Male *lom pein* to female *lom kamal:* *moma*, reciprocal *moma*
Female *lom pein* to female *lom kamal:* *pware*, reciprocal *pware*

These terms are also used between the children of *lom pein* male and
lom kamal female.

Daughter of *lom pein* male to son of *lom kamal* male: *momarue*, reciproca
momarue.

Daughter of *lom kamal* male to son of *lom pein* male: *pariong* (husband) reciprocal *asong* (wife).

Son of *lom pein* male to the son of *lom kamal* male: *polang* (brother-in-law).

Daughter of *lom pein* male to the daughter of *lom kamal* female: *ipong* (sister-in-
law).

TERMS OF AFFINITY

asong: husband
pariong: wife
nanong: father-in-law = son-in-law; also mother-in-law, son-in-law
katnarong: daughter-in-law b.s.
polang: brother-in-law m.s., reciprocal
ipong: sister-in-law w.s., reciprocal
pwongare: used between a woman and her male cross-cousin's wife, that is, to the
wife of her *moma*, reciprocal.

CONSANGUINEOUS TERMS USED IN AFFINAL RELATIONS

tuknong: husband of women called *sareng*
sareng: husband of men called *tuknong*
tering: younger sibling of spouse and of same sex as spouse
tiong: older sibling of spouse and of the same sex as spouse
teing: wife of male cross-cousin

NOTES ON THE SOCIAL ORGANIZATION

The Lou islanders follow the usual marriage pattern, including
that of forbidding marriage between all but the son of *lom pein* (male)
to the daughter of *lom kamal* (male). Name avoidance between the
betrothed pair is the only avoidance.

The father's sister, *sareng*, the husband of the father's sister, and
male cross-cousin, but not female cross-cousin, are joking-relatives.

There is patrilocal residence. Delivery is permitted in either house
of husband or father.

Villages are laid out very neatly with all the members of a gens close together. Gentile men's houses *lio* and gentile owned dancing poles *tchinals*.

A taboo, *konun*, is inherited from the father, and another, *wundru-mat*, from the mother.

Prostitutes were kept in the men's houses in the days of war.

There is only one important ear-piercing ceremony and this is for the daughter of the *luluai* who is called *pilapan*. The whole village participates.[1]

DISCUSSION

The Lou Islanders are more like the other known portions of the Admiralties than are the Balowan islanders. They share with the Balowan islanders the terminology for elder and younger sibling of the same sex, the distinctive two terms for sibling of opposite sex, the condensation of the terms for brother's child w.s. and sister's child m.s. into one term; the use of the same term for father's sister and mother's brother's wife and for mother's brother and father's sister's husband; the perpetuation of differences in order of birth between the children of male siblings. They differ from Balowan and agree with Manus in having a special term for cross-cousin, and in the presence of the joking-relationship with the father's sister and the male cross-cousin. Lou is distinctive, however, in the presence of husband and wife terms for the children of cross-cousins who are in the proper relationship for marriage, and it differs from Manus in calling the children of cross-cousins, out of the marriage road, cross-cousins again rather than brother and sister. It is also distinctive in the presence of a special term for cross-cousins of opposite sex, in the absence of joking between female *lom pein* and male *lom kamal*, and in the way in which cross-cousins of opposite sex are grouped together, regardless of which is *lom kamal* and which is *lom pein*.

It is notable that in both the Lou and Balowan system there is no perpetuation of the father's sister's line in a similar terminology and function, such as is found in the Manus system, the Ario Usiai, and the Pak system.

The presence of the men's house and the reported institution of the *pinanis* (men's house prostitute) differentiates Lou from Balowan, while with Balowan they share elaborate carving, and the use of the kava.

---

[1]Possibly the correlate of the *tchinal* feast for the skull of the dead *luluai*, which is postulated from Parkinson's account, see p. 205.

THE ARIO USIAI KINSHIP SYSTEM

The Ario Usiai were the Usiai with whom the Peri Manus traded. They lived in several small villages which stretched away inland from the southern coast. Although these Usiai were often in evidence, coming into the village to make long-time arrangements with their special trade partners and meeting the Manus people every morning at market, they were exceedingly reticent and difficult to deal with. They were frightened and ill at ease near the water, shy, and resentful of their Manus neighbors. By living in a Manus house and speaking a Manus language, we were sufficiently identified with the Manus to come in for a share of the Usiai dislike and suspicion. So although our contact with the Usiai was so much longer than with the Matankor peoples, our information is in many respects scantier.

I got a first draft of this kinship system from two stupid middle-aged men; five hours of work yielded only a very partial and unsatisfactory record. Where their genealogies were wanting they were incapable of imaginatively reconstructing the proper terminology. Later, we were fortunate enough to persuade Pokenbut, the *luluai* and most intelligent man among the Ario, to come down to Peri. He was able to give his genealogy for six generations and showed remarkable flexibility and imagination in giving terms. We worked with him twice, over an interval of four days. In some ways this is the most complete kinship system obtained—outside of that of the Manus—but it is based, with unimportant exceptions, upon the testimony of one man, as none of the others were.

buti: great-great-grandparents
salesale: great-grandparents
tumbu: mother's father, sons of all women called *tuho*
papu: father's father
nasi (or *tuho*): father's mother
nasi: mother's mother
tuho: father's father's sister and all her female descendants
tamo: father, older brother m.s.
tinai: mother, older sister w.s.
nain: father's sister, all her direct female descendants
sali: mother's mother's brother (alternative, *tumbu*); mother's brother
nyali: sibling of the same sex; father's mother's brother's child of same sex as
      speaker
pusu: sibling of opposite sex.; father's mother's brother's child of opposite sex to
      speaker
narong: child, brother's child m.s.; younger brother m.s.; younger sister w.s.; sister's
      child w.s.
yahi: sister's child m.s.; reciprocal of *sali*

nidro: brother's son w.s.; reciprocal of *nain;* mother's brother's son (reciprocal of *tuwo*)

tuwo: father's sister's son, reciprocal of *nidro;* father's mother's brother, reciprocal of *narong*

pisali: children of father's father's sister's son; reciprocal *buti*

kaiwien: children of *pisali;* reciprocal *salesale*

manambu: grandchildren

papu: children of *nidro* and *nidro's* sisters

TERMS OF AFFINITY

nyambulo: spouse

wai or *sowa:* wife's brothers; wife's mother's brothers (reciprocal *ninso*)

ninso: sister's husband

nosu: mother-in-law; daughter-in-law

nono: father-in-law; son-in-law; mother's mother's brother's daughter's husband; husband of spouse's father's sister

tomo: son-in-law w.s., mother's brother's daughter's husband

puindidro: daughter-in-law m.s.; mother's mother's brother's son's wife

puisowa: wife's brother's wife

puiwai: brother's wife w.s.; mother's brother's wife, reciprocal

puituwoe: wife of *tuwo*

pisali or *narung wai:* husband's younger sister, reciprocal *puiwai*

narong pisali: children of husband's younger sister

puituwo: father's sister's son's wife w.s.

paualo: husband of all women called *nain*

CONSANGUINEOUS TERMS USED IN AFFINAL RELATIONSHIPS

nain: wife's father sister, husband's father's sister

tamo: husband of father's sister's daughter; older sister's husband

norung: wife's mother's brother's son

tina: older brother's wife m.s.

nasi: wife of men called *pisali*

papu or *tumbu:* husband of women called *pisali* who are daughters of *tumbu*

sali: husband's mother's brother

yahi: sister's son's wife

ANALYSIS OF CROSS-COUSIN TERMS

Male *lom kamal* calls male *lom pein: tuwo*

Male *lom pein* calls male *lom kamal: nidro* (Note *nidro* is therefore the reciprocal of *nain* and of *tuwoe*, that is, male *lom pein* is completely identified with his mother and sister in the terminology which he uses to *lom kamal*)

Male *lom kamal* to female *lom pein: nain* reciprocal *nidro*

Male *lom pein* to female *lom kamal: narong* reciprocal *tuwoe*

This is the second of two ways in which ego and her mother's brother are placed in the same generation, for a man calls his wife's mother's brother, brother-in-law

Female *lom pein* to female *lom kamal: narong,* reciprocal *nain*

DISCUSSION

The Usiai system is like the Manus and unlike the Lou and Balowan systems in the attribution of one term to the father's father's sister and her female descendants, and one term to the father's sister and her female descendants. The persistence of nomenclature through three generation descendants of women called *tuho* (probably, however, only of the descendants of the true father's father's sister), in the terminology, *tumbu*, *pisali*, and *kaiwien* is unique among known Admiralty systems. The system is unusually rich in affinal terminology with the distinction between wife's brother and sister's husband and brother's wife and husband's sister. The condensation of the terms used by father's sister, father's sister's daughter and father's sister's son, into one term *nidro* is also peculiar to this system. Unique also are the several ways in which the mother's brother is equated with the sister's son in generation.

This system shows clearly the imputed seniority of the sister's line, *narun pein*, over the brother's line, *narun kamal*, otherwise it does not show any immediate reflection of the marriage arrangements. The usual Admiralty island marriage is not practised. Pokenbut stated that it was forbidden to marry into own place, mother's place, father's mother's place, and mother's mother's place. It was stated by all informants that cross-cousin marriage and marriage between the children of cross-cousins was forbidden. Our information is far from satisfactory, but it is certain that the levirate, inheritance of father's wife or father's brother's wife or elder brother's wife, is extensively practised, and that polygamy for the important older men was the rule.

THE PAK SYSTEM

The island of Pak is a most self-contained community, which combined agriculture and fishing. The closest affiliations of the Pak people seem to be with the people of Pitilu.[1] On the island of Pak itself there are only eighty households. Some preliminary and very unsatisfactory notes on the Pak system were obtained from a Pak man of poor mentality who was visiting in Peri. During the last fortnight of our stay in the Admiralties, Mr. Fortune made a flying trip to Pak and spent a few hours

---

[1]Mr. Fortune spent an evening in Pitilu where there has been a mission for many years. All attempts to take genealogies were baulked by the Pitilu natives' astute method of concealing their continued conformance to the typical marriage of cross-cousins. Mr. Fortune tried one genealogy after another, but although all had father's father's sisters, no father's father's sisters had grandchildren. The results of the inquiry were so unsatisfactory therefore, that we have decided not to publish the terms. The continued baulking of the inquiry when the crucial descent line was reached, the vehement assertions of the Pitilu people that the typical marriage was "all the same pig, all the same dog," together with the assurance of their unmissionized Pak neighbors that they followed the same marriage forms, leaves little doubt on this point at least.

working with a group of the older natives. The inquiry was carried on in Manus and pidgin English. A very full genealogy was obtained which conformed to the ideal marriage type within actual blood relationship, in strong contrast to the absence of one single perfect type marriage in all the marriages recorded among the Manus. Owing to the conformity to the marriage requirements there was a continual cross-cutting of consanguineous and affinal terminology within a given genealogy. For this reason, it was very difficult to get a full set of affinal terminology, although the presence of some affinal terms such as terms for wife's brother, wife's brother's wife, and wife's mother's brother suggest that affinal terms were available when consanguinity did not provide alternatives.

Further proof of the prevalence and importance of the type marriage was derived from notes on the functions of relatives. The functions in relation to mourning which in Manus are spoken of as being performed by the cross-cousins and the children of cross-cousins, were declared in Pak to be the functions of the brother-in-law and of the wife's mother's brother. The wife's mother's brother, rather than the wife's father, was the most important male avoidance relationship, and the brief information obtained suggested that the mother's brother played a far more significant rôle in Pak than in Manus. This agrees with Parkinson's assertion that in Pak the mother's brother buys a man his wife, a state of affairs which led Parkinson to describe the Pak people as matrilineal.

TERMS OF CONSANGUINITY

pwawariu: father's father's father; father's father; father's father's brother; father's father's sister's son; mother's father's sister's son w.s.; mother's father

hipweriu: father's mother; father's father's sister; father's father's sister's daughter; mother's mother

ndramok or *tamok:* father; father's brother; father's sister's son w.s.

hirinok: mother; mother's sisters

pahok: father's sister; father's sister's female descendants; father's father's brother's daughter and her female descendants.

yeneriu: mother's brother

ndrahik: brother m.s.; father's sister's daughter's son's son; father's sister's daughter's daughter's son's son; father's sister's son's son

tehik: sibling of the same sex

pisik: sibling of opposite sex Children of men who are called *pwaseriu* are called *tehik* and *pisik* according to sex. These terms also apply to parallel cousins.

narok: son; child of sibling of same sex, or of parallel cousin of same sex, and of all those called by sibling of same sex terms; brother's son w.s.; brother's daughter w.s.; mother's brother's daughter w.s.; mother's brother's son

asuhuk: daughter, child of sibling of same sex and sibling of opposite sex and of all those called by sibling of same sex term *yeneriu:* sister's son m.s.

wuliuk: sister's daughter m.s.

pwaseriu: male cross-cousin m.s.; sons of all women called *pahok* m.s.; father's mother's brother's son's son, and reciprocal m.s.; e.g., children of *pwaseriu,* if males call each other *pwaseriu.*

makapuk: grandchild, children of all *narok, asuhuk, wuliuk,* and *veneriu* (sister's son); mother's brother's son's child

ANALYSIS OF CROSS-COUSIN TERMS

Lom Kamal female to *Lom Pein* female: *pahok,* reciprocal *naruk*

Lom Kamal female to *Lom Pein* male; *tamok,* reciprocal *asuhuk*

Lom Kamal male to *Lom Pein* male: *pwaseriu,* reciprocal *pwaseriu*

Lom Kamal male to *Lom Pein* female: *pahok,* reciprocal *haruk*

Lom Kamal male calls the children of *Lom Pein* male, by the sibling terms of *pisik* and *tehik*

AFFINAL TERMS

A man calls his wife's female *lom kamal* (wife's mother's brother's daughter), *asuhuk*

mbuluk: spouse (The word means literally "forehead" that is "shame" corresponding to the Manus *mbule*)

mohaneriu: husband

pihineriu: wife

temwuliuk: wife's mother's brother (The most important avoidance relationship between males)

melisiuk: wife's brother (avoidance relationship)

asohuk: wife's mother (avoidance); wife's sister; sister's husband's sister's m.s.; wife of mother's brother's son. (His children are called *makapuk,* grandchildren); wife's mother's brother's daughter

mbulemelisiuk: wife's of wife's mother's brother m.s. (Most important female avoidance affinal relative).

Where the ideal marriage pattern is carried out, the wife's mother may be a relative, as there is no prohibition upon the marriage of the son of male *lom pein* to the daughter of female *lom kamal.* This may flow from the fact that marriages are said to be arranged by the mother's brothers, i.e., the contracting cross-cousins may therefore contract for their sister's children's marriage. But the wife of the wife's mother's brother would not be a relative. However, it is impossible to say whether she is avoided more stringently because she is not also a relative or because the mother's brother plays a more important rôle in arranging marriages than does the father.

Women's affinal terms missing.

The Bipi System

The following set of terms we owe to the kindness of Mr. Gregory Bateson who took two genealogies and collected a number of terms during a few hours stay in the village of Bipi, Northern Admiralties. Mr. Bateson was unable to obtain a complete set of terms, but there are points which show that the Bipi system is definitely related to the other systems recorded. Mr. Bateson found the system of double taboos which appears in both the Manus and Matankor systems as patrilineally and matrilineally inherited taboos.

TERMS OF CONSANGUINITY

pabu: grandfather and siblings of maternal grandparents

gwileo: mother's mother, father's sister, mother's brother's wife, and reciprocals. (Terms for father's mother, father's father's sisters and father's sister's daughters are missing. But a man was said to marry his *gwileo*)

tama: father, father's brothers, father's sister's son w.s.

tine: mother, mother's sisters, mother's father's sister's son's daughter w.s.

kali: mother's brother, father's sister's husband; sister's son's son w.s.

dracheu: sibling of the same sex, elder or younger b.s.; also applied to father's sister's son's daughter w.s.

we'u: sibling of opposite sex, also applied to father's sister's son's son w.s.

niato: child b.s.

asohun: daughter b.s.; mother's brother's daughter m.s.

pabu and *gwileo:* grandchild terms, used reciprocally

AFFINAL TERMS

pulu: spouse

niato: husband's brother w.s.; reciprocal *tine* m.s. (This is given for husband's elder brother as well as for husband's younger brother, but avoidance behavior was only recorded between a man and his younger brother's wife. This latter corresponds to Manus usage)

ioho: husband's sister, reciprocal

niano: wife's father, reciprocal; also wife's four grandparents

asohon or *salahon:* wife's mother (Compare *pilanasau* in Manus and *sohuk* in Pak. This is a taboo relationship)

The absence of most of the cross-cousin terms makes it difficult to analyze the Bipi system, but the use of the terms *tama*, father, and, *asohun*, daughter, between female *lom kamal* and male *lom pein*, and the perpetuation of this attributed generation difference in the next generation, as when a woman calls her father's sister's son's son, *we'u*, sibling of opposite sex, and a woman calls her mother's father's sister's, son's daughter, *tine*, mother, and that woman's brother *kali*, mother's brother, suggests the well-recognized Admiralty system by which the *lom pein* line outranks the *lom kamal* line. Furthermore, Mr. Bateson

was told that a man married his *gwileo*, translated into pidgin English
as his *tubuna*

Mr. Bateson obtained one perplexing record of terminology used
before and after the marriage of a pair who were said to have called each
other *gwileo* before marriage. The husband was said to have called his
brother-in-law, i.e., wife's brother, *kalin*, mother's brother, before marriage and his wife's sister, *tine*, mother, before marriage. It is impossible
to systematize these isolated facts with the information at our disposal
at present.

Linguistic Aspects of the Foregoing Terminologies

A detailed comparison of the actual terms used in these six systems
reveals very little more than is immediately apparent in a cursory survey
of the material. The terminology in Lou and Balowan is practically
identical in the most important terms, i.e., for the words for grandparent,
grandchild, father, mother, father's sister, mother's brother, male sibling
of a female, female sibling of a male, son, sister's son m.s., and brother's
son w.s., and grandchild. Manus and Ario show the next greatest similarity with identity of terminology[1] for the terms for mother's mother,
mother, mother's brother, sibling of opposite sex, son, sister's son, and
grandchild. The most nearly identical term in the systems under consideration is that for father, which appears in all these systems except the
Manus itself, as *tamo, tamang, tamong, tamok*, and *tama*. (Although the
Manus term for father, *papu*, is a deviant, corresponding to the Bipi and
Ario term for grandfather, the Manus retain the familiar *tama* in the
mourning term, *tamapwe*, "one whose father is dead"). The word for
mother appears as Manus *ina* term of address only, and then as *tinai,
tinang, tinong, hirinok*, and *tine*, respectively. Child is *nat, narong,
narung, narung, narok*, and *niato*. The word for daughter appears as
asaun, asohuk, and *asoʰun* in the three cases where there is a separate
term. The word for grandchild appears as *manambu, manambu*, and
makapuk. On the other hand, the greatest deviation is found in the
terms for father's sister, mother's brother, the sibling terms, and the
cross-cousin term. The term for sibling of opposite sex occurs oftenest
in a common form, as *pisio, pusu*, and *pisik*. The terms for affinal relatives reveal much the same characteristics, great similarity between Lou
and Balowan and great variability among the other groups.

---

[1]The term identity is used advisedly with such allowance for dialectic variation as a knowledge of
only one Admiralty Island language will permit. It is probable that a few more terms might be shown
to be related if a complete knowledge of Admiralty Island linguistics could be brought to a comparative
study of these kinship terms.

It is interesting to note that the terms which show the greatest similarity are those which are least subject to modification from different kinship structures; grandparent, mother, father, child, and grandchild. On the whole, the evidence of the terms themselves is less convincing of important relationship—except in the case of Lou and Balowan, than is the structure of the systems, for the similar terms contain widespread roots which occur also thousands of miles from the Admiralties.

CONCLUDING STATEMENT

In the introductory statement, I indicated that the Manus system belonged in some respects to that type which Professor Lowie has called "bifurcate merging," designating the matrilineal type as the Crow system and the patrilineal type as the Omaha system. I reproduced in Fig. 5 a diagram from *Omaha Secret Societies* in which Mr. Fortune has combined these two types into one diagram. It has been very plausibly suggested by Professor Lowie[1] that the Crow system in which the father's sister and her female descendants are grouped together under one term and the children of the brother in addressing the children of the sister use terms overriding generation, is correlated with matriliny, and that the Omaha system in which the converse condition holds is correlated with patriliny.

The Manus are patrilineal, yet the father's father's sister's female descent line and also the father's sister's female descent line are grouped under common terms. This treatment of the father's sister's line is found for example among the Crow, in Dobu, and the Trobriands, and among the Twi[2] of the West Coast of Africa. The elevation of the children of the father's sister is obscured in the Manus system by the use of special cross-cousin terms, but is unmistakably present in the Balowan, Ario, and Pak systems where such elevation occurs. In both African and Oceanic systems, the primary stress lies between cross-cousins, between the inheriting and the non-inheriting lines.

It is possible to regard kinship forms from the standpoint of limited possibilities of emphasis.[3] Within the biological family the possible emphases are husband-wife, father-son, mother-daughter, father-daughter, mother-son, father to both son and daughter and mother to both son and daughter. With emphasis upon the husband and wife relationship comes a bilateral system, with the effective groups re-forming with each new marriage. Where the chief relation is between a parent and children of one sex, the relationship between siblings of the same sex becomes the important one after the death of the parent, giving the typical picture of unilateral descent. Where the chief relationship is between a parent and the children of both sexes, after the parents' death it is the relationship between siblings of opposite sex which assumes prominence. An emphasis on father to son, results in pure

---

[1] Article on "Relationship Terms." 14th edition, *Encyclopedia Britannica.*
[2] Mead, Margaret, A Twi Relationship System (Journal of the Royal Anthropological Institute of Great Britain and Ireland, in proof).
[3] I have discussed this point, briefly, in The Primitive Family (*Encyclopedia of the Social Sciences,* vol. 6) and in Contrasts and Comparisons from Primitive Society (*The Annals of the American Academy of Political and Social Science,* Publication 2499, Philadelphia, March, 1932).

patriliny, such as East African systems; on mother to daughter, pure matriliny such as Zuñi or the Nairs. Father to daughters and mothers to sons, as pivotal points in the social organization of a people have not been recorded, although it is possible that son-in-law inheritance such as that found in Omaha and Kwakiutl may be an aspect of the former, and the combination of matrilineal inheritance and residence in the husband's village found in the Trobriands and in Basima, Fergusson Island, may be an aspect of the latter.

From an almost equally balanced emphasis upon the relationship of one parent to children of both sexes, can be derived those systems which may be called modified unilateral descent, or double unilateral descent. Societies like Dobu and the Trobriands are not properly speaking mother-right societies at all, they are rather sister's son right. Nor can a society like Tonga where a man must defer to the will of his eldest sister be called father-right or pure patriliny. So in Dobu, by being the son of his mother, a man has a right to his mother's brother's inheritance; it is not a case of the inheritance passing from mother to daughter as in Zuñi. And it is because she is the daughter of her father that the sister exercises her power in Tonga. The claims of children of both sexes upon the parent who is legally ascendant, in Dobu, the mother, in Tonga, the father, are recognized. This results in a special relationship between the brother and sister, and between the cross-cousins, one of whom is partially disinherited. In its typical Oceanic form, under this system, neither line is completely disinherited; one inherits temporal powers, the other spiritual. The extent and importance of this balance of inheritance, of the relative status of cross-cousins, is reflected in the terminology of the systems under consideration. The categories may be interpreted as a recognition of superior status, or merely as a perpetuation of one status throughout several generations. That is, it can be said, as say the Dobuans and as said my Twi informant, "one calls a father's sister's son father because he takes one's father's place." Or it can be stated more generally, that all the members of a descent line who stand in the same relationship to ego, will be called by a common term, regardless of generation.

The Admiralty systems in which, under patriliny, the children of the female line are elevated to a parent status seems, at first sight, contradictory. If this attribution of parent status be interpreted in the Admiralties as expressing not inheritance and temporal ascendancy, but the inheritance of spiritual ascendancy over the male and inheriting descent line, the incongruity vanishes. So, where the descendants of the father's sisters possess similar powers, they are called by a similar term, and the terminology expresses the spiritual dominance of *lom pein*.

From this standpoint, the relation of one parent to children of both sexes has its reverberations in the relationships between brother and sister and between the next generation, the cross-cousins. If the principal relationship is to the father, in such matters as inheritance of property, status, residence, etc., modified patriliny is the result, if to the mother, modified matriliny. Where there is a definite division of the inheritance, as among the Twi-speaking peoples, a completely dual system results, with the patrilineal unilateral group claiming one inheritance and the matrilineal unilateral group claiming a different one. The terminology of the kinship system may express either type of inheritance. So in the Twi system which I recorded, all the emphasis is upon the inheritance of land and status, which come, with the blood (the *abusua*), from the mother's side; and a man calls his father's sister's son *adya*, father, "because he will take his father's place," as head of the family. But in Manus, a man calls his father's sister's daughter *patieyen*, which is primarily "father's sister," because she will inherit her mother's place of spiritual dominance towards him. It is not a question of matriliny or of patriliny, but of a division of privilege between the two descent lines, and the expression of this division in various ways in the kinship terminology. In Manus children of both sexes stand in a special relationship to each parent; the kinship terminology has emphasized only those privileges which descend from mother to children of both sexes, and which can only be transmitted by the daughter.

Although the parallels between widely separated variants of this type of kinship system are sometimes so minute as to be startling, like the occurrence of the term "female father" in Ifugao, Manus, and Bathonga, or the application of the same term to brother and mother's mother's brother in Dobu and among the Hidatsa, if all of these systems be regarded as flowing from one of a limited number of possible interfamilial emphases, it is not necessary to postulate historical connections among the very distant areas in which strikingly similar systems are found.

In closing I should like to refer to one other theoretical point upon which the mixed nature of Manus descent throws some further light. Professor Radcliffe-Brown[1] explained the occurrence of similar attitudes of awe and respect towards the father's sister and of familiarity and

---

[1]Radcliffe-Brown, A. R., The Mother's Brother in South Africa (*South African Journal of Science,* vol. 21, 542-546, 1924).

license towards the mother's brother in Tonga and Bathonga, on the hypothesis that the father's sister shared the austere regard in which the father was held, while the mother's brother partook of the indulgent kindness characteristic of the mother. In Manus, however, the father's sister is a jesting relative, the mother's brother a respect relative. This is not, however, a contradiction of Professor Radcliffe-Brown's hypothesis, for in Manus it is the father who is the kind indulgent parent, and the father's sister shares his familiar relationship to the child, while the mother's brother shares the more distant, more austere character of the mother. The Manus situation simply adds one more complication to the known pictures of social organization, that of an indulgent father combined with patriliny.

Perhaps the greatest historical interest of the Manus kinship system lies in the completeness and explicitness with which the sanctions which support the power of the father's sister's line are preserved. An institution which is found in Samoa, Tonga, Fiji, Tikopia, New Caledonia, and undoubtedly in many other parts of Oceania also, is illuminated and made intelligible, shown to be an expression of a well-integrated ancestral ghost cult.

The chief functional interest of the Manus system lies, I believe, in the way in which the Manus, while preserving the formal categories appropriate to status determined by birth, have developed a system through which temperament and individual endowment are given great freedom of expression. The Manus culture is one which sets a premium upon individual gifts, intelligence, foresight, energy, aggressiveness, and gives to these far more play than is usual in a primitive society.

GLOSSARY

aiyo, Effective generation, ten year period

arakeu, Small coral rubble platforms

ato ndriasi, They brothers; collective reference to a group of relatives classified together

ilamutu, (Samoan) Titular father's sister

Kalat, A clan name (probably same word as *Karat*, turtle)

kaleal, An affinal relative who must be avoided

Kalo, A clan name (a bamboo walled fish trap)

Kano, Indemnity payment

Kan tchinitchini poenpalan, Feast for hair cutting for a boy

Kapet, A clan name (net)

kau, Two-man fishing net, two-handled, three-sided

kawas, Trade

kendrol, Omen birds or omen fish

kiap, District officer

komambut, Betrothal payments by bridegroom's kin

Kopkops, Breast ornaments of tridacne shell

Kor, Village; literally, place

kuin um, Rear of house

lapan, A designation of rank, meaning those with noble blood

lau, A designation of rank meaning commoner; sometimes used to mean economic dependents

lavalava, (Pidgin) Length of trade cloth worn by men, wrapped around waist, falling to knee

liklik, (Pidgin), for gens or "(small) place belong me"

Lo, A clan name (a coconut leaf fish barrier)

lon um, Interior or central section of house

luluai, Head man, hereditary war leader, a designation of rank

mamandra, Large pre-marriage payment by bridegroom's kin

mana, Ovalis shells

matiruai, Post marriage payment by bridegroom's kin

Mbuke, Name of a village (clam shell)

memandra Pre-marriage segregation and feast for a girl about to be married

metcha, Late marriage payment; final great exchange in marriage of people of wealth

moen, A prefix meaning man or sir

moen kawas e io, A trade friend

musui, Part of wife payment which is given secretly and need not be returned

mwandrin, House of mourning

mwelamwel, Payment by bride's kin at actual marriage; ornament

mwengo, Sir Crazy

mwere, Middle space; an open space; avoidance resulting from a quarrel

mwetchels, Mats; used to partition a house

nambu-n, Gentile taboo

ndrengen, any pair of economic vis-à-vis

ngang, Institutionalized plunder after death

Palan um, Front section of house; men's section of house

palu, Co-wife

patandrusun, Taboo associated with a matrilineal descent line, used in this paper to designate a matrilineal descent line

patapat, A carved bed

Pataran, Two contracting parents or chief entrepreneurs in initiating marriage

petitchol, Central beam of house floor

pilapan, A female *lapan,* or person of noble blood

Ponopon, A hand net

pwitch, A fish

pwoeakni, To finance an individual's marriage payments; literally, "to strengthen"

ramʉtan um, Owner of the house

ramus, Charm tied to middle post of house, consists of pigs' tusks and straw

sobalabalate, Accusation of incest (directed towards husband and one of his female relatives)

sowal, A term sometimes used for gens, literally meaning side, as north side; more exactly, parties to one side of an affinal exchange

ta-mana, To dance; literally, "to make or put *mana*"

tandritanitani, Ceremonial blessing or cursing exercised by woman's line upon members of collateral male line; used in this paper to designate cult of ghosts so invoked

tchamoluandras, Feast following mourning

tchani, Ceremonial blessing of a young man by his grandfather giving him power in war, in wealth getting, and to live a moral life

tchelingen, Formal partners in affinal exchange, synonym of *ndrengen*

tchinal, Inter-village feast; dancing platform pole

wari, Mourning over those injured in war

Date Due

		FEB 0 1 1994	
JAN 2 8 1994		FEB 2 8 1994	
NOV 2 6 1974		MAR 2 7 1994	
JAN 30 1981		DEC 0 6 1995	
FEB 10 1981		DEC 6 1995	
MAR 27 1981		MAR 0 6 1996	
		FEB 2 5 1998	
APR 5 1980			
NOV 1 1983			

Printed in the USA
CPSIA information can be obtained
at www.ICGtesting.com
LVHW060011070823
754368LV00003BA/195